A geographical map that is a map of the earth, and there are distinguished the seas in it and the adjacent land areas

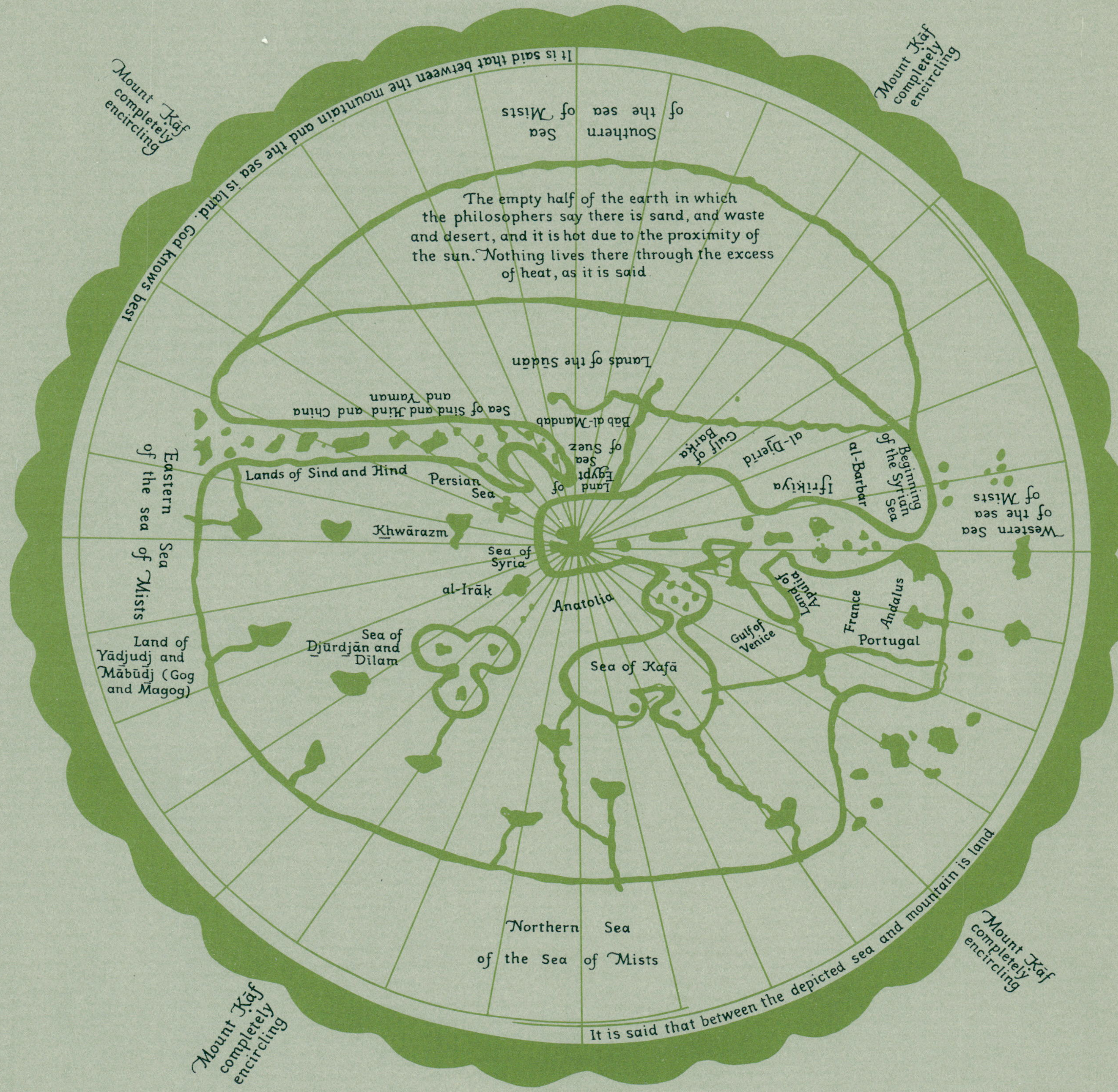

Transcribed from the World Sketch in the Sea-Atlas of Ahmad al-Sharfī of Sfax (Marsh 294) by courtesy of the Bodleian Library, Oxford

AN HISTORICAL ATLAS OF ISLAM

AN HISTORICAL ATLAS OF ISLAM

EDITED BY WILLIAM C. BRICE
under the patronage of the Encyclopaedia of Islam

TUTA SUB AEGIDE PALLAS · EJB ·

E. J. BRILL - LEIDEN - 1981

PREFACE

The idea of this Historical Atlas of Islam was first suggested in 1958 by the late Donald Edgar Pitcher. He had completed a thesis at the School of Oriental and African Studies in the University of London on the Historical Geography of the Ottoman Empire—a work which was published posthumously in 1968—and this larger enterprise followed naturally. In 1959 it was agreed that the new Atlas should be prepared under the aegis of the Encyclopaedia of Islam. Most regrettably Pitcher, a teacher by profession and a talented musical composer as well as a meticulous cartographer, died unexpectedly in the summer of 1963. The present editor was asked to take over his Atlas later that same year.

Pitcher's plan was to compile the Atlas himself. When he died, he had completed and proofed two specimen sheets; and these form the basis of the present pages 37 and 35 (lower half). It was then decided to request specialists to design or advise on particular maps, and those involved are mentioned on the relevant sheets. Wherever such an acknowledgement does not appear, the map was constructed by the editor. It will be evident that without the magnanimous help of the consultants, and above all of Professor Charles F. Beckingham who has throughout rendered general advice on historical points, this Atlas could never have been completed.

The superb line-work and hand-lettering are by the hand of Mr Kenneth Jordan, and the editor has drawn thankfully on his experience, and on that of Mr Neil Balmer at the press, in matters of lay-out and presentation.

Gratitude is due to the Rockefeller Foundation which awarded Pitcher a grant for work on the project from 1959 to 1963, and also to the Bollingen Foundation, to Columbia University, to Princeton University, and to the University of California at Berkeley and at Los Angeles which gave financial aid for the later stage of the undertaking.

Manchester, W. C. B.
October, 1980

LIST OF COLLABORATORS

Nicholas N. Ambraseys, London (Imperial Coll.)
Charles F. Beckingham, London (S.O.A.S.)
A. Frederick L. Beeston, Oxford
C. Edmund Bosworth, Manchester
Claude Cahen, Savigny-sur-Orge
Simon Digby, Oxford
Andrew Forbes, Leeds
Lucien Golvin, Aix-en-Provence
H. J. de Graaf, Wassenaar
Nigel St. J. Groom, London
Michael Hendy, Birmingham
Colin Heywood, London (S.O.A.S.)
Richard J. Holmes†, Aden/Harpenden
Peter M. Holt, London (S.O.A.S.)
J. F. P. Hopkins, Cambridge
Colin Imber, Manchester
Arthur K. Irvine, London (S.O.A.S.)
Mohammad A. Al- Jerash, Jidda
Jacques Jomier, Cairo
Paul Kunitzsch, Munich
Robert Mantran, Aix-en-Provence
Raymond Mauny, Paris
Charles P. Melville, London (Imperial Coll.)
Donald E. Pitcher†, Reading
Jean-François Salles, Lyon
Robert B. Serjeant, Cambridge
Henri Terrasse, Madrid
Gerald Tibbetts, London (Senate House)
Roger le Tourneau†, Aix-en-Provence

ISBN 90 04 06116 9

PRINTED IN THE UNITED KINGDOM
BY JOHN BARTHOLOMEW AND SON LTD., EDINBURGH

CONTENTS

Page

iv. Preface.

v. Contents.

vi. Introduction.

Part I. The Early Muslim Earth and Sky

1. The World according to Idrīsī, A.D. 1154.
   The World Map of al-Sharfī, A.D. 1579.
2. Arabic Constellations.
3. Star-names used by Arabs in the Indian Ocean.

Part II. The Extension of the Muslim World

4. The linguistic regions of the Islamic World.
5. The pre-Muslim World, *c.* A.D. 600.
6. Muslim expansion until A.D. 661.
7. The Umayyad Empire, *c.* A.D. 750.
8. The Late Abbasid Caliphate, *c.* A.D. 900.
9. Almoravid, Saldjūk and Ghaznāvid expansion *c.* A.D. 1100.
10. The Muslim World, *c.* A.D. 1300.
11. The Muslim World, *c.* A.D. 1500.
12. The Muslim World, *c.* A.D. 1700.
13. The Muslim World, *c.* A.D. 1900.

Part III. Early Arabia

14. Classical Arabia according to Ptolemy.
    Arabia in Classical Times.
15. S.W. Arabia before the 4th Century A.D.
    Arabia in the 6th Century A.D.

Part IV. The Near and Middle East

16/17. Iran, Afghanistan, Makran, Sind in the 10th and 11th Centuries.
18. Seismic Map of the Middle East.
19. The Middle East at Hidjra (A.D. 622).
20. The Middle East, CC 8–11 (the Abbasids and their successors).
21. The Middle East: dynastic changes, C 9–C 13 A.D.
22. The Near East in the C 12 A.D. (the Crusades and Ṣalāḥ al-Dīn).
    The Pilgrim routes of Arabia.
23. The Holy City of Makka.
    The Holy City of al-Madīna.
24. Transoxiana in the 10th and 11th centuries.
    The Khwārazm Shāhs and Ghūrids, CC 12–13.
25. The Middle East in the later C 14: the campaigns of Timur.
26. The Middle East in the mid–C 18 A.D.
27. The Middle East, C 19–early C 20 (encroachment by the great powers: strategic railways).

Part V. Anatolia and the Balkans

28. Byzantine Anatolia, CC 8–11.
    Anatolia, 1116–1204. Byzantine campaigns and Turkish penetration.
29. Anatolia in the C 13: Seljuk roads and Crusader routes.
    Anatolia *c.* A.D. 1300. The expansion of the Ottomans to A.D. 1362.

Page

30. Ottoman expansion, A.D. 1362–1402. The first conquest of Rumelia and Anatolia.
31. Anadolu and Rumeli in the later C 17.
32. Ottoman Naval Power in the 16th Century.
    Istanbul.
33. Sectaries in Anatolia, CC 13–16.
    The spread of the Anatolian sectaries, CC 15–17.
34. Anadolu and Rumeli in the later C 19.

Part VI. Muslim Spain

35. Spain and the Maghrib, CC 7–8. The Arab Conquest (with dates).
    The Western Mediterranean in the 9th Century.
36. The Muslim Conquest of Spain: early C 8.
37. Spain under the Umayyads, *c.* A.D. 890.
38. Spain *c.* A.D. 1035. The Party (*Taifa*) Kings.
39. Spain. The Christian Reconquest (A.D. 1035–1482).

Part VII. North Africa

40. North Africa, C 14.
    The Barbary States—C 17.
41. North Africa and the Sudan *c.* A.D. 1610.
42. North Africa, A.D. 1700–1830.
    North Africa, A.D. 1830–1912.
43. North Africa since 1912.

Part VIII. India and the Indian Seas

44. The Indian Ocean, *c.* A.D. 1000.
45. The Indian Ocean in the 15th Century.
46. The Turks and Portuguese in the Indian Ocean.
47. Early Muslim penetration of India, C 8–C 13.
48. The Greater Delhi Sultanate (Khalji and Early Tughluk) A.D. 1290–1335 (first Muslim conquest of the Deccan).
49. India 1335–1415. Contraction of Muslim rule under the Tughluk and Sayyid dynasties.
50. India *c.* A.D. 1530 (the death of Babur). The first Mughul conquest.
51. India *c.* A.D. 1605 (end of reign of Sultan Akbar).
52. India *c.* A.D. 1690. Maximum extent of the Mughul Empire under Aurangzeb (second conquest of the Deccan).
53. India *c.* A.D. 1770: Maratha expansion and the beginning of British administration.

Part IX. The Far East

54. Indonesia/Java. The first Muslim Empires.
55. Indonesia/Java, A.D. 1500–1750.
56. Indonesia/Java. European colonisation.
57. Islam in China.

Indices

58. Index of place-names and ethnics.
70. Astronomical Index (ref. pp. 2/3).
71. Economic Index.

INTRODUCTION

The broad divisions of the Atlas are regional, and within each division the maps are arranged in chronological order. Relief features are conveyed by means of contours and hill-shading, so that trade-routes, military campaigns, migrations and the like may be related to topography. Conventional signs and colours are kept as standard as possible, but the maps are not rigidly uniform in style and content: for as the work proceeded it soon became clear that different maps would stress different features, economic, strategic or ethnic, according to what was most important at the time and place concerned.

The Atlas comes down just to the period of the First World War, since there are many sources of information for the years since then. Firm lines are used for only those political frontiers that were clearly defined and surveyed, that is roughly those of the last hundred years: for the most part the Atlas endeavours to portray, through graduated stippling, the broad zones of uncertain loyalty that separated one country from another.

When the distinction seemed useful, in the maps of India for example, the names of political units that were under Muslim rule are shown in black, others in red. Italicized red names are ethnics, that is tribes rather than states, though the distinction is not always easy to make. In records of battles, the victor is named first.

The system of transliteration used by the Encyclopaedia of Islam has in general been adopted for Arabic names, but modern Turkish orthography has been considered more appropriate for Ottoman Anatolia and the Balkans, and conventional spellings have been used for those times when and places where Islam did not prevail. Alternative forms are given in the Index.

Part I. The Early Muslim Earth and Sky (Pages 1–3 and End-papers)

Two Arabic world maps (Page 1). Idrisi compiled his geographical treatise and map of the world in A.D. 1154, to the order of King Roger II of Sicily, and his work acquired much the same authority among Arab scholars as did that of Ptolemy in the academies of Europe. This outline is taken from the maps in the Paris MS, as reduced and copied by F. Schrader (*Atlas de Géographie Historique*, Paris 1922, Map No. 18).

'Ali ibn Aḥmad ibn Muḥammad al-Sharfi of Sfax was the author of a sea-atlas of the Mediterranean of which two copies survive; one in Paris dated to 1551, the other in Oxford to 1571/2. From the Oxford version (MS Marsh 294) have been traced the four sheets which are reproduced on the end-papers of this book. He also drew, in A.D. 1579, a world map which he says that he copied from one (which has not survived) drawn by his uncle Muḥammad; and his own map was copied in turn by his son Muḥammad, whose version is preserved in the Bibliothèque Nationale in Paris (Geography Section, dated A.D. 1600/1).

Al-Sharfi's world map of A.D. 1579 is here rendered in simplified form from the reduced photograph in the publication by Carlo A. Nallino in the *Bolletino della Società Geografica Italiana* V, 1916, 721–736, since in spite of assiduous inquiries the writer has not been able to trace the present whereabouts of the original. In the inscription on the east side the author mentions that his uncle copied the coasts of the 'Syrian Sea' (the Mediterranean) and its ports from a *kunbāṣ* drawn by an inhabitant of Majorca; and in the inscription on the west side he uses the same term, this time in the plural, *kanābiṣ*. These two contexts confirm the well-known observation of ibn Khaldun (Kitāb al-'Ibar, Cairo 1867, I, 10, 11. 11–15), that the Mediterranean sea-charts (now usually referred to as 'Portolan charts') were called in his time (the late 14th or early 15th century) 'compass [charts]'. The word 'compass/*kunbāṣ*' used in this sense can have had nothing to do with the mariner's magnetic compass which was not so called until A.D. 1515: it doubtless derives from the much earlier use of the word to mean a pair of dividers, such as must have been employed to mark out circles and subdivisions of their circumferences, as a guide for the patterns of rhumb or direction lines which were superimposed on these charts and were manifestly their most distinguishing feature.

The Star-charts (Pages 2, 3). The first of these shows the orthodox Arabic names of the constellations and their Classical equivalents: for particulars refer to P. Kunitzsch, *Arabische Sternnamen in Europa* (Wiesbaden, 1959). The twenty-eight *anwā'* or stations along the Ecliptic, through which moved the moon, the planets, and the sun on its annual cycle, are numbered in red, and the particular stars, or star-pairs or clusters, which acted as their markers are pointed out by red arrows. As the sun passed through each *naw'*, the star or constellation involved was thought to influence climatic and other events for a certain number of days. There are many versions of this time-scheme, though they differ only in details: the one which is listed here is taken from the calendar diagram in the sea-atlas of al-Sharfi which is re-drawn and translated on the right-hand back end-paper of this book. Al-Sharfi's diagram shows the date of the dawn setting of each constellation, exactly six months from the rising.

The second chart (Page 3) shows the traditional names of stars and constellations used by Arab sailors in the Indian Ocean. The twenty-eight *anwā'* or stations along the Ecliptic are written with underline. The insets in the middle below show how the simple 'string and board' sextant (*kamāl*) was used to measure the altitudes, or equal altitudes, of stars, with a view to determining the ship's latitude. The risings and settings of particular stars on the horizon were used to ascertain direction, and the points of the Arabic mariner's compass were named after these stars; the corresponding Mediterranean instrument by contrast named its points after the local winds. See G. R. Tibbetts, *Arab Navigation in the Indian Ocean before the entry of the Portuguese* (London, Roy. Asiat. Soc., 1971).

The End-Papers. All four are traced and translated from the Oxford copy (Bodleian—MS Marsh 294) of the Mediterranean Sea-Atlas of 'Ali ibn Aḥmad ibn Muḥammad al-Sharfi of Sfax, dated to A.D. 1571/2.

The al-Sharfis of Sfax were, like Bartholomews of Edinburgh, a family firm of cartographers. They enjoyed a long reputation as map-makers and scientists in Tunisia and Egypt, and Nallino has traced their publications from the sixteenth century to the eighteenth. Each of their two surviving sixteenth-century atlases contained, in addition to sea-charts, a world diagram, and information in the form of tables and text about calendars and also about how to ascertain the time and direction for prayers. The sea-charts show the Mediterranean and Black Sea in segments, in a style that was current in the Mediterranean at least from the late thirteenth century A.D.

Part II. The Extension of the Muslim World (Pages 4–13)

Islam arose near the centre of the Old World, and this series is intended to illustrate its spread and the connections, linguistic, economic and cultural, between the regions where it prevailed and the further parts of Europe, Asia and Africa.

The broad line which shows the limits of the Muslim world must be understood generally as a transitional zone, as should most political boundaries before the time of the final map. The Muslim territories as here recognised usually fall within this category through conquest or political allegiance, but in the case of some regions, such as East Africa, because the influence of Muslim traders was so powerful and pervasive.

Because of the important part played by Muslim countries in the transport of commodities, inventions and ideas between peoples at the extremities of the old continents, special attention is given throughout this series to routes of travel and what moved along them. By the year 1900 (Page 13) railways have become more important than roads, especially as instruments of conquest and control.

In the compilation of this series, the following atlases have proved helpful: H. W. Hazard, *Atlas of Islamic History*, Princeton 1951; R. Roolvink, *Historical Atlas of the Muslim Peoples*, Djambatan, Amsterdam 1957; A. M. Magued, *Atlas Historique du Monde Islamique au Moyen Age*, Cairo 1960; R. Reichert, *A Historical and Regional Atlas of the Arabic World*, Univ. Bahia, Salvador 1969.

Part III. Early Arabia (Pages 14, 15)

Pre-Islamic (Classical) Arabia (Page 14). Ptolemy's map of Arabia—his sixth Asian sheet—is reduced from the original compilation by A. Sprenger (*Die Alte Geographie Arabiens*, Bern 1875). This version reproduces precisely the original of Ptolemy, unlike the many manuscript and printed versions which are usually roughly copied at several removes from an original which may itself have been inaccurately plotted. Ptolemy himself appreciated the danger and intended that his work be handed down in the form of lists of co-ordinates which could be re-plotted with precision at any time.

It will be evident from a comparison with the modern outline that Ptolemy in his map exaggerated east–west or longitudinal distances by comparison with his north–south or latitudinal measures. In particular, he placed Dianae Oraculum (Salala) much too far east of Arabia Emporium (Aden), and effectively excluded the long desert stretch of the south Arabian shore opposite the Island of Masira. This persistent error stems from Ptolemy's under-estimate of the size of the Sphere, which led him to exaggerate all linear measures when they were plotted on his globe. In the north–south dimension he would automatically correct this exaggeration when he used direct measurements of latitude; but there were at that time no means of making regular and accurate measurements of arcs of longitude, so his east–west distances remained uncorrected.

The route for transporting the frankincense from Dhufar to Gerra on the Gulf is reconstructed from the evidence of Pliny and Ptolemy, as interpreted by the compiler in "The Construction of Ptolemy's map of South Arabia", *Proceedings of the Seminar for Arabian Studies*, 4, 1974, 5–9. Ptolemy seems to advance his inland locations consistently too far from the coast, with the result that he leaves no space for the great southern sand-sea of the Rub' al-Khali. This error is doubtless one result of his persistent exaggeration, explained in the preceding paragraph, of longitudinal distances. Another such effect may be his widening of the Sinus Persicus: but the whole configuration of this Gulf and its islands is wildly awry, and it is hard to understand the considerable space that Ptolemy leaves between the island of Ichara (Failaka) and Coromanis Oppidum (Kuwait), if these conventional identifications are accepted. Perhaps Ptolemy was here working beyond the limits of reliable information.

The extensive classical remains at Thadj in al-Hasa, a site not yet identified but possibly to be correlated with Ptolemy's Phigeia, are discussed by W. E. James, "On the location of Gerra", in F. Altheim and R. Stiehl, *Die Araber in der alten Welt* V 2, Berlin 1969, 36–57 (see p. 54). It seems to have lain on a road between the Gulf and the oases of the district of Yamama. Likewise the road connecting Nadjran with Yamama is drawn with more confidence following the excavations of Dr. A. R. al-Ansari at al-Faw (Saudi Arabian Dept. of Antiquities and Museums, *An Introduction to Saudi Arabian Antiquities*, Riyadh 1975, 157, 175). Ptolemy's Nagara, which must correspond with Nadjran, is well out of place in longitude—it would be more acceptable in the position of Mara or even Amara (a duplicated name?) to the west in the same latitude—and there may be some confusion here.

Pre-Islamic SW Arabia (Page 15, above). The toponyms in block letters are transliterations from the South Arabian alphabets, which leave the vowels uncertain; the modern names as written with a hard *jīm*, according to the local pronunciation. The roads are by no means certain, and are largely inferred from circumstantial evidence. Note two source-maps: H. von Wissmann, *Southern Arabia*, 2 sheets, London, Roy. Geog. Soc. 1957/8; N. St. J. Groom, *South-West Arabia*, London, Roy. Geog. Soc.

Arabia c. A.D. 600 (Page 15, below). Henri Lammens, *L'Arabie occidentale avant l'Hégire*, Beyrouth 1928, describes the fairs, which were held in an annual cycle clockwise round the peninsula; see also Ign. Guidi, *L'Arabie antéislamique*, Paris 1921; Sa'id al-Afghānī, *Aswāq al-'Arab*, Damascus 1960; R. B. Serjeant, "Hud and other pre-Islamic prophets", *Le Muséon* 1954, 121. For the site of the dam and the road across the eastern Rub' al-Khālī, see the *Introduction to Saudi Arabian Antiquities* quoted with reference to Page 14.

Part IV. The Near and Middle East

Abbasid Iran (Pages 16/17). A. Sprenger, *Die Post- und Reiserouten des Orients*, Leipzig 1864; G. le Strange, *The Lands of the Eastern Caliphate*, Cambridge 1905; C. E. Bosworth, *Sistan under the Arabs*, IsMEO, Rome 1968.

Seismic Map of the Middle East (Page 18) is based on the interpretation and analysis of historical records, carried out at Imperial College, London. See N. N. Ambraseys, "Studies in historical seismicity and tectonics", in W. C. Brice (ed.), *The Environmental History of the Near and Middle East*, London 1978, Chap. 12.

The Near East, C12 (Page 22, above). René Dussaud, *Topographie historique de la Syrie antique et médiévale*, Paris 1927. The early drainage system of Irāḳ is reconstructed by Rashid al-Fil (al-Feel), *The Historical Geography of Iraq . . . 1258–1534*, Baghdad 1967.

The Pilgrim Routes of Arabia (Page 22, below). For the Egyptian road see J. Jomier, *Le mahmal et la caravanne égyptienne des pèlerins de la Mecque*, Cairo 1953. The Darb Zubeida from Irak has been explored by Dr. S. Rashid of Riyadh. The late Richard Holmes kindly obtained itineraries of the Hadramaut road from friends who had made the journey long ago.

The Holy Cities of Makka and Madīna (Page 23). The outlines are modern and precise. The best of the older published plans are those of Eldon Rutter, *The Holy Cities of Arabia*, 1928: these are copied, without acknowledgement, in the Naval Intelligence Division's *Western Arabia and the Red Sea*, Geographical Handbook Series 1945, 558, 562; they are recognisable but not accurate.

Transoxiana and the Ghurids (Page 24). See the references to Pages 16/17.

The Middle East, C14 and C18 (Pages 25, 26). On strategic matters the *Historical Atlas of Iran*, Univ. Tehran, 1971 is especially informative.

The Middle East, CC19–20 (Page 27). This sheet shows the new railways. They enabled the Russians to annex and hold the Caucasus and Trans-Caspia, and the British to take over the Sudan and Sind. Abd al-Hamid built a railway to strengthen his hold on Arabia, and the Germans had almost completed the line to Baghdad at the outbreak of the First World War. Then the aeroplane ended the era of the strategic railway.

Part V. Anatolia and the Balkans

The Turkish immigration to Anatolia (Pages 28, 29). These four maps are the work of Dr Michael Hendy. W. M. Ramsay (*A Historical Geography of Asia Minor*, London 1890) made some brief but perceptive remarks on the subject, but his interest was mainly in earlier periods.

The first map on Page 28 illustrates the lines of communication that supported the broad natural frontier of the Taurus and Anti-Taurus Mountains and enabled the Byzantine Empire to withstand the pressure from Arab Syria for several centuries.

The second map on Page 28 shows the completely changed state of affairs after the crucial battle of Manzikert (A.D. 1071—see Page 9), following which the Turkish tribes were able to outflank the Anti-Taurus barrier on the north. The former imperial system of roads and commerce substantially collapsed along with the cities, the plateau was 'nomadized', and the Byzantines pressed back on to the coasts.

The upper part of Page 29 records the more settled conditions when Selçuk rule was established. Some towns were re-founded and some roads re-opened; but as Ramsay remarked the numerous and heavily-fortified *hans* along these roads are an indication of the insecurity of the countryside and the need to protect the traffic against the still unsettled tribes.

The lower half of Page 29 shows the further constriction of the Byzantine realm into the west and north-west of the peninsula during the early phase of Ottoman expansion. The next stage of Ottoman conquest is recorded on Page 30.

Ottoman expansion, A.D. 1362–1402 (Page 30). The trade-routes of Anatolia converged at this time on Bursa. The Ottoman advance into the Balkans outflanked Constantinople by way of Gallipoli, and thereafter followed the main valleys and mountain passes.

Anadolu and Rumeli in the later C17 (Page 31) relies on three main sources, to which Dr. Colin Heywood has kindly drawn attention:

K. Kemal Özergin, "Rumeli Kadılıklarında 1078 Düzenlemesi", in *İsmail Hakkı Uzunçarşılıya Armağan* (*Türk Tarih Kurumu Yayınları* VII Dizi Se. 70), Ankara 1976. This is a gazeteer of Rumeli dated 1078/1667–8.

Riza Bozkurt, *Osmanlı İmparatorluğunda Kollar, Ulak ve İaşe Menzilleri*, Ankara 1966—an edition of several itineraries in Anatolia and Rumelia, dated between A.D. 1698 and 1756.

Faik Reşit Unat, "Ahmet III. devrinde yapılmış bir Önasya haritası, H. 1139/D. 1726", *Tarih Vesikaları* I. 2, 1941–42, 160—a clear facsimile of a large-scale contemporary map.

Ottoman Naval Power in the C16 (Page 32, above) is based on a study by Colin Imber of Ottoman naval archives.

Istanbul (Page 32, below). Historic buildings are shown in relation to the main modern thoroughfares. A large-scale plan of the city in the last century is reproduced in segments by Ekrem Hakkı Ayverdi, *19. Asırda İstanbul Haritası*, İstanbul, Şehir Matbaası, 1958. See also J. J. Hellert, *Atlas de l'Empire ottomane*, Paris 1843, Pl. 37.

Sectaries in Anatolia and the Balkans (Page 33). See F. W. Hasluck, *Christianity and Islam under the Sultans*, 2 vols., Oxford 1929; J. K. Birge, *The Bektashi Order of Dervishes*, London 1937. J.-L. Bacqué-Grammont has generously loaned a copy of his study "Notes et documents sur la révolte de Şah Veli b. Şeyẖ Celāl (Etudes turco-safavides III)" in advance of its appearance in *Archivum Ottomanicum* 7, 1975.

Anadolu and Rumeli in the later C19 (Page 34). See Fr. Taeschner, *Das anatolische Wegenetz*, Leipzig 1926, also art. 'Anadolu', *Encyc. Islam*[1]; J. J. Hellert, *Atlas Historique de l'Empire ottomane*, Paris 1843 (with Joseph de Hammer's *Histoire de l'Empire ottomane*).

Part VI. Muslim Spain (Pages 35–39)

The two maps on Page 35 show the general circumstances of the establishment of Muslim rule in Spain, and they correspond with those on a larger scale on Pages 36 and 37. The Umayyads used an existing mesh of mediaeval roads, which themselves were inherited from the Roman administration. The main road junctions of Muslim Spain were Seville and Cordoba in the south, and Mérida and Toledo on the frontier. Further north a broad depopulated zone separated the two peoples. It may be assumed that the earlier roads still existed between the eleventh and the fifteenth centuries when local kings took over and the reconquest slowly advanced (Pages 38 and 39); but they were evidently in poor repair, and the armies of the reconquest made much use of the 'green tracks' that the shepherds followed on their seasonal migrations. These are shown on Page 39.

There are historical sections in two general atlases of Spain:

Aguilar, Departamento de Cartografia, *Nuevo Atlas de España*, n.d., historical maps pp. 158–9.

Instituto Geografico y Catastral, *Atlas Nacional de España*, Madrid 1965, Lamina 81, "Historia de los Caminos".

Reference may also be made to two books of history: Luis Garcia de Valdeavallano, *Historia de España* (Madrid 1952) and Ramon Menéndez Pidal, *The Cid and his Spain* (London 1934).

Part VII. North Africa (Pages 40–43)

The five maps on Pages 40, 42 and 43 follow those of Page 35, and make up a sequence from the fourteenth century onwards. Page 41 shows the same Mediterranean coast, together with the Sahara, the Sudan and West Africa, early in the seventeenth century. The links between these territories at other times can be seen, on a smaller scale, in the series of Part II. Recent work on African history is summarized in F. D. Fage and R. A. Oliver (eds.), *Cambridge History of Africa* (1975–8).

From the latest excavations it is evident that Old Jenne was smelting iron already in the third century B.C., and by the ninth century A.D. had grown into a great city at the head of the inland delta of the Niger. Gold, slaves and kola nuts (a permitted stimulant) were brought together here from the rain-forests further south and floated down the Niger to the lower part of the inland delta, where Timbuktu was founded, according to tradition, about A.D. 1100. From here the trade moved overland along the trans-Saharan tracks. It is possible that metallurgy and distant commerce were practised equally early in the towns of the other West African empires, which can be traced eastwards from Mali along the Sudan road on Page 41.

Part VIII. India and the Indian Seas (Pages 44–53)

Pages 44–46 show three phases of navigation in the Indian Ocean. The techniques of sailing are analysed in Gerald R. Tibbetts, *Arab Navigation in the Indian Ocean before the entry of the Portuguese* (London, Roy. Asiat. Soc., 1971). James Prinsep earlier published translations of excerpts from the *Muḥīṭ* of Seydī 'Alī concerning the shipping routes of the Arabian Sea (*Jnl. Asiat. Soc. Bengal*, 1834/6/7/8/9). Evidently the dhow captains in order to find their ways (Page 45) relied not only on astronomy but also on natural indications, sea-birds, marine fauna, the set of the waves, cloud banks, coastal silhouettes and the like. In 1498 da Gama was guided by ibn Madjid on a standard route, but subsequently the Portuguese fleet was able to pioneer a more direct line of sailing to the Cape of Good Hope (Page 46). In this general field at least two questions remain to be answered. First, according to the account of the sixteenth-century historian Jeronymo Osorio, Bishop of Sylves (Book I of his *Life and Deeds of King Manuel*, section on the island of Egesimba), the Arab navigators whom da Gama and his crews met in the vicinity of Madagascar had magnetic card-compasses with gimbal suspension. Did they invent this elaborate version of the mariner's compass and pass it on to the Mediterranean mariners? Second, three manuscript maps of A.D. 1502, the Canerio and Cantino charts and the anonymous Portuguese 'Munich' parchment, show the coasts and islands of the Indian Ocean with high precision, and are a vast improvement on the best versions of Ptolemy and Idrisi that we know from before then. Da Gama returned from his first voyage in 1499 and did not go back to India until 1502. So these charts of 1502 must be based on specimens which da Gama brought back in 1499. He had certainly not surveyed these coasts himself, so did he acquire some Arab sea-charts, of a kind which we know from the chroniclers certainly to have existed, but not one of which has survived, so far as we know?

For Islam in India see E. J. Rapson *et al.*, ed., *The Cambridge History of India*, 6 vols., 1922–53; R. C. Majumdar, ed., *The History and Culture of the Indian People*, 10 vols., Bombay 1951–65; Colin Davies, *An Historical Atlas of the Indian Peninsula*, Oxford 1949; Joseph E. Schwartzberg (ed.), *A Historical Atlas of South Asia*, Chicago Univ. 1978. The demographic inset on Page 50 has been prepared with the help of Professor T. O. Ling; see K. S. Lal, *Growth of Muslim Population in Mediaeval India*, Delhi 1973: other insets show the uncertainties about the breadth of the Deccan.

Islam entered India at the time of the Umayyad Caliphate through conquest, first by way of the Makran coast and subsequently over the frontier passes into the Northern Punjab. Meanwhile Muslim traders settled along the coast of the far south-west in Travancore. Sind and Punjab were converted early, and the plains of the Upper Ganges brought under Muslim rule by the Abbasids in the ninth century A.D. The Ghaznavids and later the Sultans of Delhi controlled the northern plains and the plateau of Malwa, but by-passed the Rajput strongholds of the Aravalli range which remained Hindu enclaves through Mughul times. The mountains and jungles of Khandesh and Gondwana were a barrier against conquest of the Deccan, which could best be outflanked through Gujarat along the west coast (Page 48). The Muslim Sultanates of the Deccan (Page 50) occupied the 'trapps' of the North-Western Deccan with their level stretches of fertile black volcanic soils, and left the more broken terrain of the Southern Deccan to Vijayanagar. The roads on Pages 52 and 53 are taken from contemporary sources, and show the growing importance of the ports and coastal cities as the European powers extended their trade.

Part IX. The Far East (Pages 54–57)

Indonesia and Java (Pages 54–56). Islam reached the northern tip of Sumatra, the region of Atjen (Atchin), through the medium of merchants from Gujarat in the thirteenth century A.D., but only spread widely through the Indonesian archipelago some two hundred years later, just before the arrival of the Portuguese. At that time the islands were very vaguely known to European cartographers, who had only Idrisi and Polo to help them; and until well into the sixteenth century the Portuguese revealed the outlines only of certain limited stretches of island shores around the Celebes Sea, where they collected the spices. H. J. de Graaf, who has compiled the three charts of Indonesia, is the author of *Geschiedenis van Indonesië* ('s-Gravenhage—Bandoeng, 1949).

Islam in China (Page 57). Islam penetrated China by two main routes: from the south-east, following the well-established maritime communication lines to Canton; and from the north-west, passing over the Pamirs and through the Tarim Basin to Kansu and Shensi, following the ancient Silk Road.

Many of the Muslim merchants, soldiers and freebooters who entered China via these routes (predominantly Arabs and Persians in the south-east, and Turks and Persians in the north-west) settled down and took Chinese wives, thus giving rise to the Hui (Chinese-speaking) Muslim community which is today scattered throughout China. Besides the Hui and the Turkic Muslims, China also has a small Iranian community of Tadjiks in the far west, and a group of Muslims with Mongol blood, the Tung-hsiang, in Kansu. All Chinese Muslims are Sunnī Ḥanafī, with the single exception of the Tadjiks, who are Nizārī Ismā'īlī, or followers of the Aga Khan. Chinese Muslims, and in particular the Hui, are divided into numerous local sects. The most important Sufi group is the Nakshbandiyya.

Sources for the early coming of Islam to China are: Isaac Mason, *When and How Muhammadanism Entered China*, London, the China Society, 1932, and Tadeusz Lewicki, "Les Premiers Commerçants arabes en Chine", *Rocznik Orientalistyczny* XI (1935), 172–86. For the north-west see: H. A. R. Gibb, *The Arab Conquests in Central Asia*, New York 1923; AMS reprint 1970. For the south-west (Yunnan) see: G. Cordier, *Les Musulmans de Yunnan*, Hanoi 1927. For the great mid-nineteenth century rebellions see: Chu Wen-djang, *The Moslem Rebellion in North-West China 1862–1878*, The Hague 1966; also W. L. Bales, *Tso Tsung-t'ang, Soldier and Statesman of Old China*, Shanghai 1937; the latter is particularly useful for maps. For more recent works see: François Joyaux, "Les Musulmans en Chine Populaire", *Notes et Etudes Documentaires*, 2, 915 (22nd August 1962); also see the very useful map in *Chinese Muslims in Progress*, Peking, China Islamic Association, 1957, similarly in Nagel's *Encyclopaedia Guide China*, Geneva 1968.

THE WORLD ACCORDING TO IDRISI, A.D. 1154

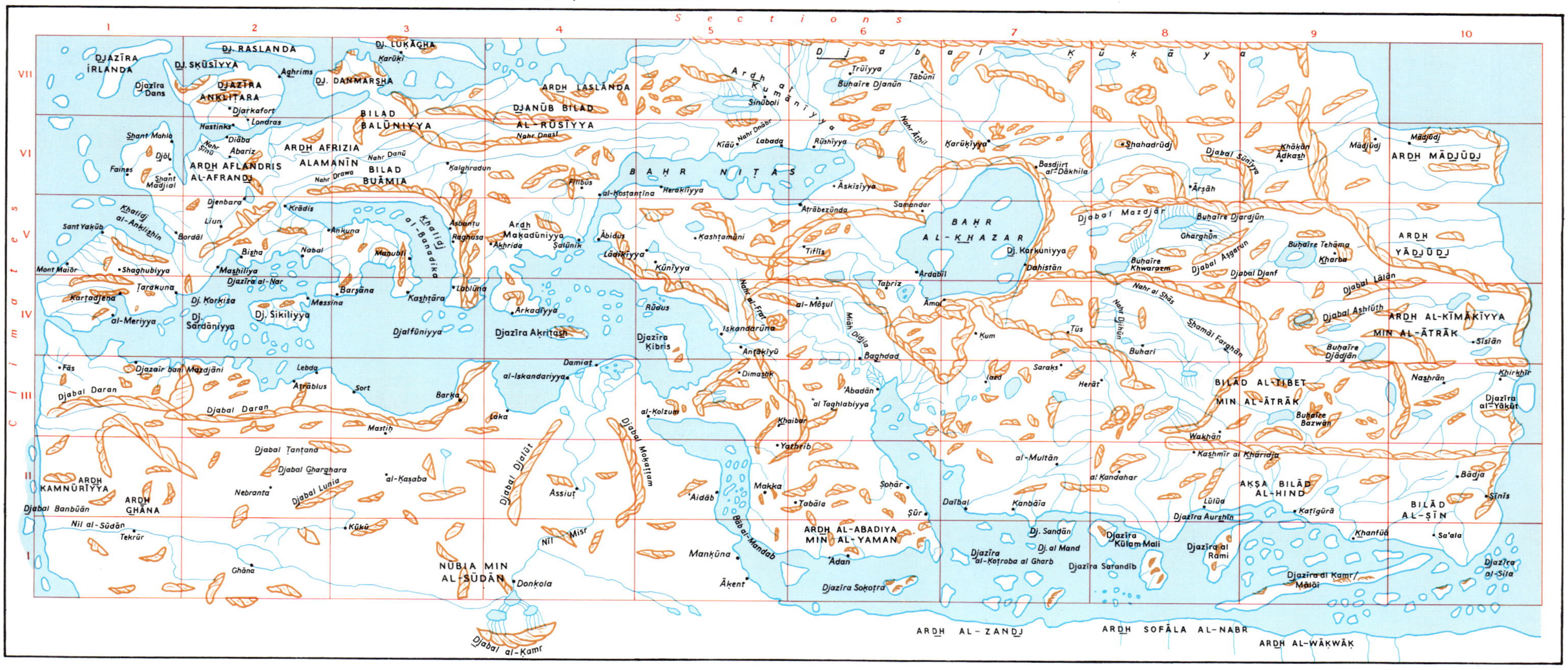

AL-SHARFI WORLD MAP A.D. 1579

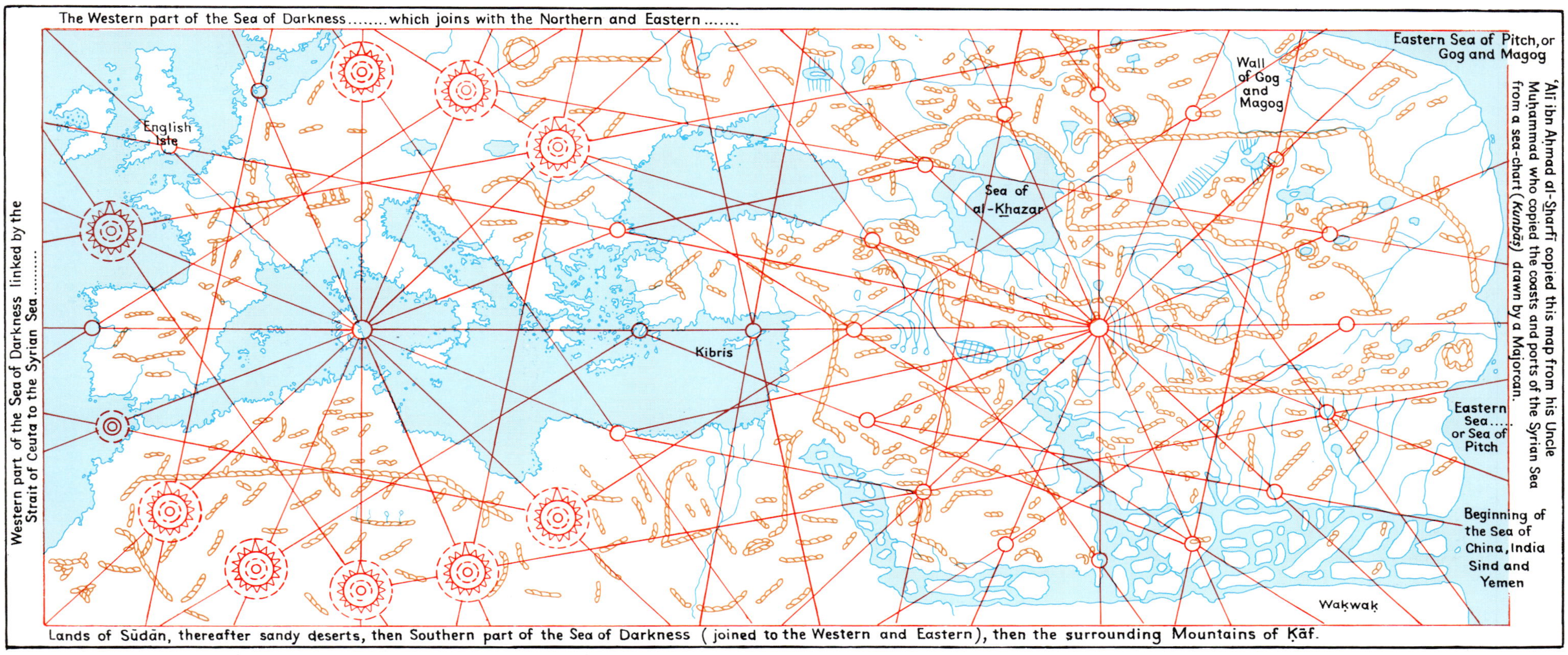

Idrisi's world map owes much to that of Ptolemy, except in the Far East: the Arabs were early aware of the sea-route to China, and Idrisi therefore opened a passage eastwards from the enclosed lake by which Ptolemy had represented the Indian Ocean. The numerous islands of this ocean and the long extension of the African coast to form its southern shore, in both Idrisi's scheme and al-Sharfi's copy, bear little resemblance to reality: but there is reason to think—as argued in the Introduction (p. viii) in connection with Pages 44–46—that there were in early use in the Indian Ocean, as also in the Mediterranean, practical sea-charts of an accuracy greatly superior to that of their 'academic' counterparts.

It will be evident that al-Sharfi has here combined two sources: an outline of the Mediterranean and Euxine derived from a sea-chart, and a representation of the rest of the *œcoumene* in the standard Idrisi style. In a similar way, European cartographers of the time sometimes inserted a 'Portolan' version of the Mediterranean into a world-map taken essentially from Ptolemy.

Al-Sharfi has also abandoned the rectangular partition of Idrisi's scheme and repeated in Asia the circle of rhumb-lines that overlies the Mediterranean.

It will be apparent that the shape of his Mediterranean, which al-Sharfi says was taken from a Majorcan sea-chart, is considerably more accurate than that which Idrisi copied from Ptolemy. The Majorcan chart acknowledged by al-Sharfi was evidently in the 'Portolan' style of which many examples have survived from about A.D. 1275 to 1600. Most were inscribed in Italian or Catalan, some in Greek, Turkish or Arabic, but all used outlines which were virtually identical, even as to their defects: for example, the west coast of the Iberian peninsula was regularly drawn on a smaller scale than the east, as also in the case of the Balkan promontory. It seems clear that all these charts were derived from a standard format which was established, possibly as early as Classical times, by piecing together numerous fragments of detailed coastal surveys undertaken from shipboard.

ARABIC CONSTELLATIONS

Stars of the Middle Heavens

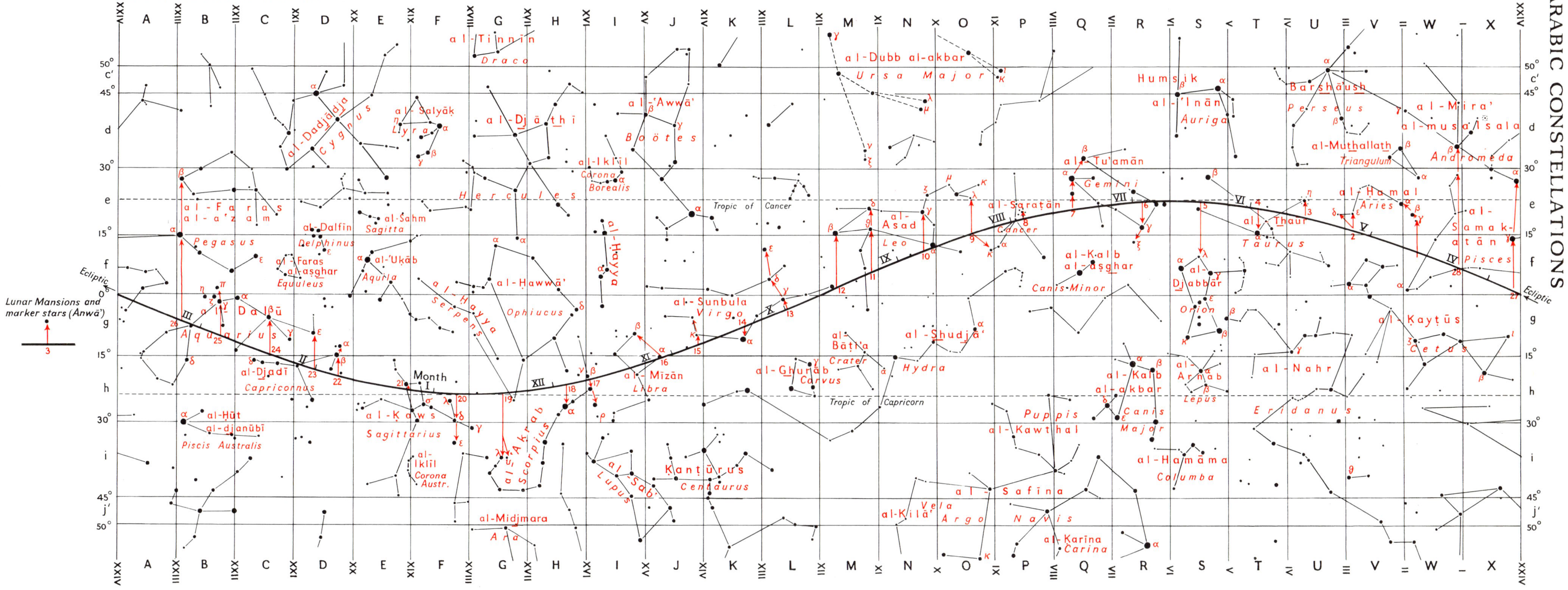

Northern Circumpolar Stars

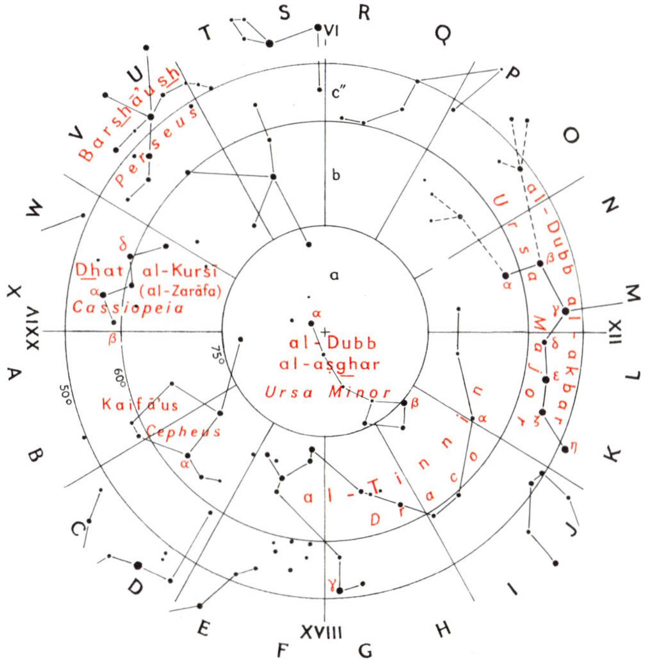

Southern Circumpolar Stars

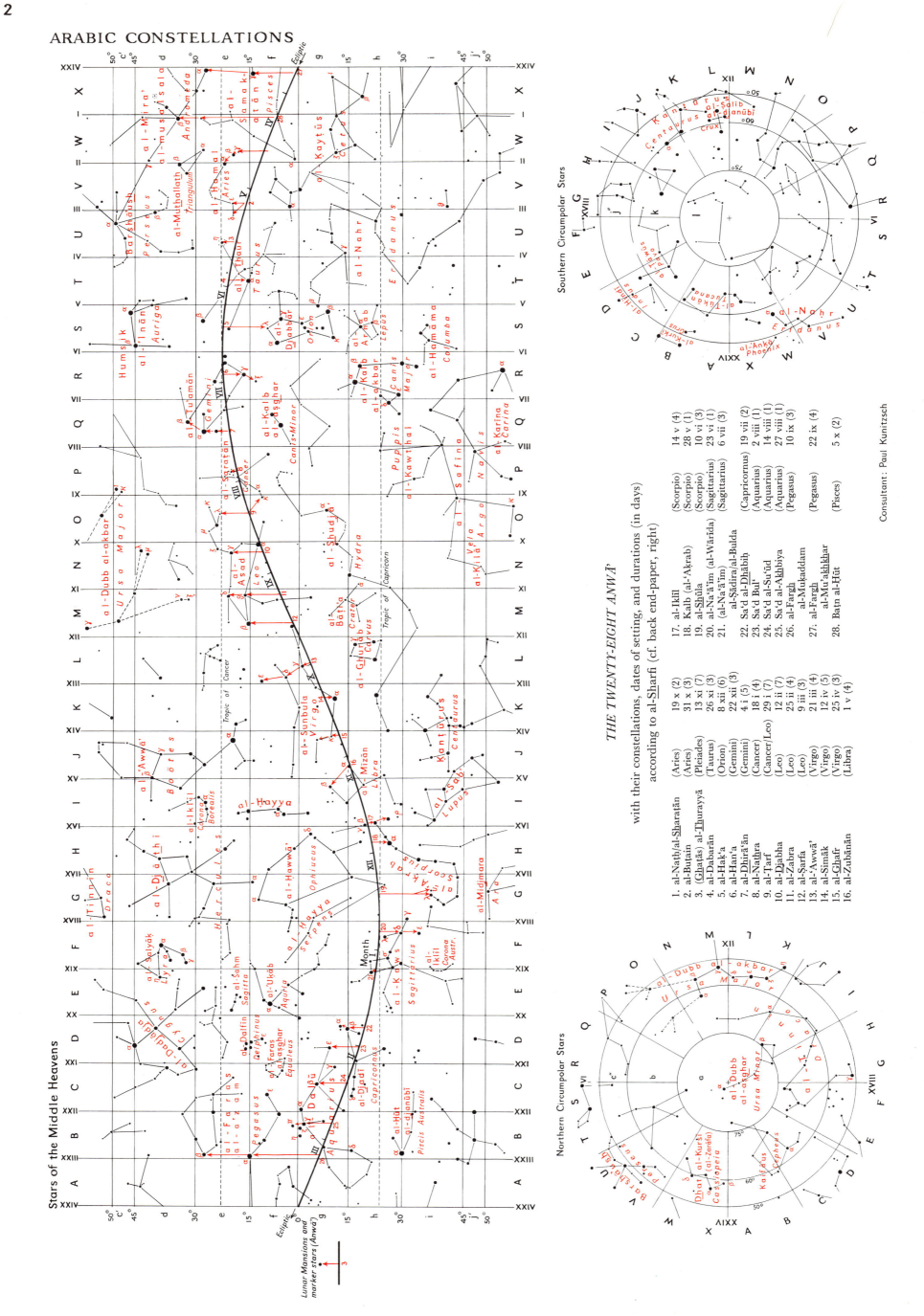

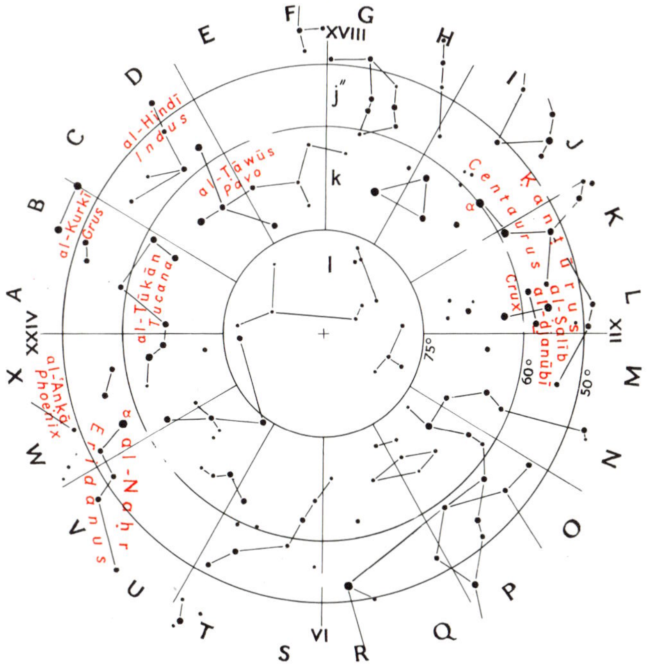

THE TWENTY-EIGHT ANWĀ'

with their constellations, dates of setting, and durations (in days) according to al-Sharfi (cf. back end-paper, right)

1. al-Naṭḥ/al-Sharaṭān	(Aries)	19 x (2)	17. al-Iklīl	(Scorpio)	14 v (4)
2. al-Buṭain	(Aries)	31 x (3)	18. Kalb (al-'Aḳrab)	(Scorpio)	28 v (1)
3. (Ghaṭās) al-Thurayyā	(Pleiades)	13 xi (7)	19. al-Shūla	(Scorpio)	10 vi (3)
4. al-Dabarān	(Taurus)	26 xi (3)	20. al-Na'ā'im (al-Wārida)	(Sagittarius)	23 vi (1)
5. al-Haḳ'a	(Orion)	8 xii (6)	21. (al-Na'ā'im) al-Ṣādira/al-Bulda	(Sagittarius)	6 vii (3)
6. al-Han'a	(Gemini)	22 xii (3)	22. Sa'd al-Dhābiḥ	(Capricornus)	19 vii (2)
7. al-Dhirā'ān	(Gemini)	4 i (5)	23. Sa'd Bul'	(Aquarius)	2 viii (1)
8. al-Nathra	(Cancer)	18 i (4)	24. Sa'd al-Su'ūd	(Aquarius)	14 viii (1)
9. al-Ṭarf	(Cancer/Leo)	29 i (7)	25. Sa'd al-Akhbiya	(Aquarius)	27 viii (1)
10. al-Djabha	(Leo)	12 ii (7)	26. al-Fargh al-Muḳaddam	(Pegasus)	10 ix (3)
11. al-Zabra	(Leo)	25 ii (4)	27. al-Fargh al-Mu'akhkhar	(Pegasus)	22 ix (4)
12. al-Ṣarfa	(Leo)	9 iii (3)	28. Baṭn al-Ḥūt	(Pisces)	5 x (2)
13. al-'Awwā'	(Virgo)	21 iii (4)			
14. al-Simāk	(Virgo)	12 iv (5)			
15. al-Ghafr	(Virgo)	25 iv (3)			
16. al-Zubānān	(Libra)	1 v (4)			

Consultant: Paul Kunitzsch

STAR NAMES USED BY THE ARABS IN THE INDIAN OCEAN

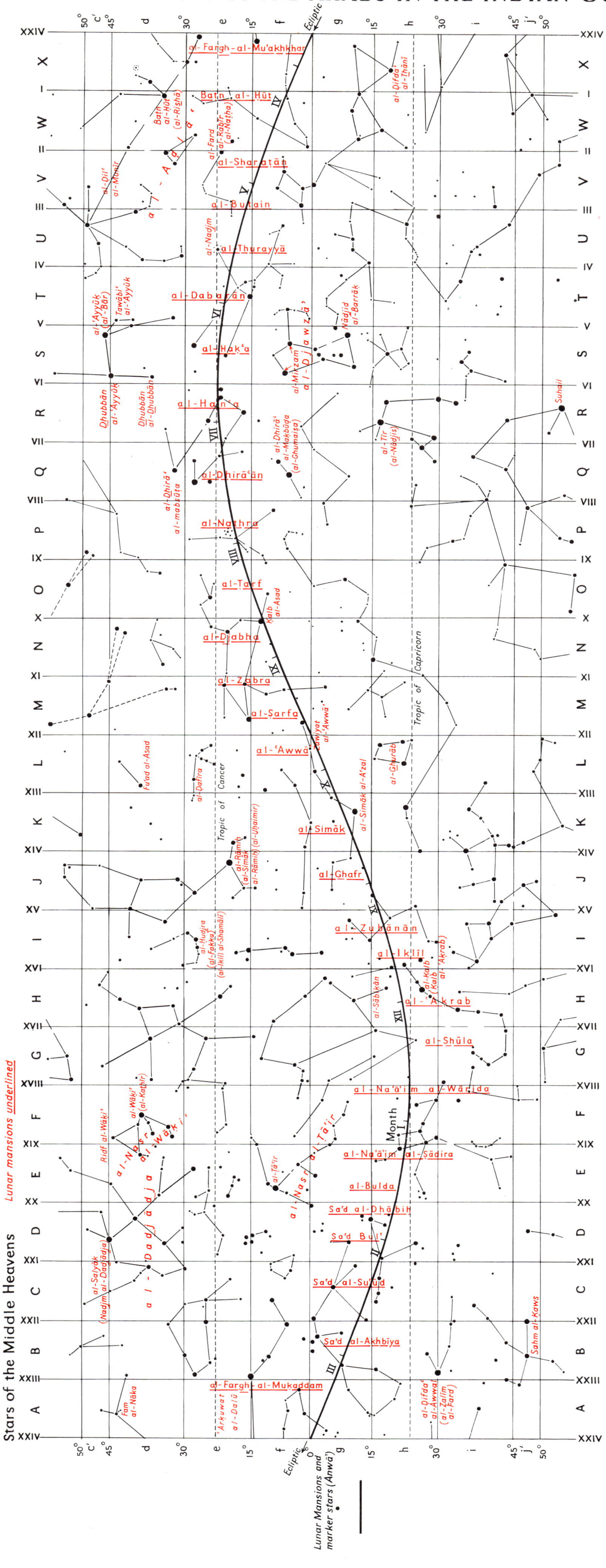

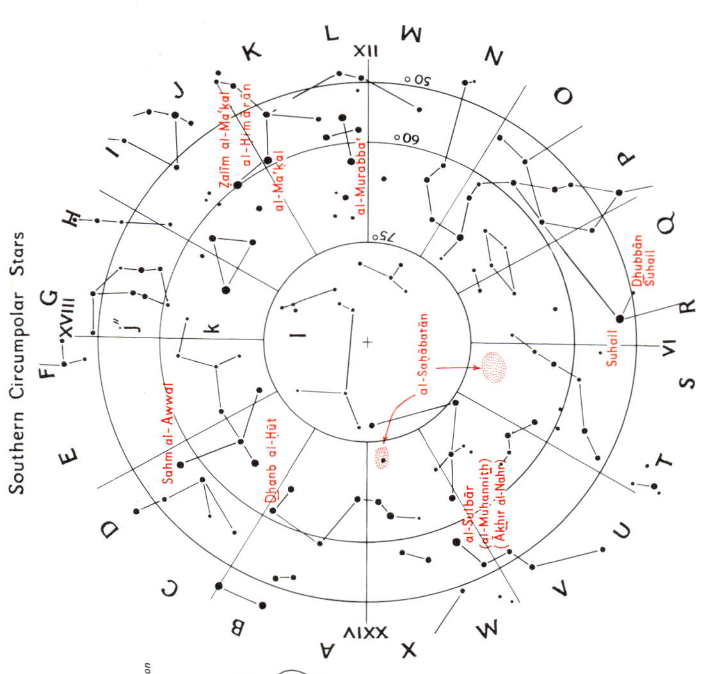

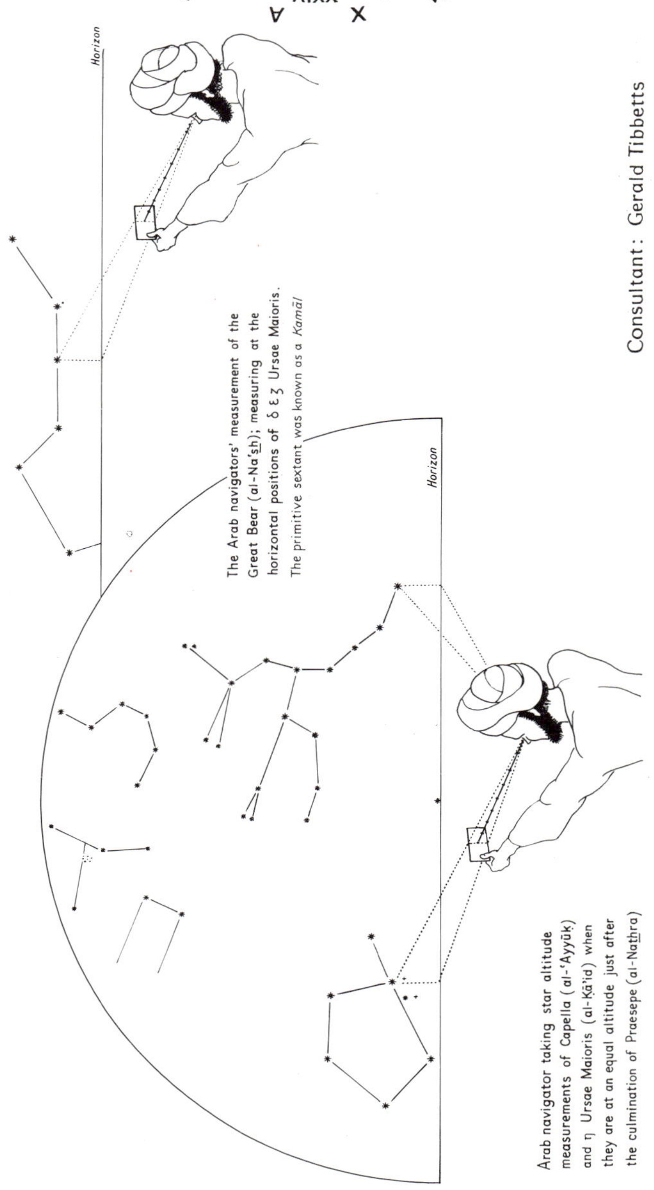

The Arab navigators' measurement of the Great Bear (al-Na'sh); measuring at the horizontal positions of δ ε ζ Ursae Maioris. The primitive sextant was known as a *Kamāl*

Arab navigator taking star altitude measurements of Capella (al-'Ayyūk) and η Ursae Maioris (al-Kā'id) when they are at an equal altitude just after the culmination of Praesepe (al-Nathra)

Consultant: Gerald Tibbetts

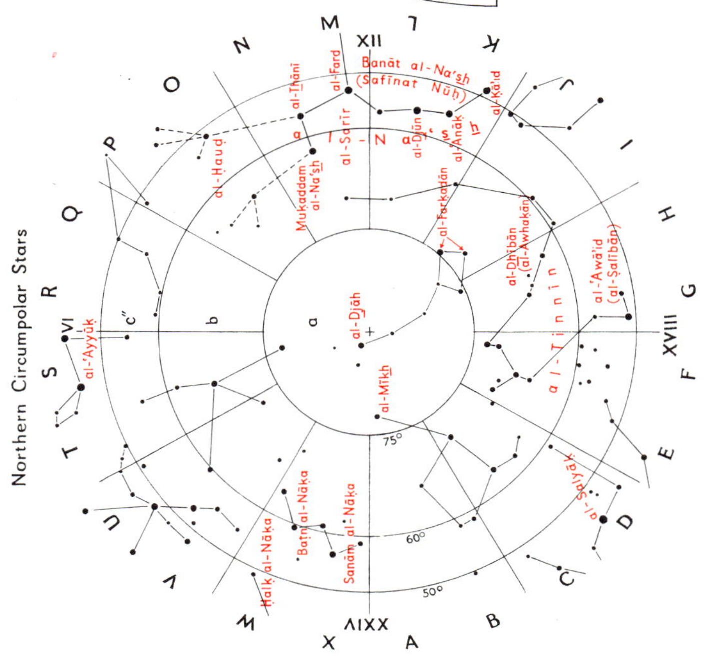

THE LINGUISTIC REGIONS OF THE ISLAMIC WORLD

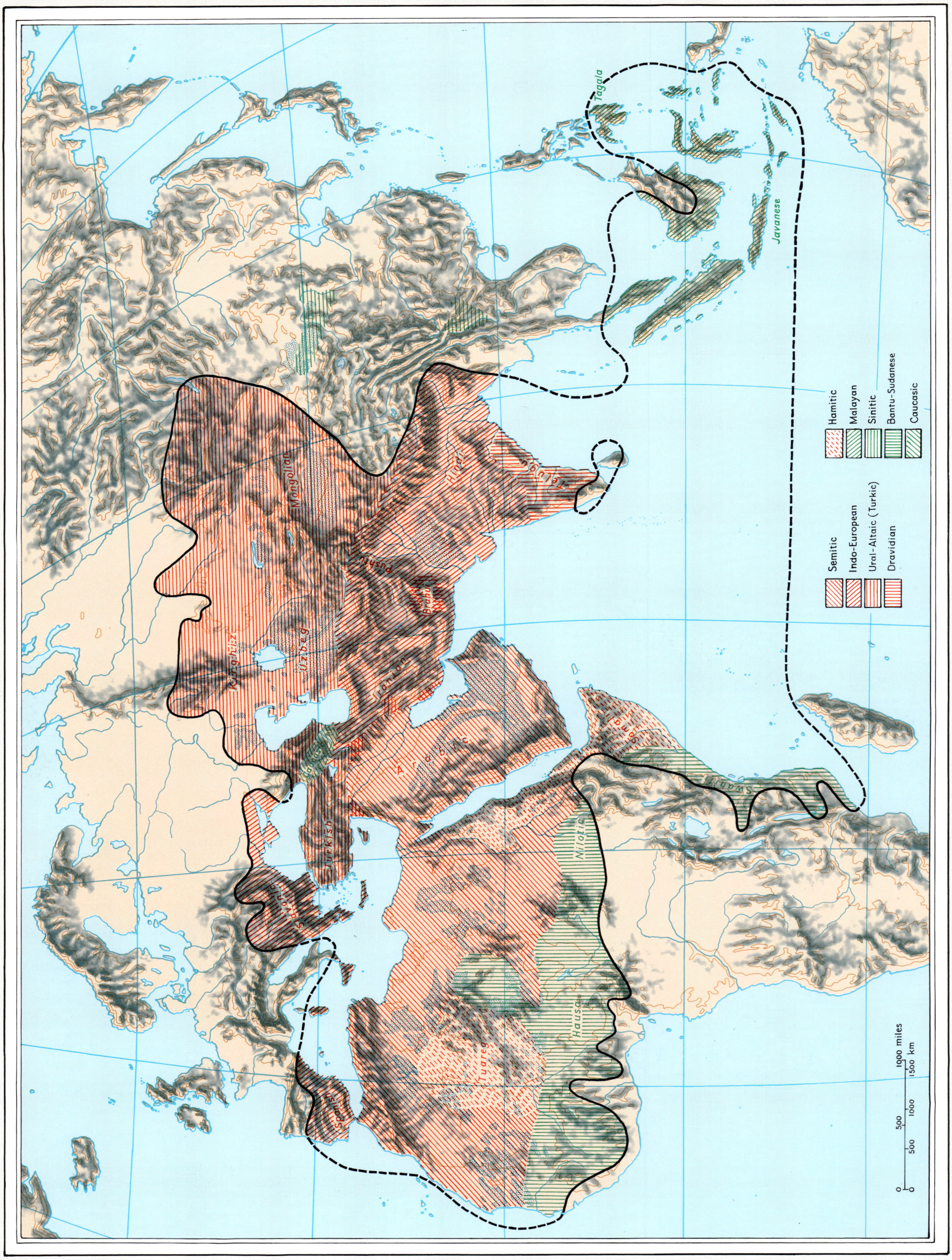

THE PRE-ISLAMIC WORLD c. A.D. 600

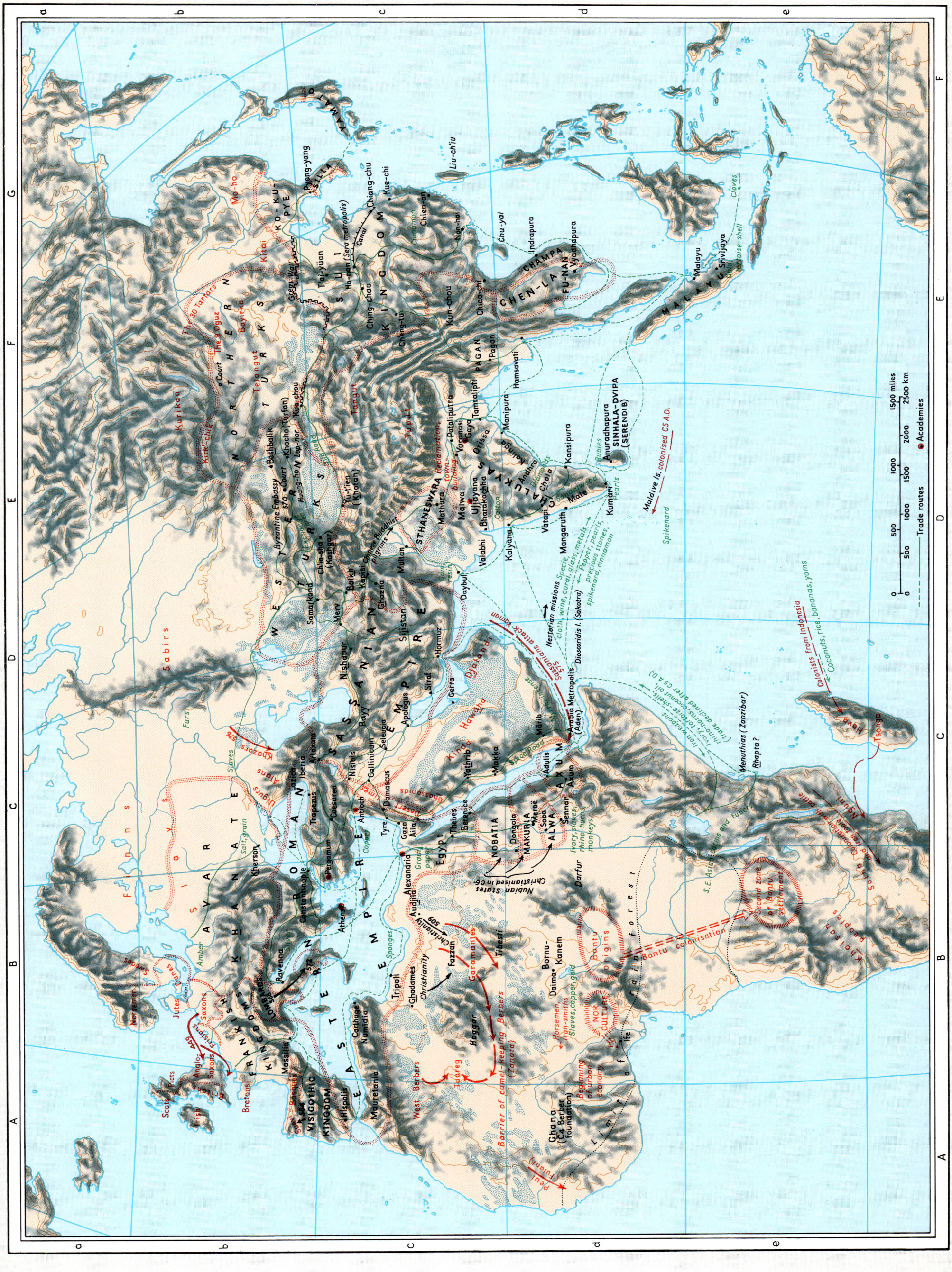

MUSLIM EXPANSION until A.D. 661

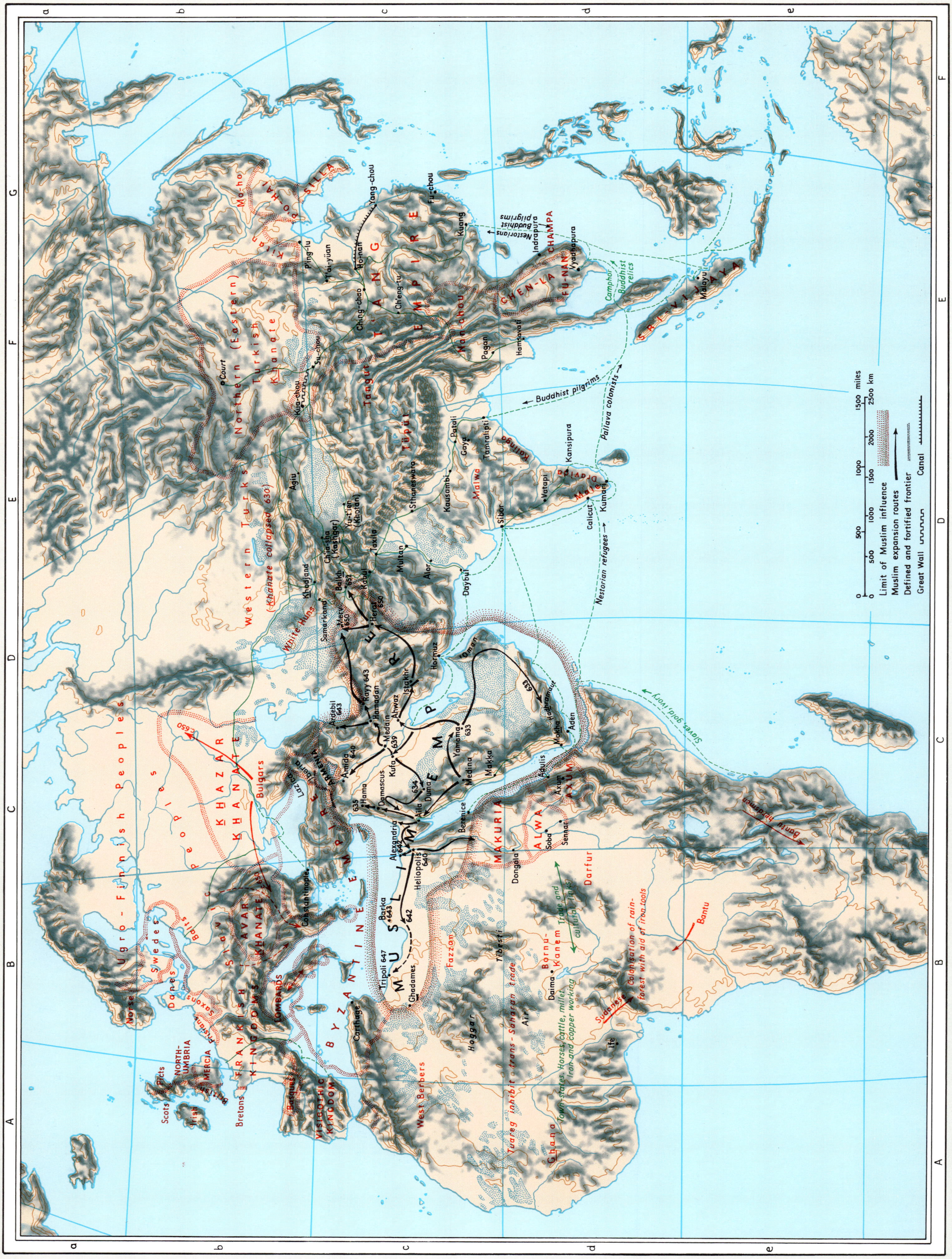

THE UMAYYAD EMPIRE c. A.D. 750

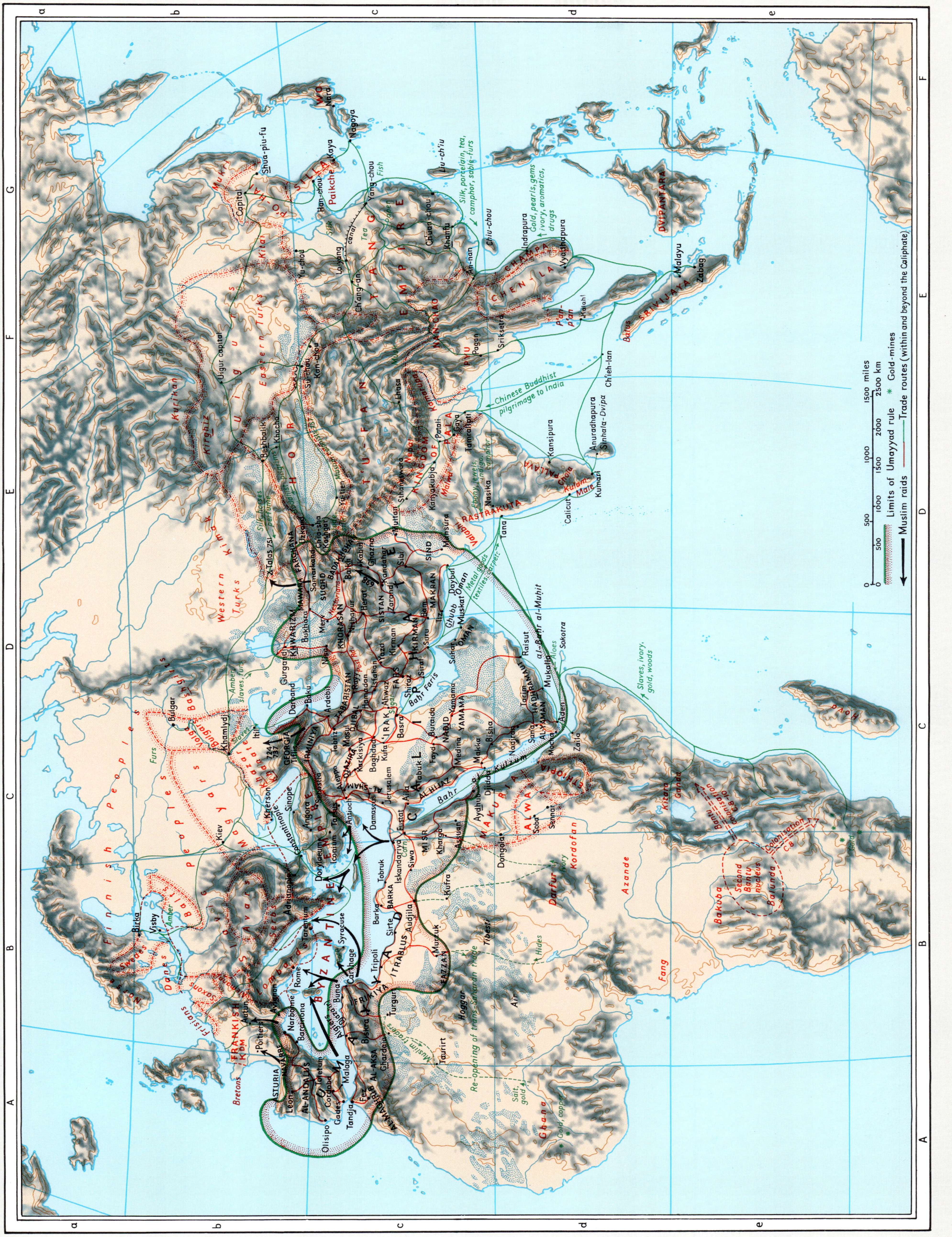

THE LATE ABBASID CALIPHATE c.A.D. 900

ALMORAVID, SALDJUK AND GHAZNAVID EXPANSION c. A.D. 1100

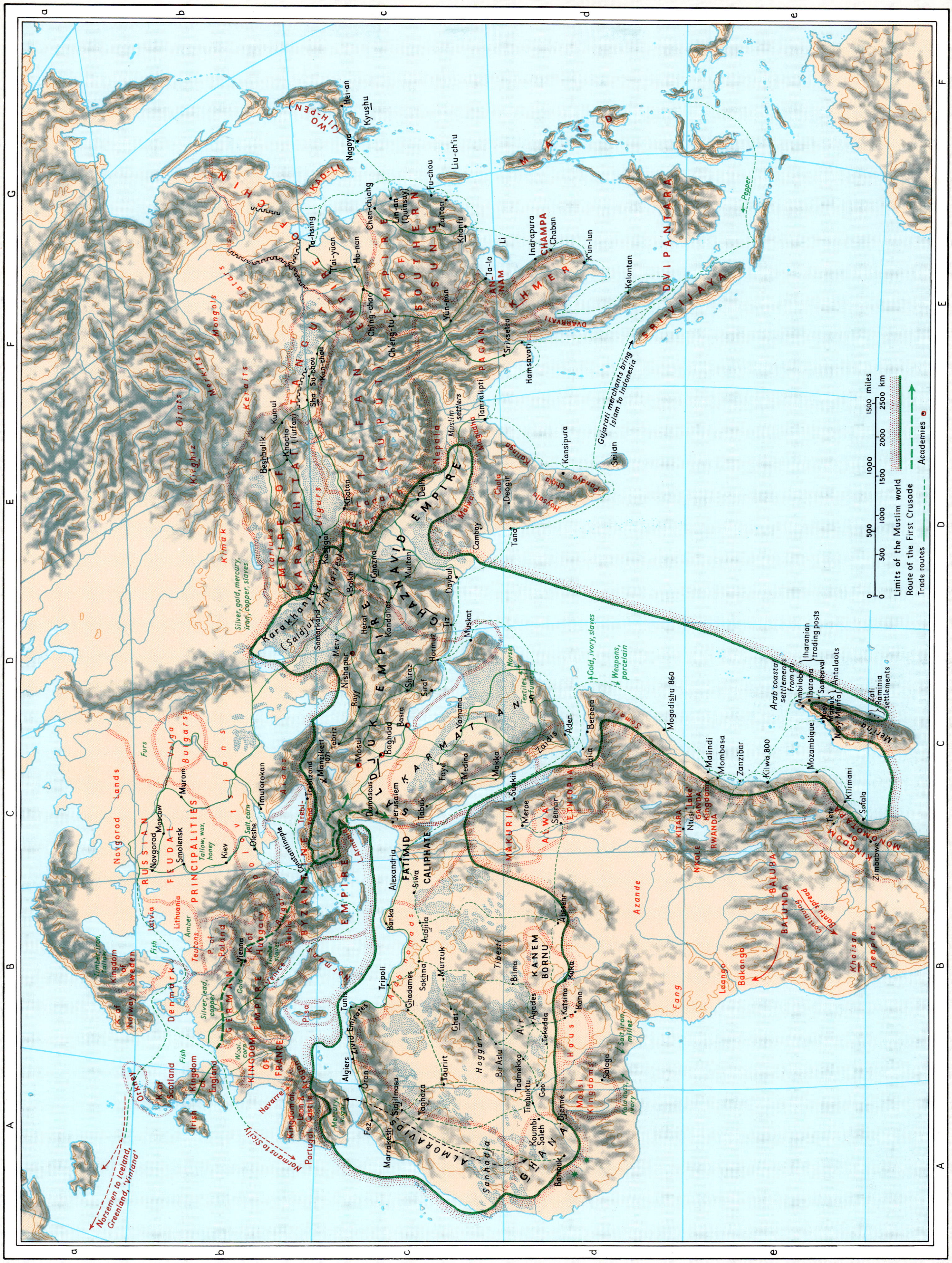

THE MUSLIM WORLD c.A.D. 1300

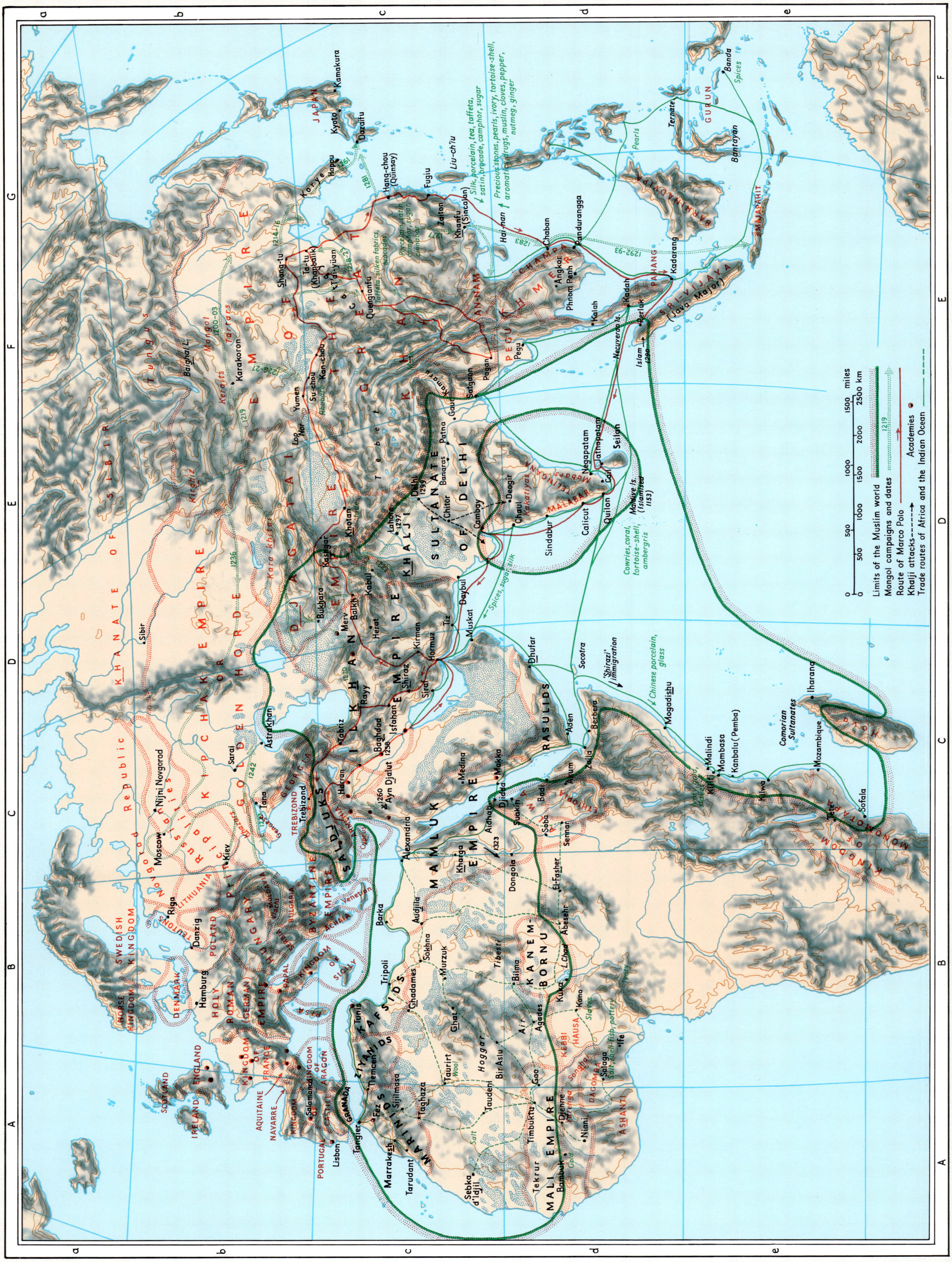

THE MUSLIM WORLD c. A.D. 1500

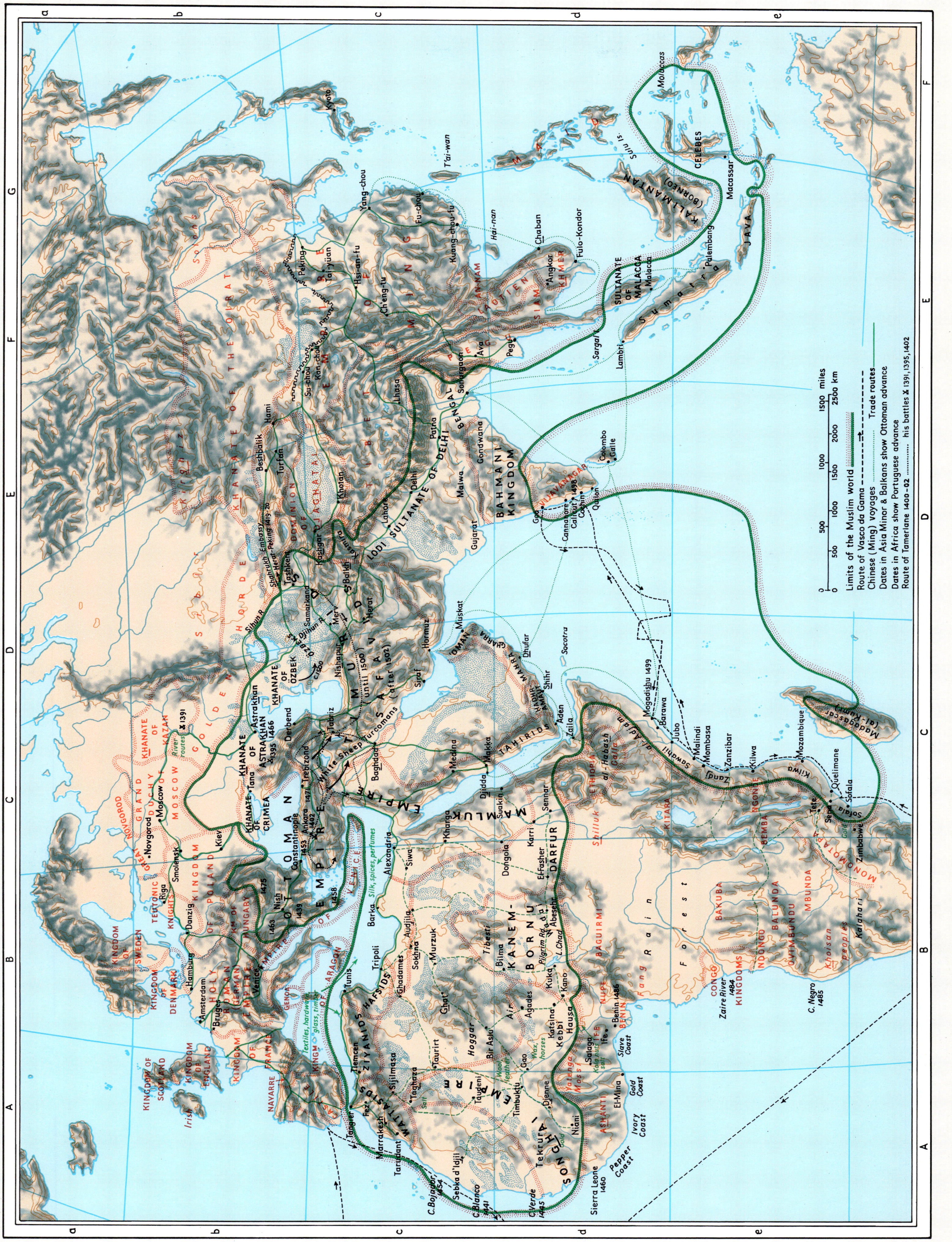

THE MUSLIM WORLD c. A.D. 1700

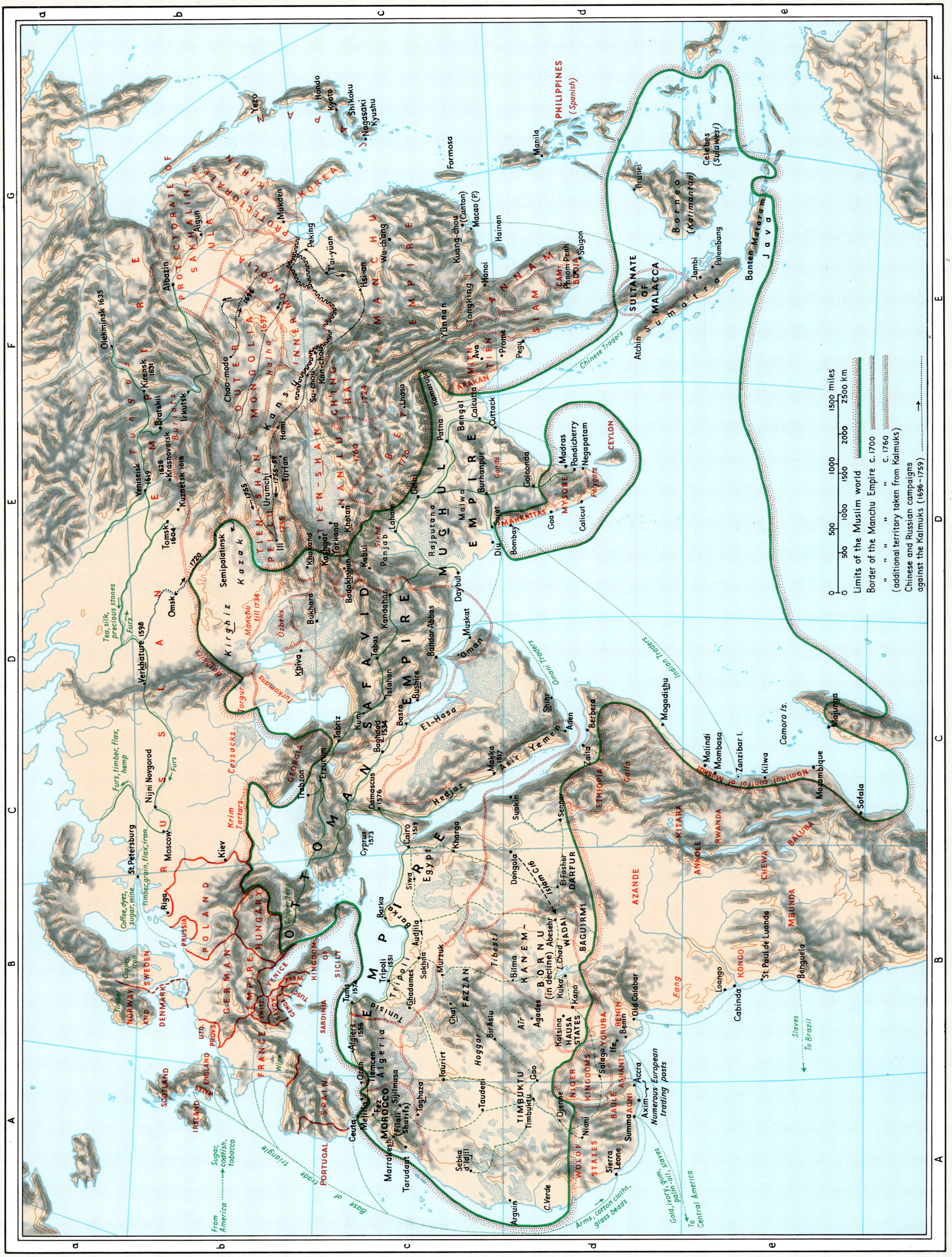

THE MUSLIM WORLD c. A.D. 1900

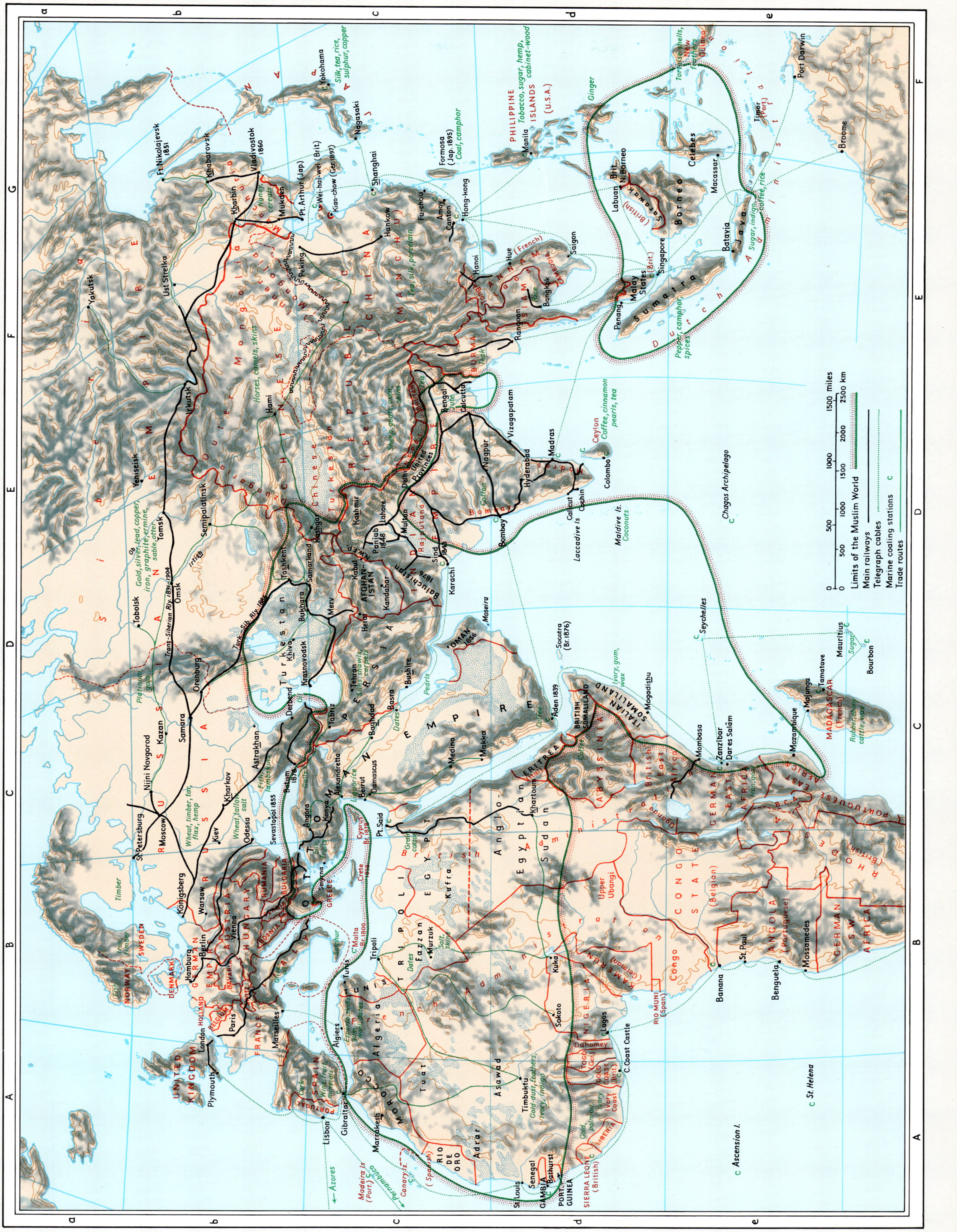

CLASSICAL ARABIA ACCORDING TO PTOLEMY c. A.D. 150

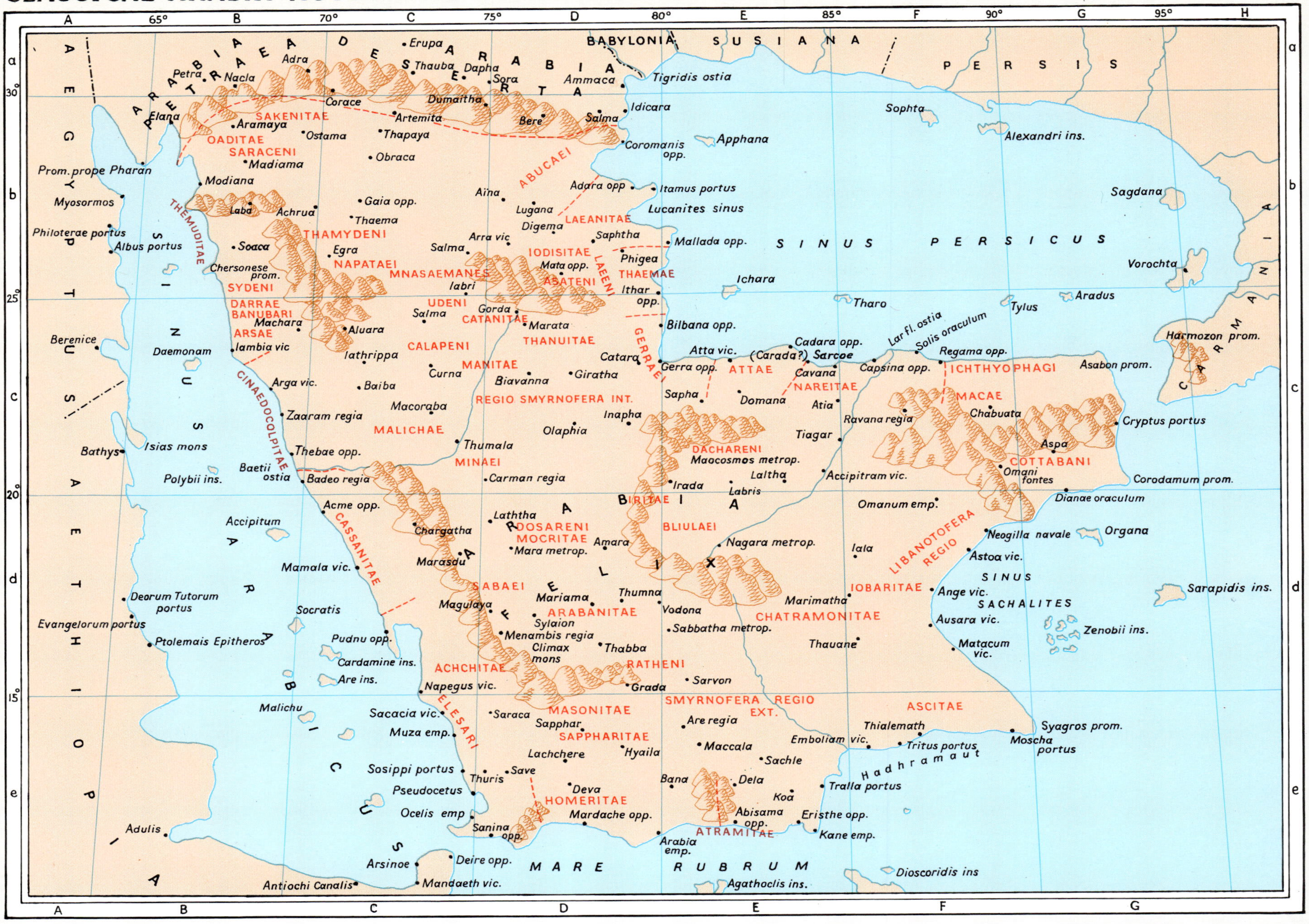

ARABIA IN CLASSICAL TIMES

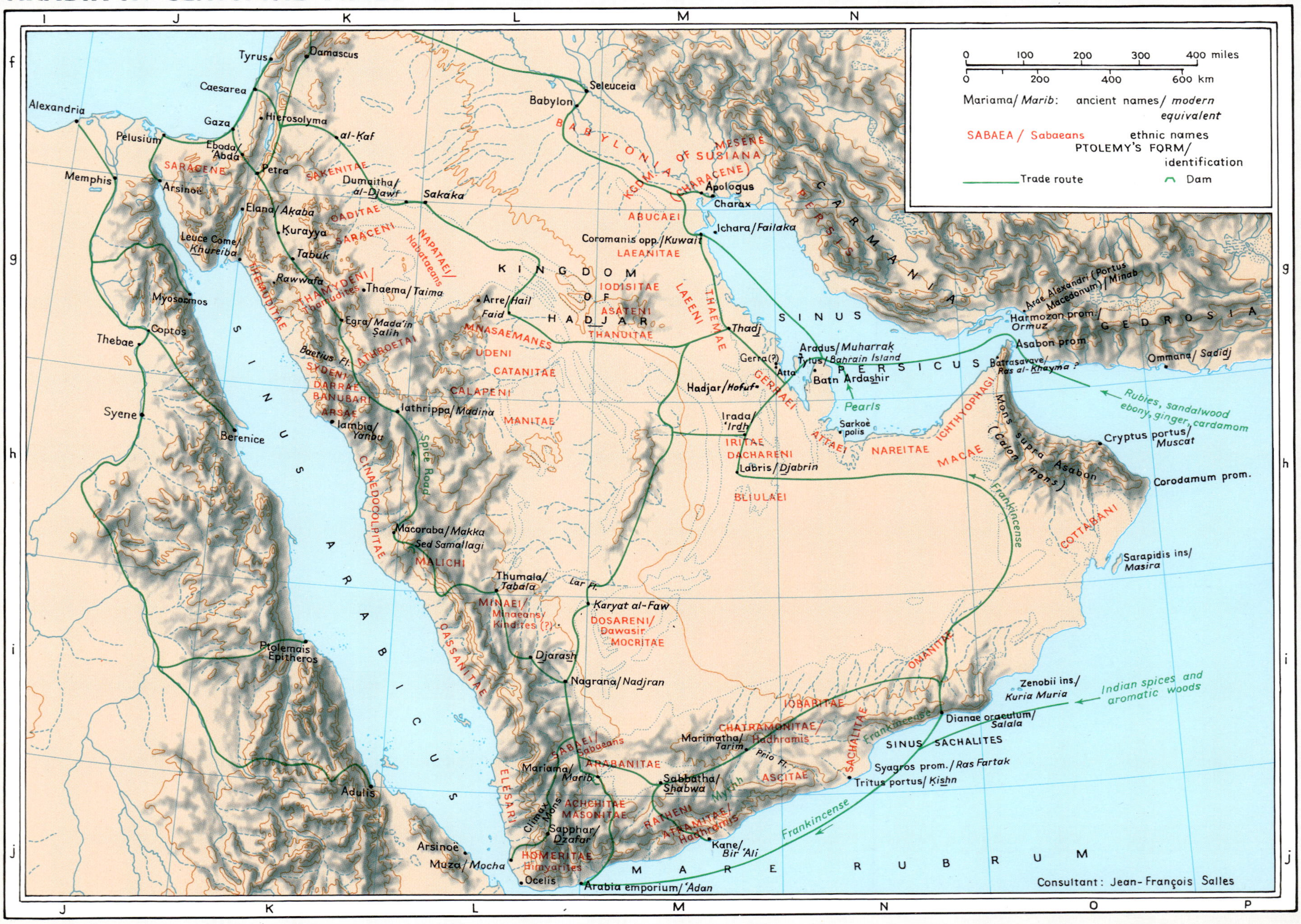

S.W. ARABIA BEFORE THE 4TH CENTURY A.D.

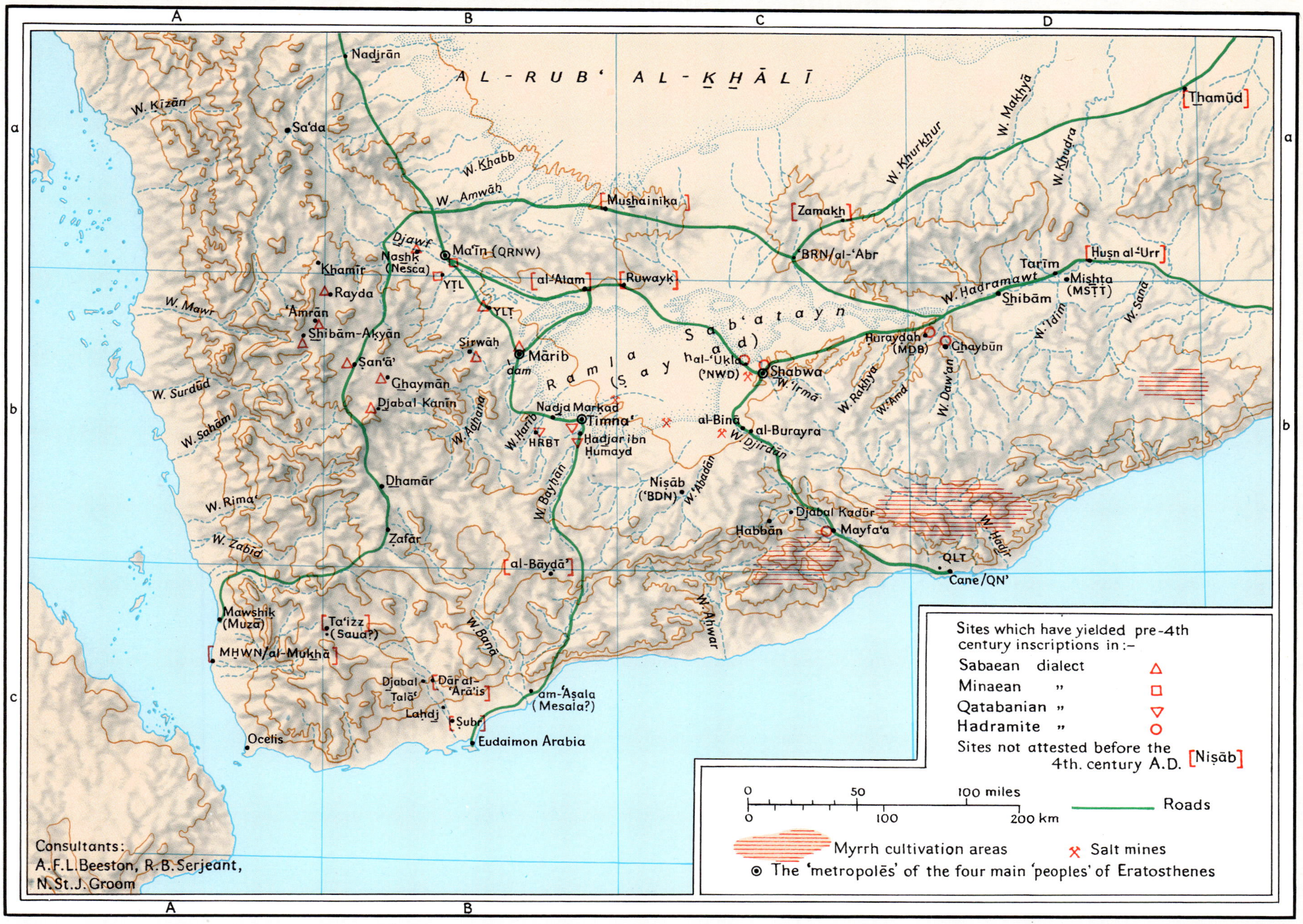

ARABIA IN THE C6 A.D.

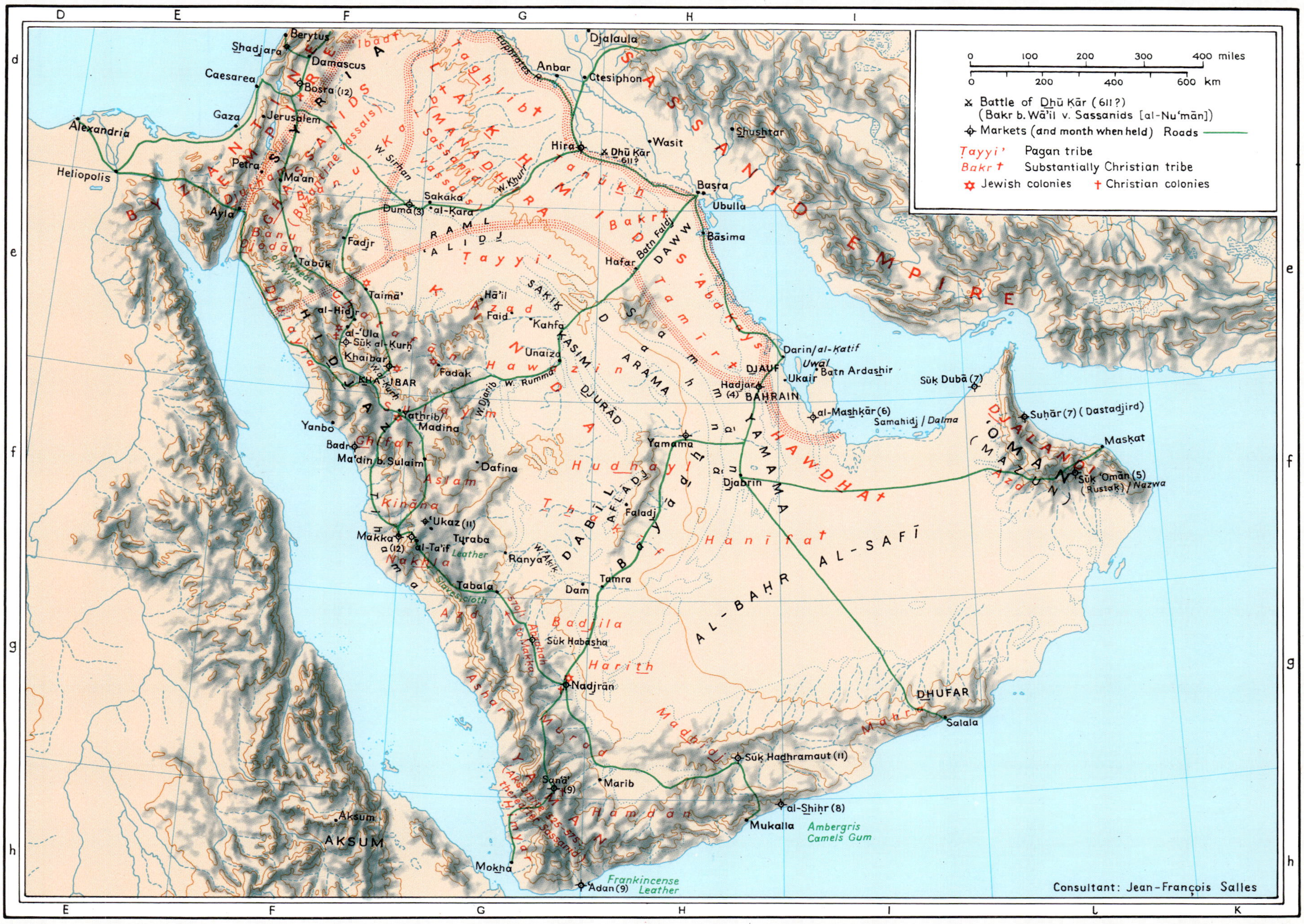

IRAN, AFGHANISTAN, MAKRAN, SIND IN THE 10TH & 11TH CENTURIES

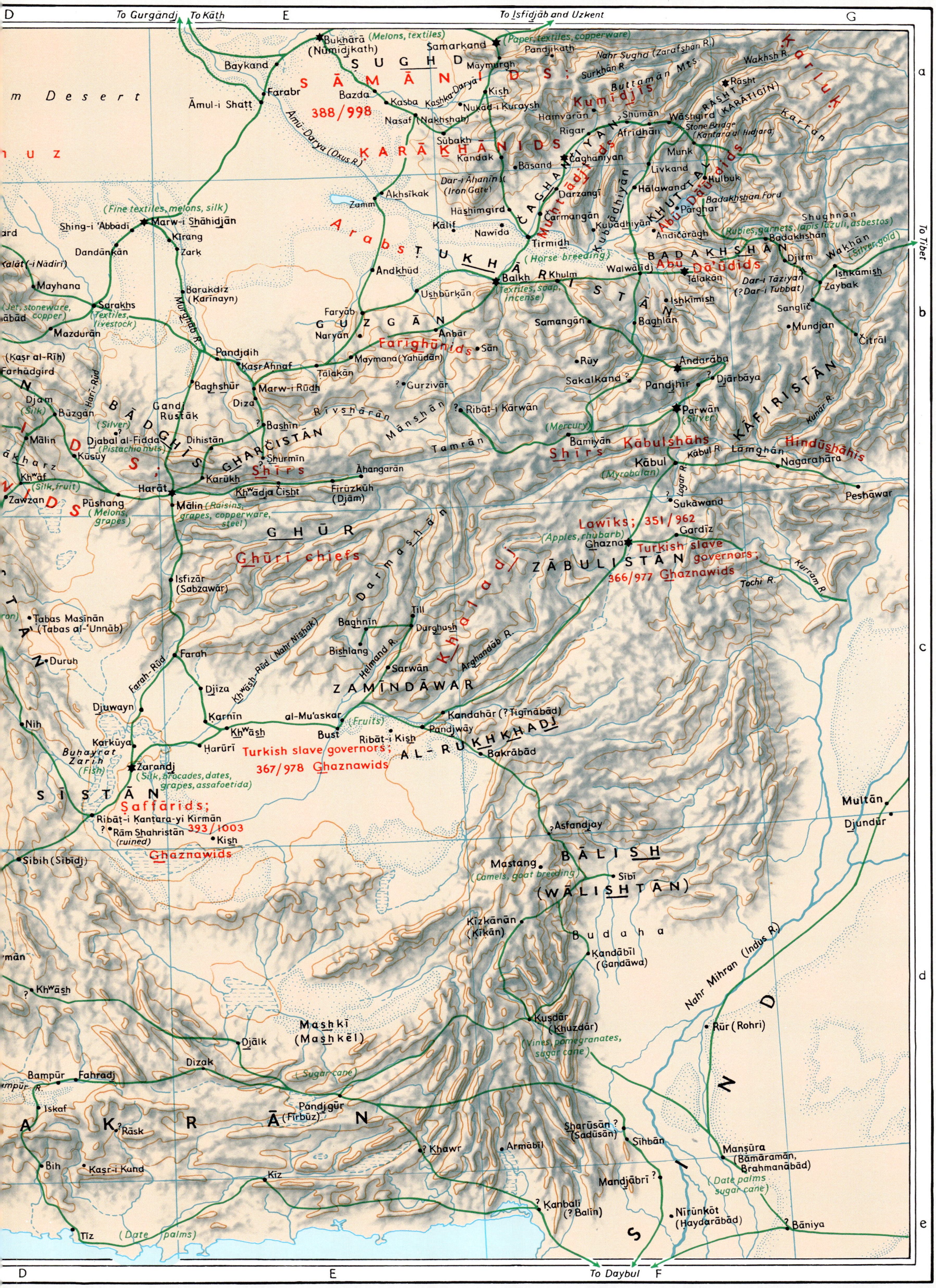

To Gurgāndj
To Kāth
To Isfidjāb and Uzkent
To Tibet
To Daybul
Bukhārā (Numidjkath)
(Melons, textiles)
Samarkand
(Paper, textiles, copperware)
SUGHD
SĀMĀNIDS;
388/998
KARĀKHĀNIDS
Baykand
Farabr
Āmul-i Shaṭṭ
Bazda
Kasba
Nasaf (Nakhshab)
Kish
Maymurgh
Pandjikath
Nahr Sughd (Zarafshān R.)
Surkhān R.
Buttamān Mts
Kumīdjīs
Rāsht
RĀSHT (KARĀTIGĪN)
Karluk
Wakhsh R.
Nūkad-i Kuraysh
Hamvarān
Shūmān
Wāshgird
Stone Bridge (Kanṭara al-Ḥidjāra)
Rigar
Afrīdhūn
Ṣubakh
Kandak
Bāsand
Ṣaghāniyān
ČAGHĀNIYĀN
Muḥtādjids
Dar-i Āhanīn (Iron Gate)
Akhsīkak
Zamm
Āmū-Darya (Oxus R.)
Munk
Hulbuk
Livkand
Hālawand
KHUTTAL
Abū Dā'ūdids
Badakhshān Ford
Pārghar
Darzangī
Hāshimgird
Čarmangān
Kubādhiyān
Andīčārāgh
Shughnān
(Rubies, garnets, lapis lazuli, asbestos)
Badakhshān
BADAKHSHĀN
Wakhān
(Silver, gold)
Ishkāmish
Zaybak
Djirm
Ṭālakān
Dar-i Tāziyān (?Dar-i Tubbat)
Sanglič
Mundjan
Čitrāl
Kālif
Nawīda
Tirmidh
(Horse breeding)
Arab
TUKHĀRISTĀN
Andkhūd
Balkh
(Textiles, soap, incense)
Khulm
Walwālidj
Ishkimish
Baghlān
Samangān
Ushbūrkān
Faryāb
GUZGĀN
Naryān
Anbār
Farīghūnids
Sān
Maymana (Yahūdān)
Ṭālakān
Gurzivān
Rūy
Sakalkand
Andarāba
Pandjhīr
Djārbāya
KĀFIRISTĀN
Kunar R.
Parwān
(Silver)
(Mercury)
Ribāṭ-i Karwān
Rivshārān
Mānshān
Tamrān
Bāmiyān
Shīrs
Kābulshāhs
Hindūshāhīs
Kābul
Kābul R.
Lamghān
Nagarahāra
Peshāwar
(Myrobalan)
Logar R.
Sukāwand
Lawīks; 351/962
Gardīz
(Apples, rhubarb)
Ghazna
Turkish slave governors;
366/977 Ghaznawids
ZĀBULISTĀN
Kurram R.
Tochī R.
Khaladj
Darmashān
Āhangarān
Fīrūzkūh (Djām)
GHŪR
Ghūrī chiefs
(Fine textiles, melons, silk)
Marw-i Shāhidjān
Shing-i 'Abbādī
Kīrang
Zark
Dandānkān
Barakdiz (Karīnayn)
Murghāb R.
Kalāt (-i Nādirī)
Mayhana
Sarakhs
(Textiles, livestock)
(Jet, stoneware, copper)
Mazdurān
(Kaṣr al-Rīḥ)
Farhādgird
Pandjdih
Kaṣr Aḥnaf
Marw-i Rūdh
Baghshūr
Dizā
Bashīn
GHARČISTĀN
Shurmīn
Gandj Rustāk
Hari-Rūd
BĀDGHĪS
Djām
(Silk)
Būzgān
(Silver)
Djabal al-Fiḍḍa
(Pistachio nuts)
Mālīn
Kūsūy
Dihistān
Karūkh
Harāt
Mālīn (Raisins, grapes, copperware, steel)
Khwādja Cisht
Khwāf
(Silk, fruit)
Zawzan
Pūshang
(Melons, grapes)
Isfizār (Sabzawār)
Tabas Masīnān (Tabas al-'Unnāb)
Duruh
Farah
Farah-Rūd
Djiza
Khwāsh-Rūd (Nahr Nīshak)
Baghnīn
Till
Durghush
Bishlang
Helmand R.
Sarwān
Arghandāb R.
ZAMĪNDĀWAR
Djuwayn
Karnīn
Khwāsh
al-Mu'askar
(Fruits)
Bust
Kandahār (? Tigīnābād)
Pandjwāy
Ribāṭ-i Kish
AL-RUKHKHADJ
Bakrābād
Nih
Karkūya
Buhayrat Zarih
(Fish)
Zarandj
Harūrī
Turkish slave governors;
367/978 Ghaznawids
(Silk, brocades, dates, grapes, assafoetida)
SĪSTĀN
Ṣaffārids;
393/1003
Ghaznawids
Ribāṭ-i Kanṭara-yi Kirmān
Rām Shahristān (ruined)
Kish
Sibih (Sibidj)
Asfandjay
Multān
Djundūr
Mastang
(Camels, goat breeding)
BĀLISH (WĀLISHTĀN)
Sībī
Kīzkānān (Kīkān)
Budaha
Kandābīl (Gandāwa)
Nahr Mihran (Indus R.)
SIND
Rūr (Rohri)
Khwāsh
Mashkī (Mashkēl)
Djālk
Kuṣdār (Khuzdār)
(Vines, pomegranates, sugar cane)
Dizak
(Sugar cane)
Bampūr
Fahradj
Iskaf
Rāsk
MAKRĀN
Pandjgūr (Firbūz)
Sharūsān ? (Sadūsān)
Sihbān
Manṣūra (Bāmarāmān, Brahmanābād)
Khawr
Armābīl
Bih
Kaṣr-i Kund
Kīz
Mandjābrī
(Date palms, sugar cane)
Kanbalī (? Bālin)
Nīrūnkōt (Haydarābād)
Bāniya
Tīz
(Date palms)
D
E
F
G
a
b
c
d
e

SEISMIC MAP OF THE MIDDLE EAST

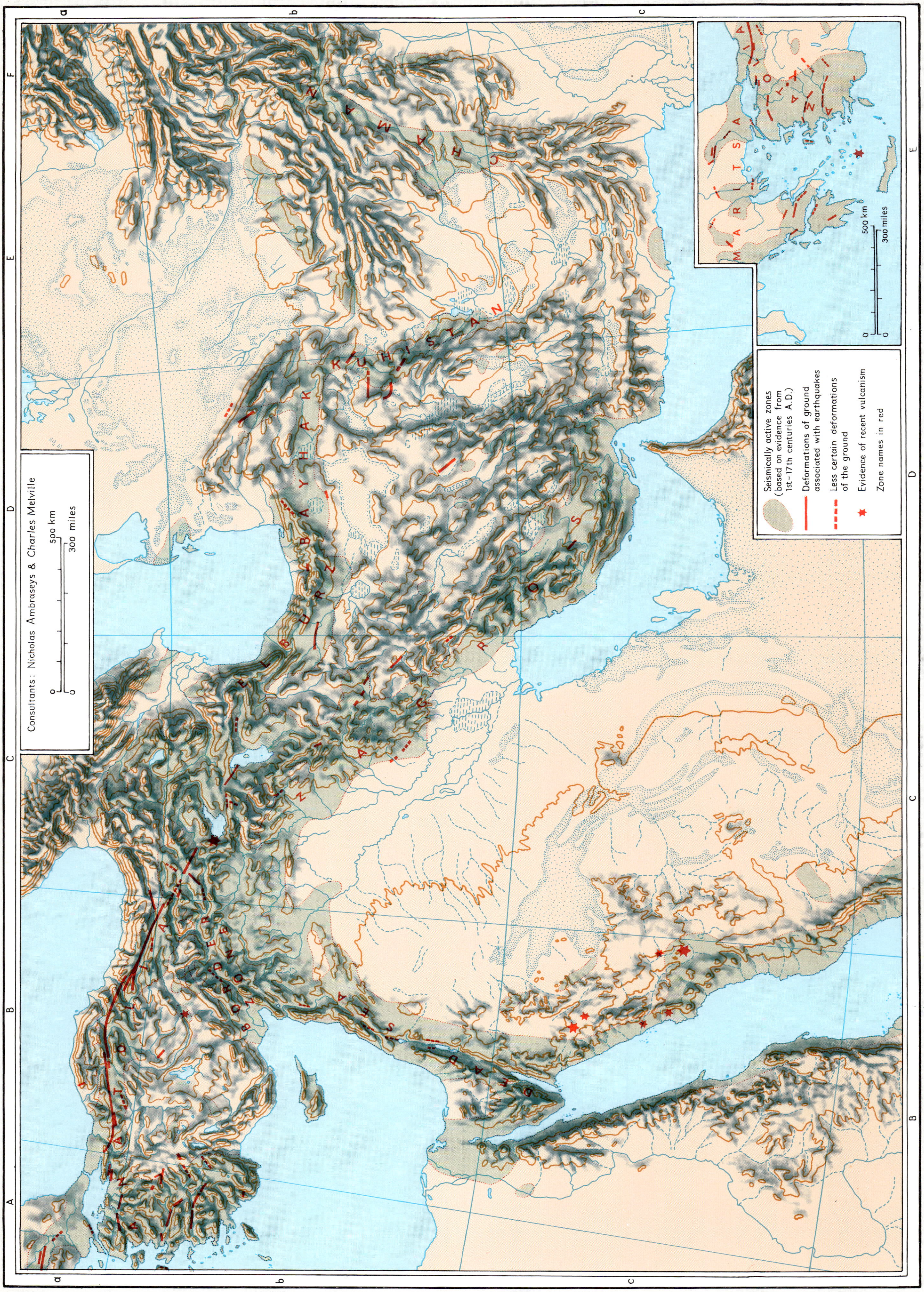
Consultants: Nicholas Ambraseys & Charles Melville
0 500 km
0 300 miles
Seismically active zones (based on evidence from 1st–17th centuries A.D.)
Deformations of ground associated with earthquakes
Less certain deformations of the ground
Evidence of recent vulcanism
Zone names in red

THE MIDDLE EAST AT HIDJRA (A.D. 622)

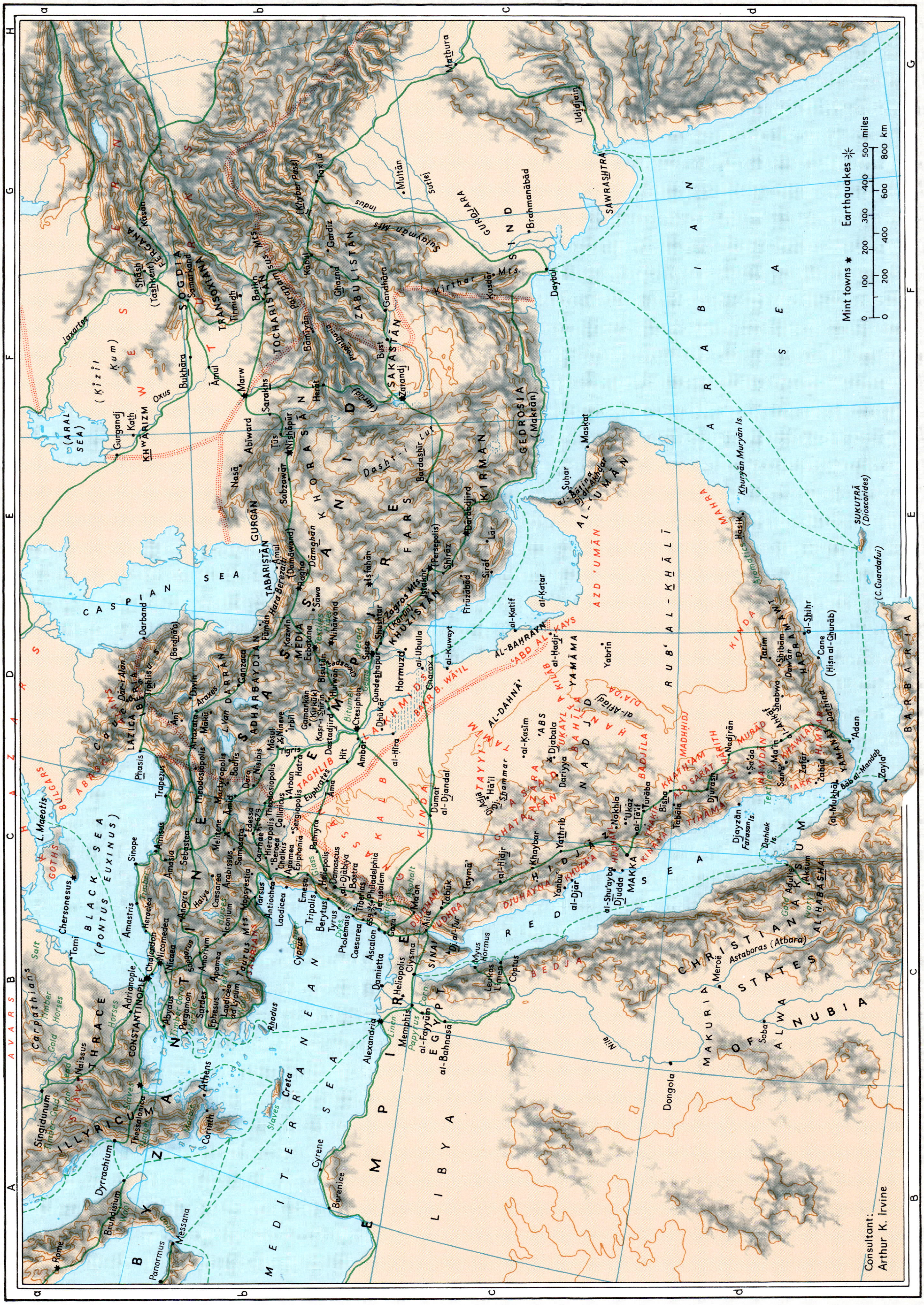

THE MIDDLE EAST cc8-11 (THE ABBASIDS AND THEIR SUCCESSORS)

THE MIDDLE EAST - DYNASTIC CHANGES, C9-C13 A.D.

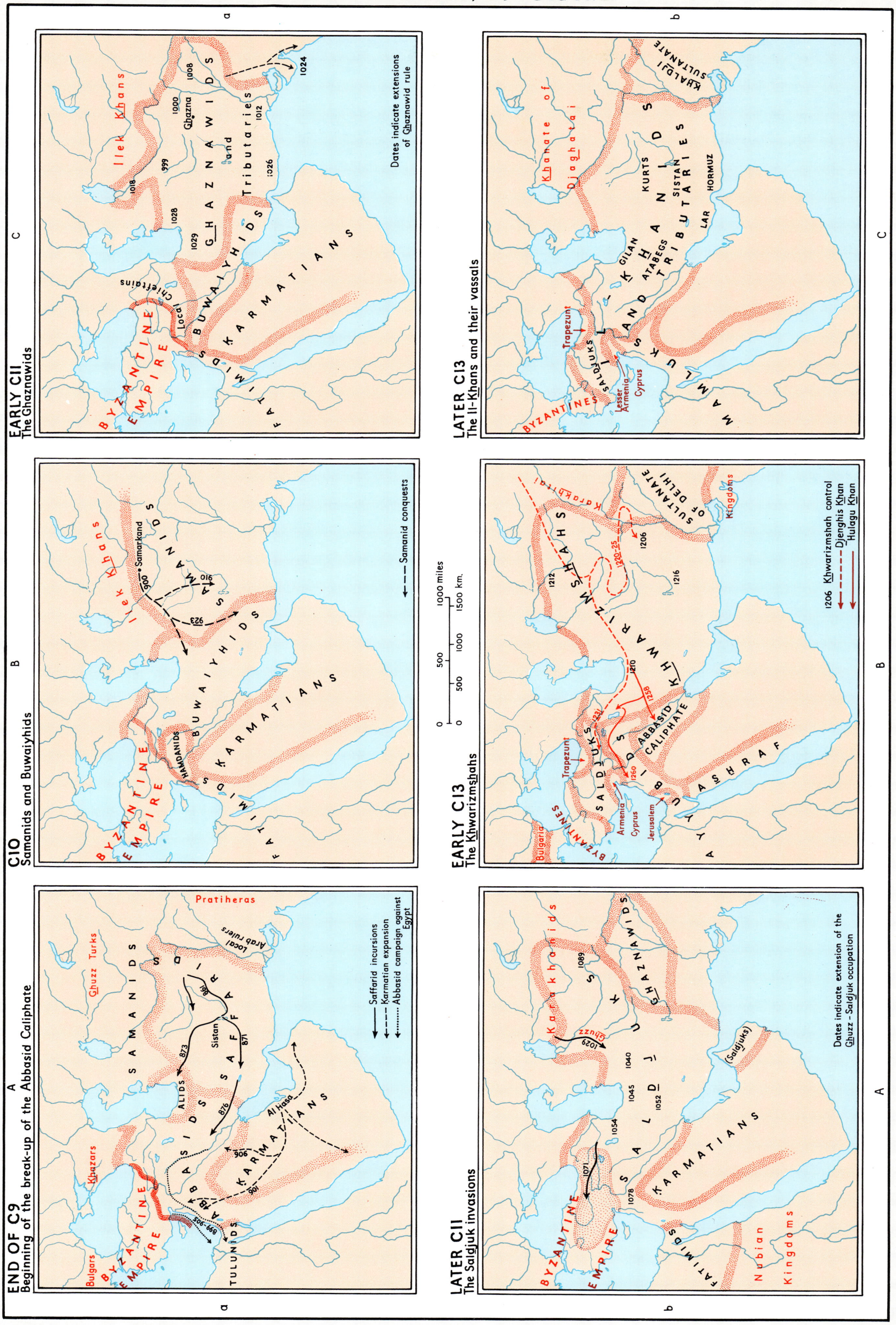

THE NEAR EAST IN C12 A.D. (THE CRUSADES AND ṢALĀḤ AL-DĪN)

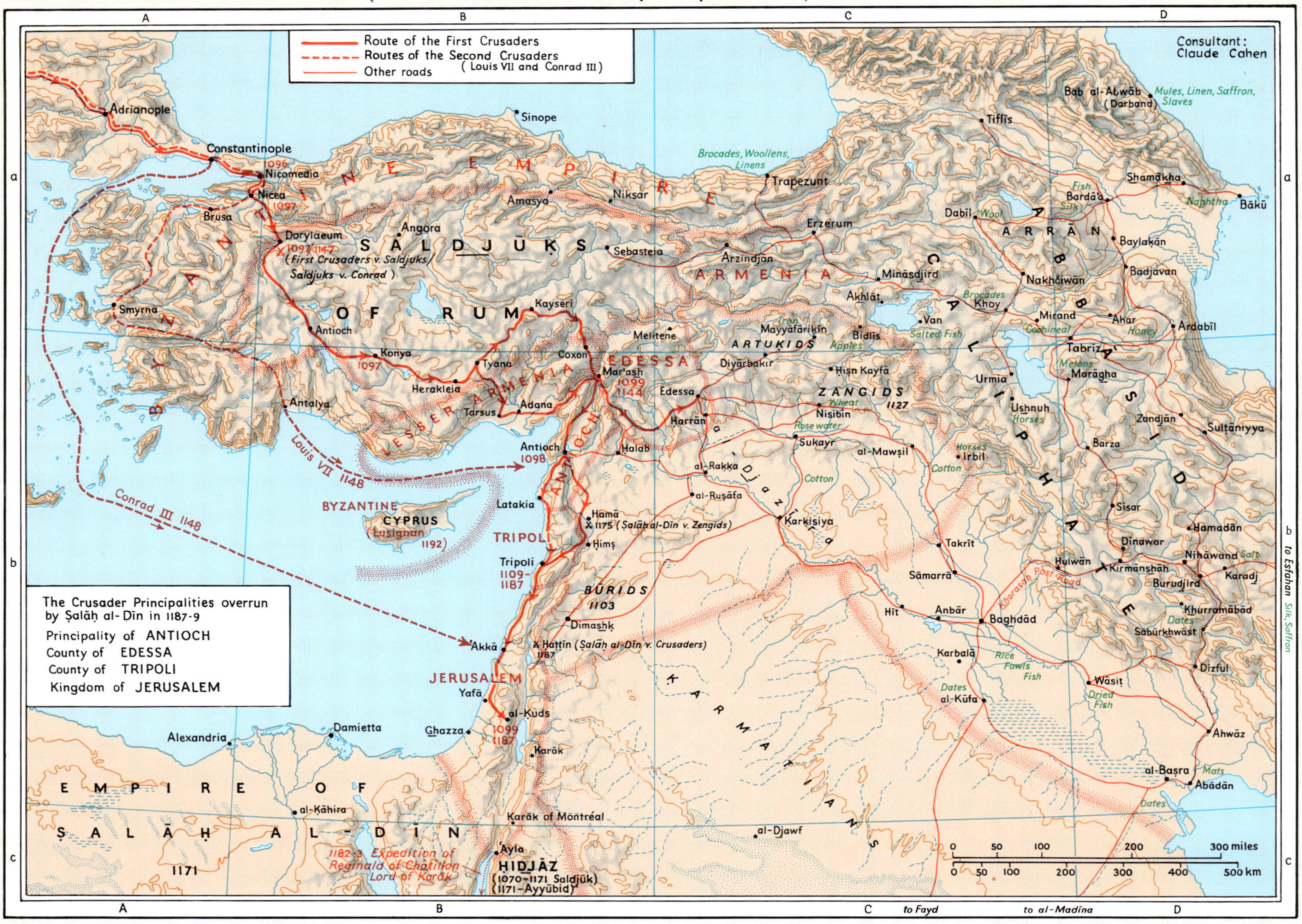

THE PILGRIM ROUTES OF ARABIA

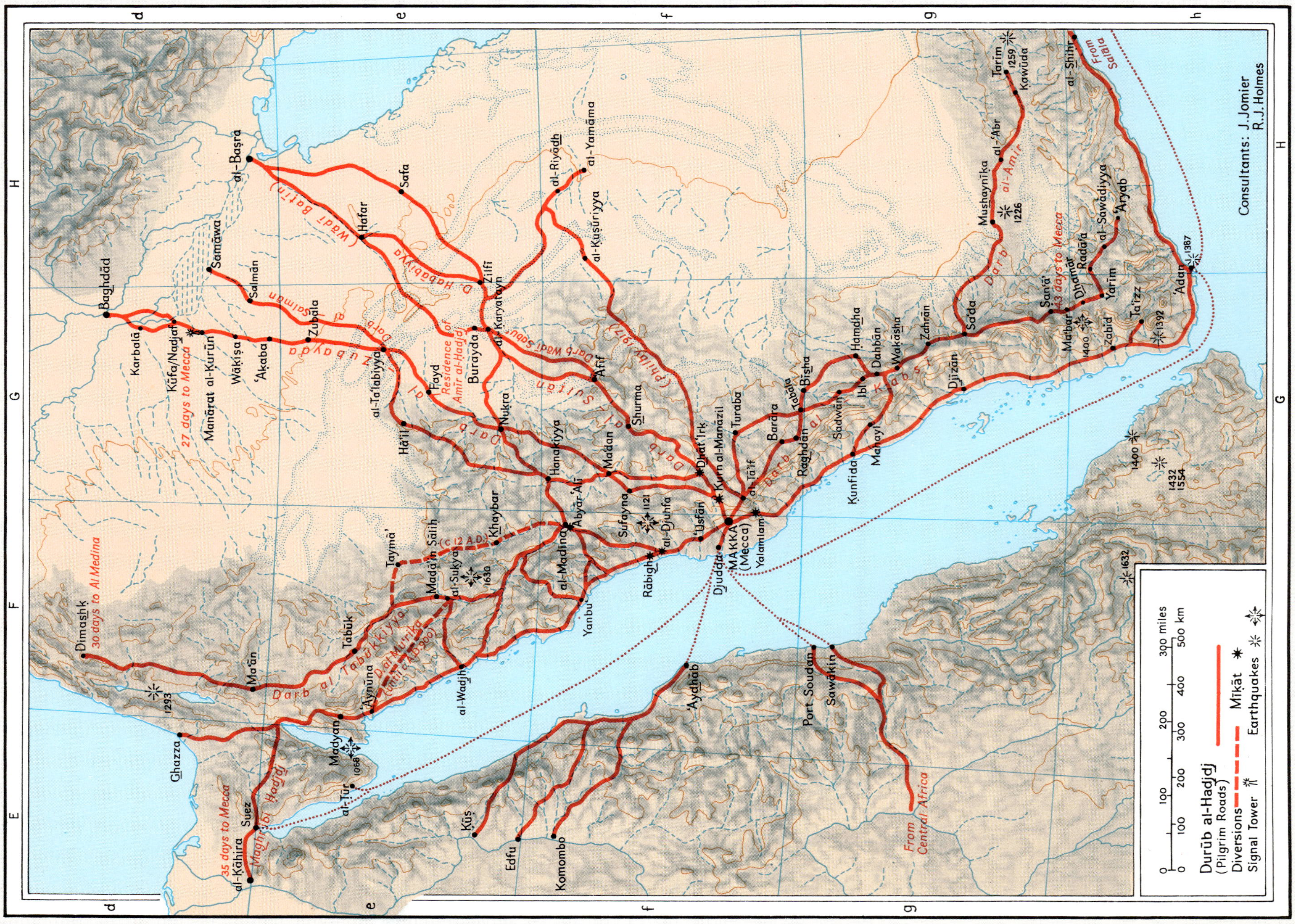

THE HOLY CITY OF MAKKA

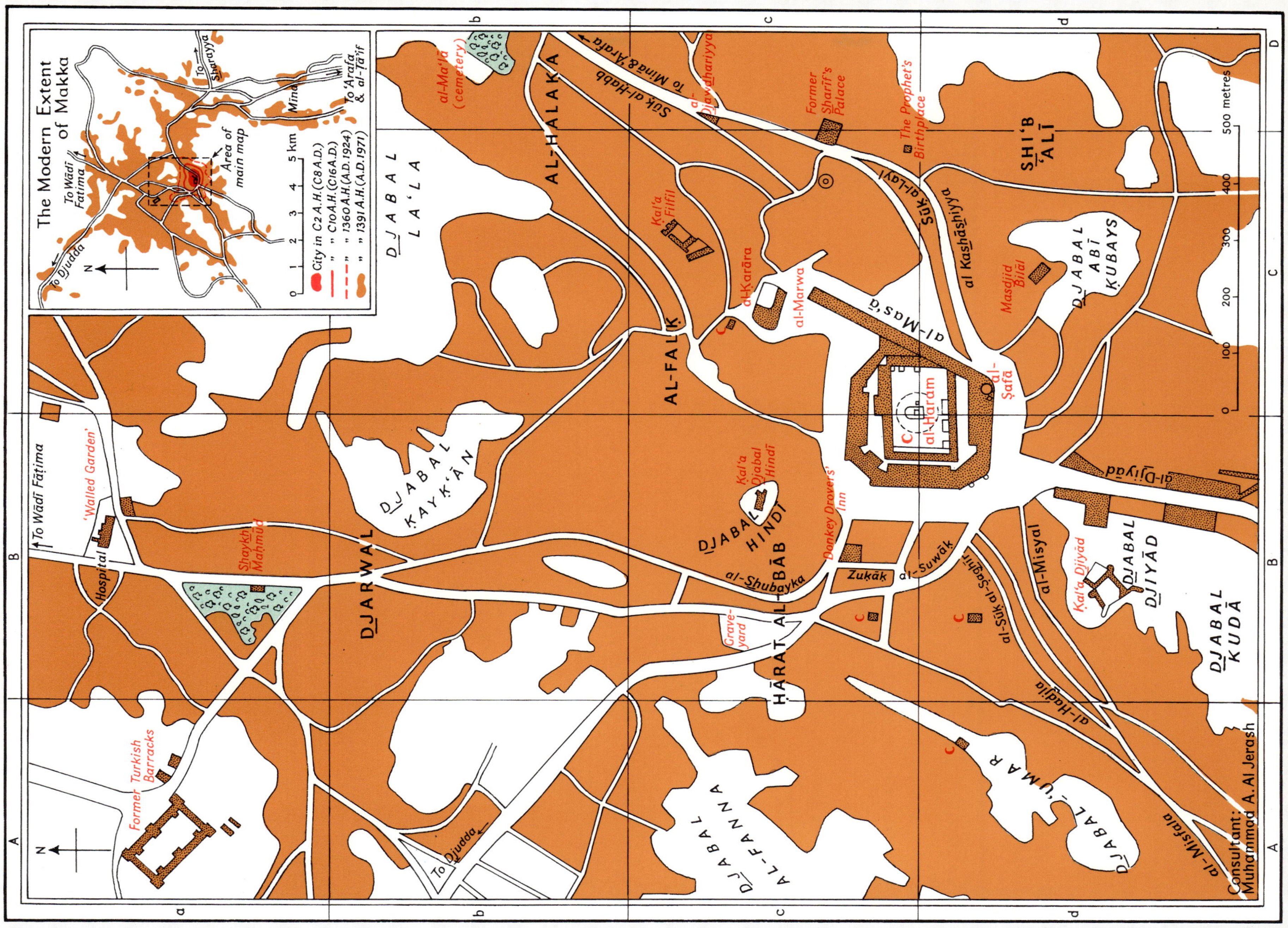

THE HOLY CITY OF AL MADĪNA

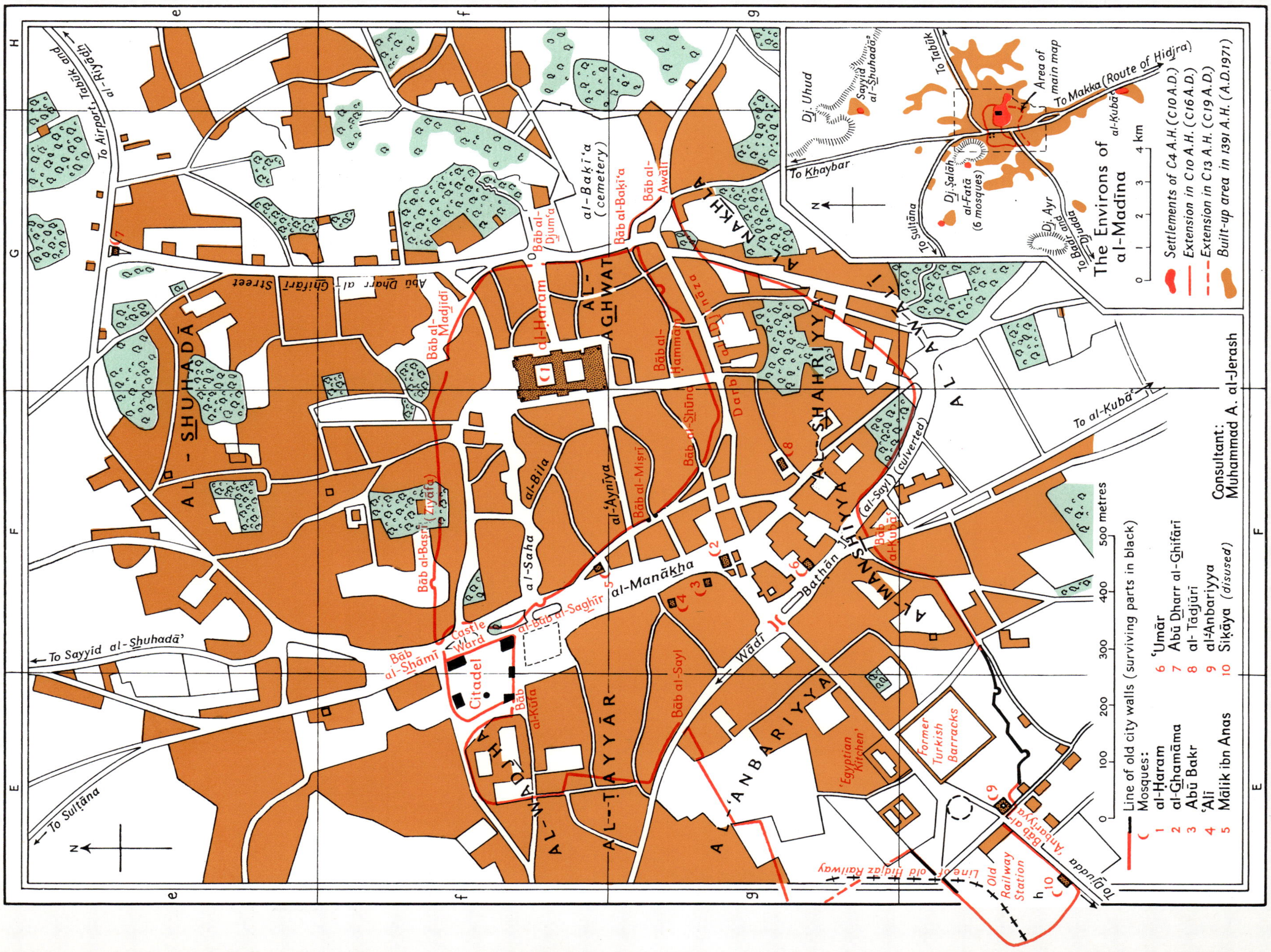

TRANSOXIANA IN THE 10TH & 11TH CENTURIES

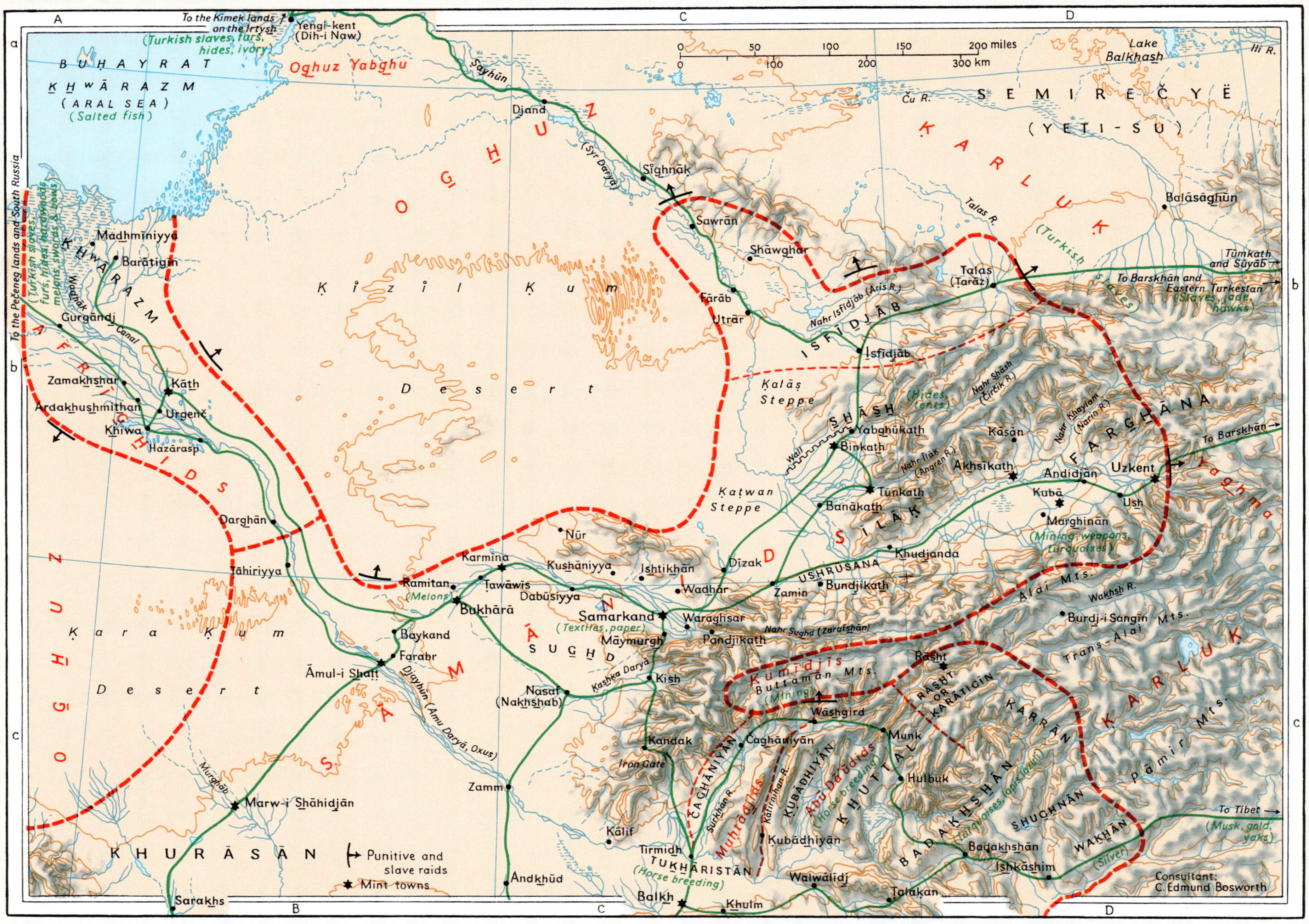

THE KHWĀRAZM SHĀHS AND GHŪRIDS

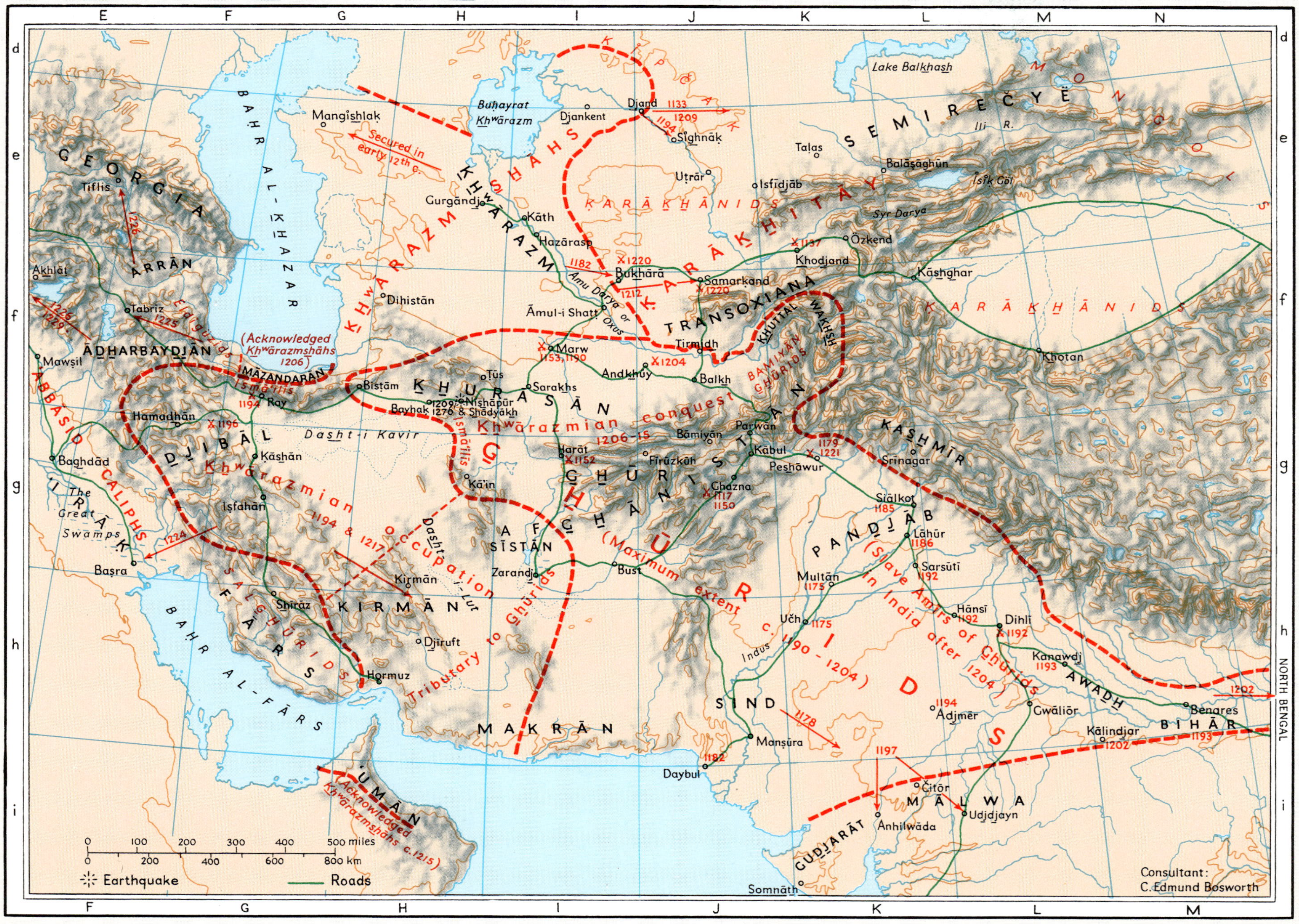

THE MIDDLE EAST IN THE LATER C 14
THE CAMPAIGNS OF TIMUR

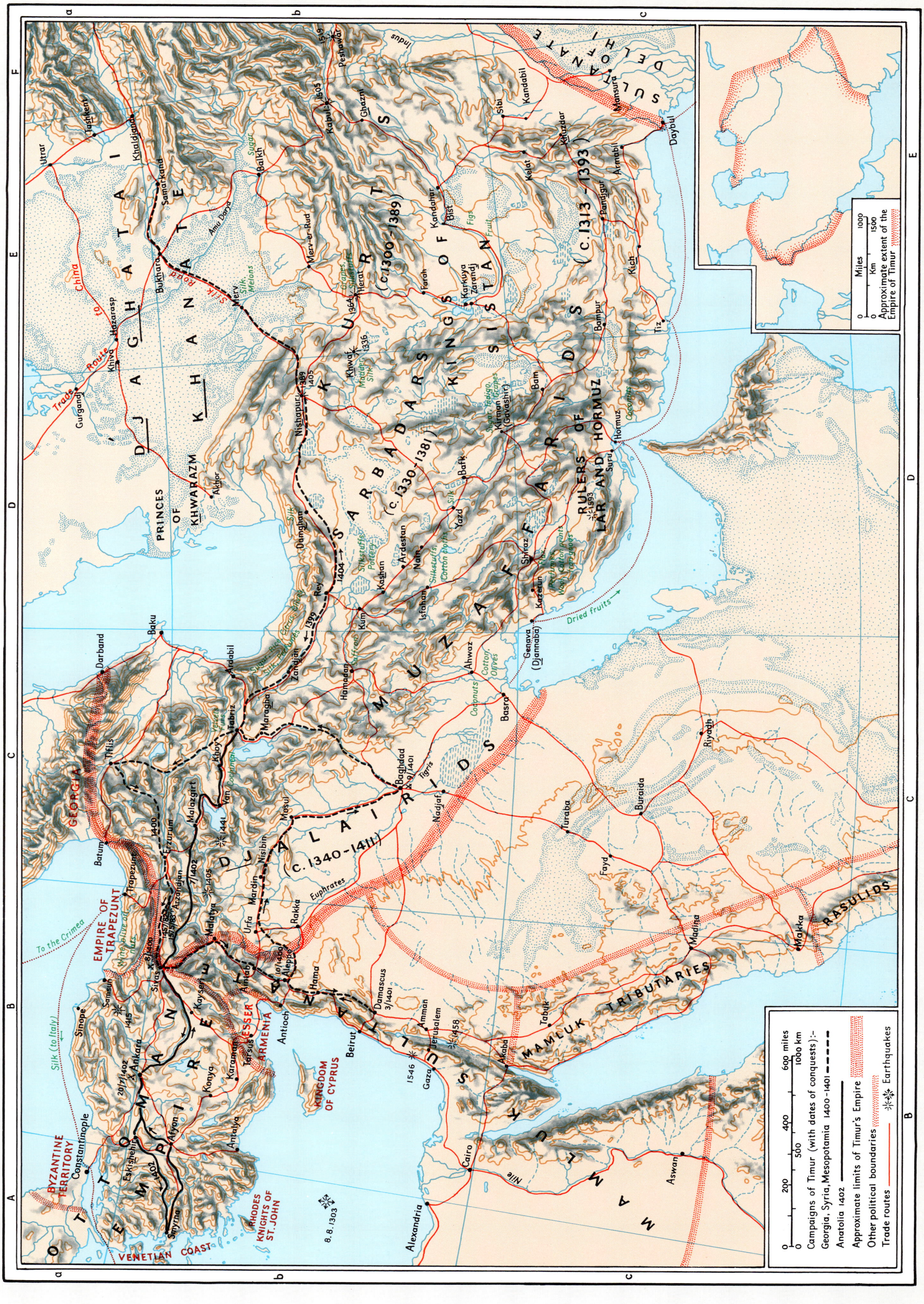

THE MIDDLE EAST IN THE MID-C18 A.D.

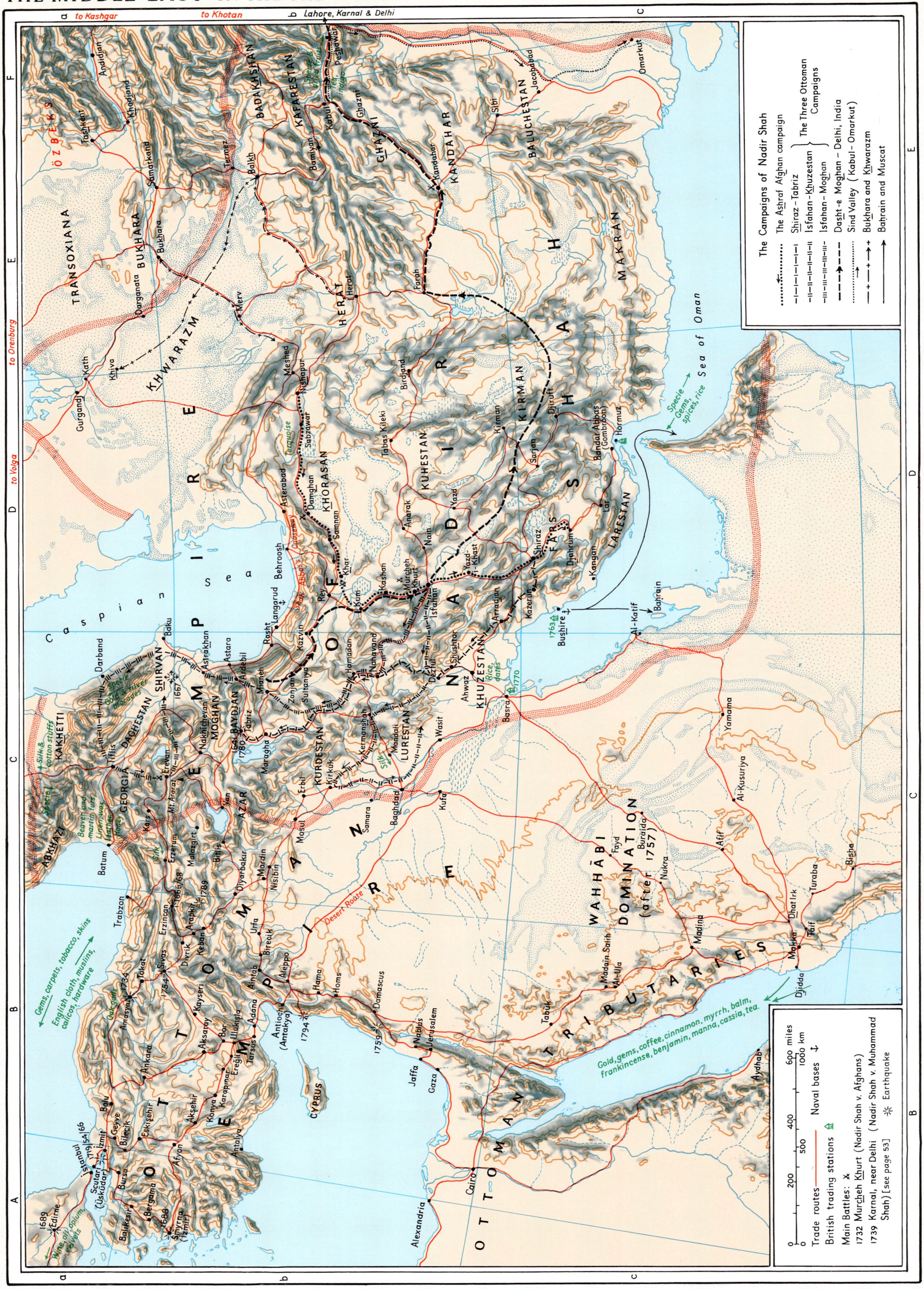
The Campaigns of Nadir Shah
The Ashraf Afghan campaign
Shiraz - Tabriz
Isfahan - Khuzestan
Isfahan - Moghan
The Three Ottoman Campaigns
Dasht-e Moghan - Delhi, India
Sind Valley (Kabul - Omarkut)
Bukhara and Khwarazm
Bahrain and Muscat
Trade routes
British trading stations
Naval bases
Main Battles:
1732 Murcheh Khurt (Nadir Shah v. Afghans)
1739 Karnal, near Delhi (Nadir Shah v. Muhammad Shah) [see page 53]
Earthquake
600 miles
1000 km
to Kashgar
to Khotan
Lahore, Karnal & Delhi
to Orenburg
to Volga
OTTOMAN EMPIRE
EMPIRE OF NADIR SHAH
WAHHĀBI DOMINATION (after 1757)
OTTOMAN TRIBUTARIES
Caspian Sea
Sea of Oman
TRANSOXIANA
BUKHARA
KHWARAZM
KHORASAN
KANDAHAR
BALUCHESTAN
MAKRAN
KIRMAN
FARS
LARESTAN
KHUZESTAN
LURESTAN
KURDESTAN
AZAR
GEORGIA
DAGHESTAN
SHIRVAN
MOGHAN
Gems, carpets, tobacco, skins
English cloth, muslins, calicos, hardware
Specie
Gems, spices, rice
Gold, gems, coffee, cinnamon, myrrh, balm, frankincense, benjamin, manna, cassia, tea.
Desert Route
CYPRUS

THE MIDDLE EAST C19-EARLY C20 (ENCROACHMENT BY THE GREAT POWERS: STRATEGIC RAILWAYS)

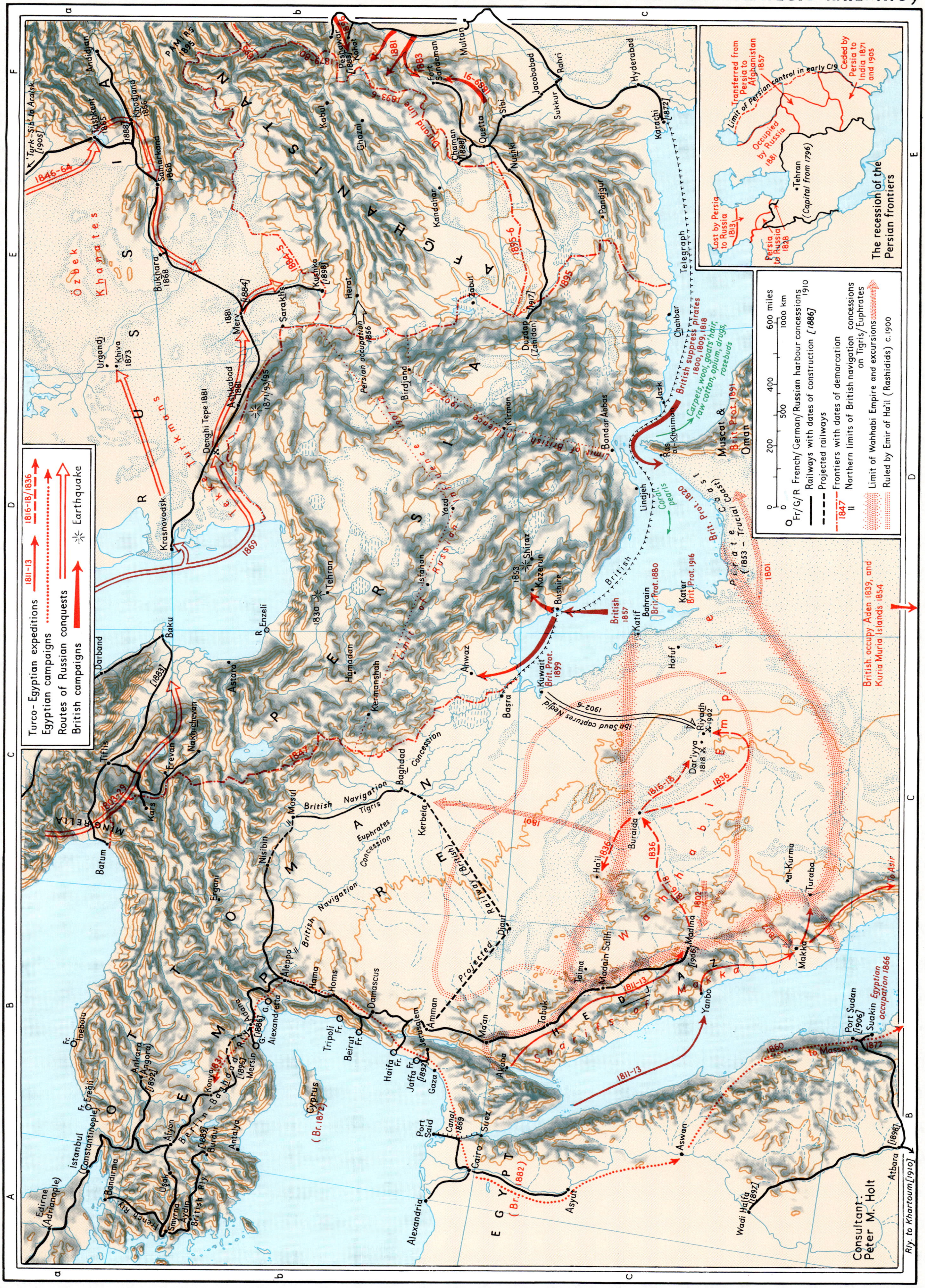

BYZANTINE ANATOLIA CC 8-11

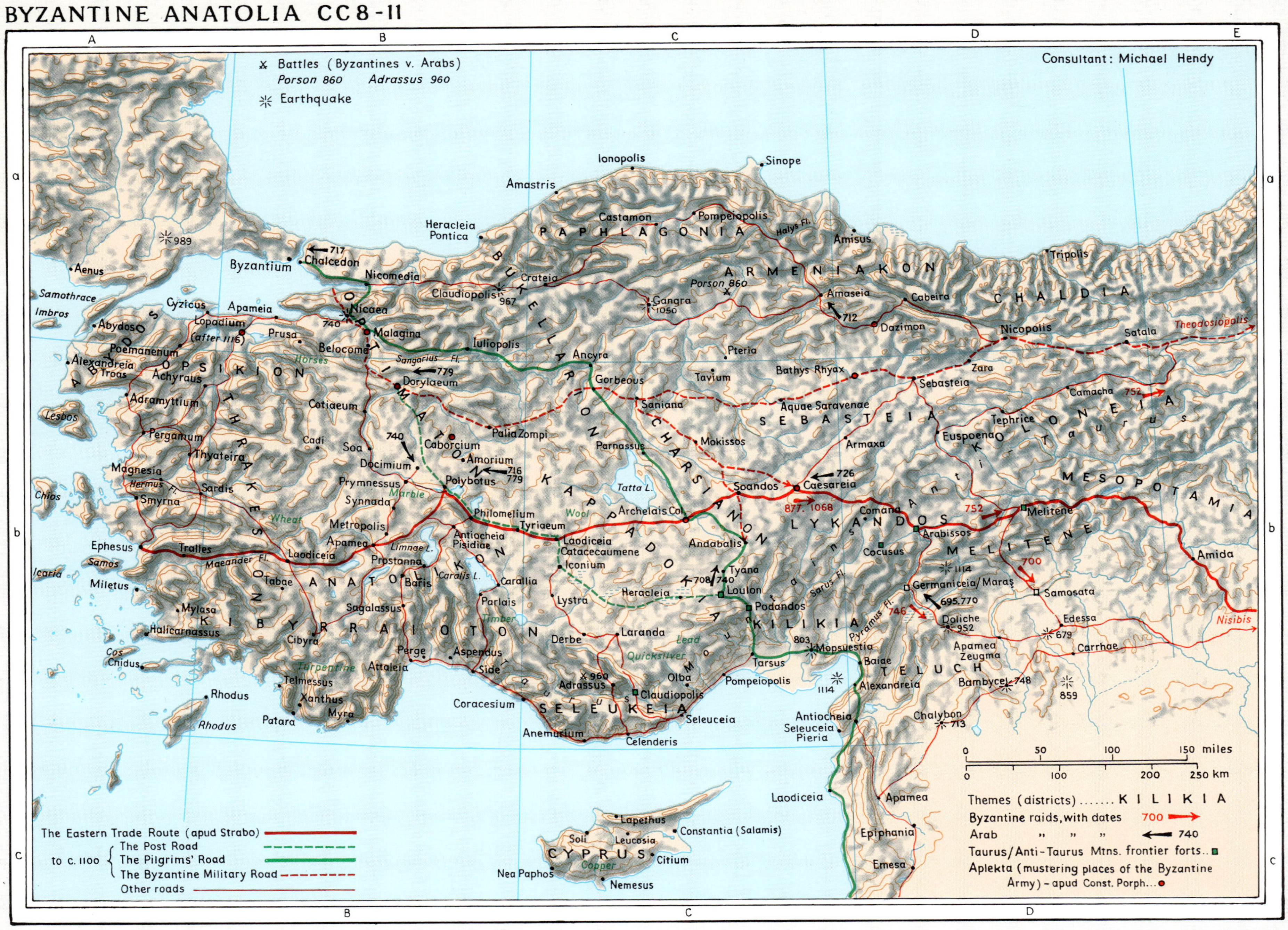

ANATOLIA 1116-1204. BYZANTINE CAMPAIGNS AND TURKISH PENETRATION

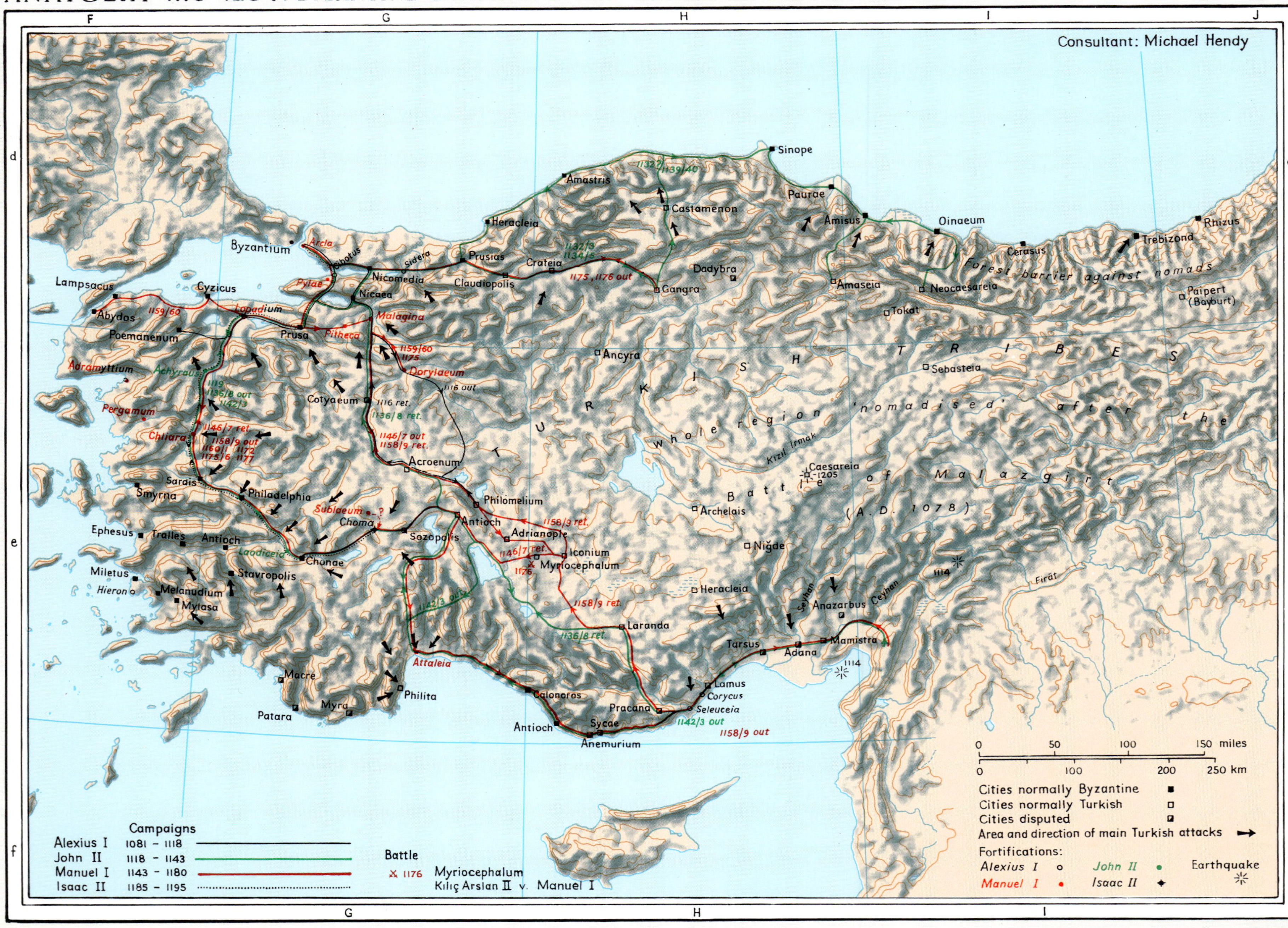

ANATOLIA C 13 SELÇUK ROADS & CRUSADE ROUTES

Consultant : Michael Hendy

Crusade Routes

First Crusade 1097-8 { Main army / Baldwin of Boulogne →

Second Crusade 1147-8
Third Crusade 1189-90

Han (caravanserai) and date
Major city with han
Roads and other cities or nodal points
Approximate limit of Selçuk occupation c.1243
Earthquake

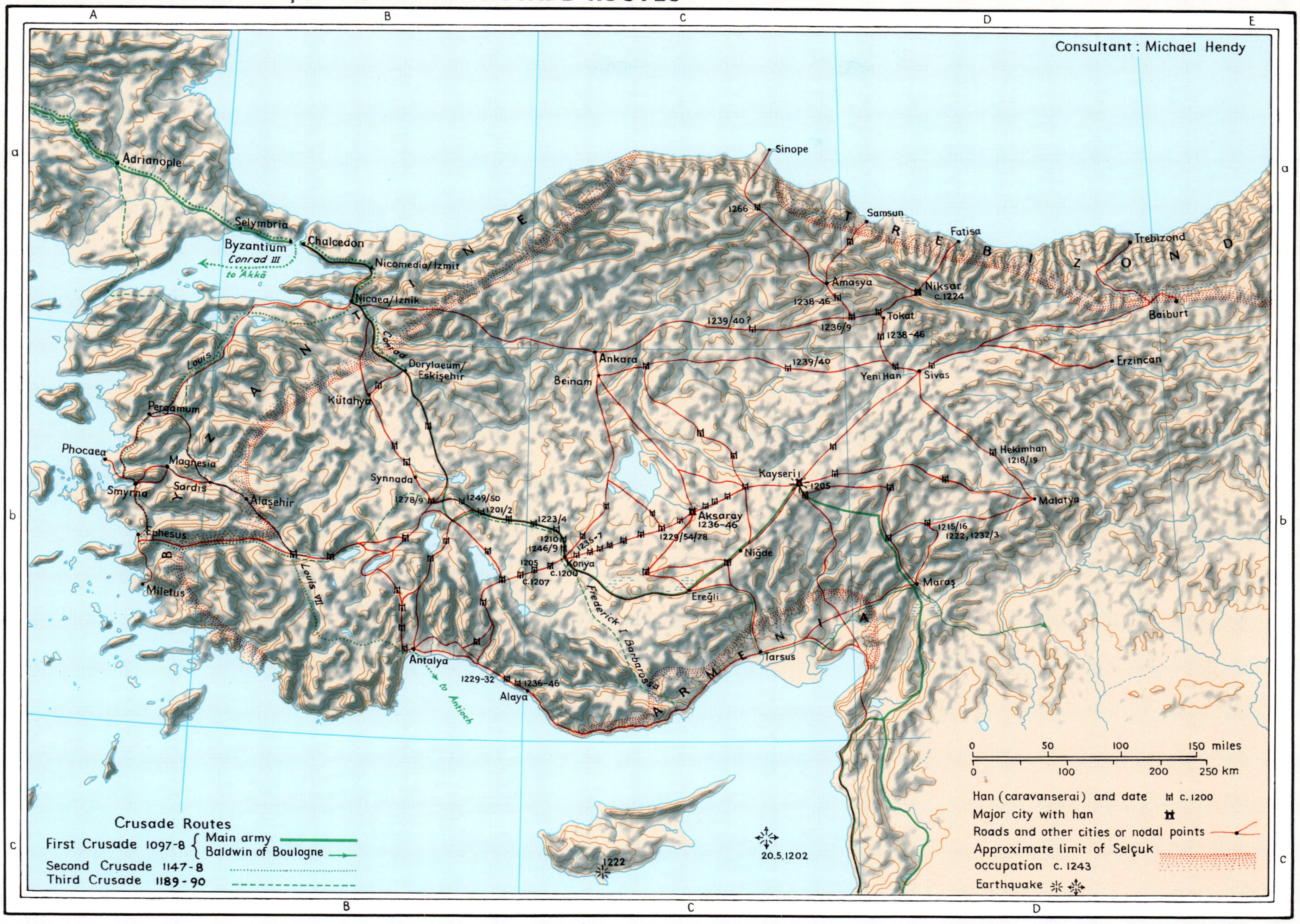

ANATOLIA c. A.D.1300 THE EXPANSION OF THE OTTOMANS TO A.D. 1362

Consultants: Roger le Tourneau / Robert Mantran / Lucien Golvin

✕ 1301 Baphaeon, Osman Gazi v. Byzantines
✕ 1347 Imbros (naval), Knights of Rhodes v. Ottoman Fleet
✳ Earthquake

Frontier zone of *gaza* or Holy War between Byzantium and the Turkish Principalities.
Main Principalities succeeding the Selçuk state, with approximate dates
Other frontiers

TEKE 1300-1426
Raids by Turkish corsairs
Conquests and raids of Orhan (1326-62)
Trade routes

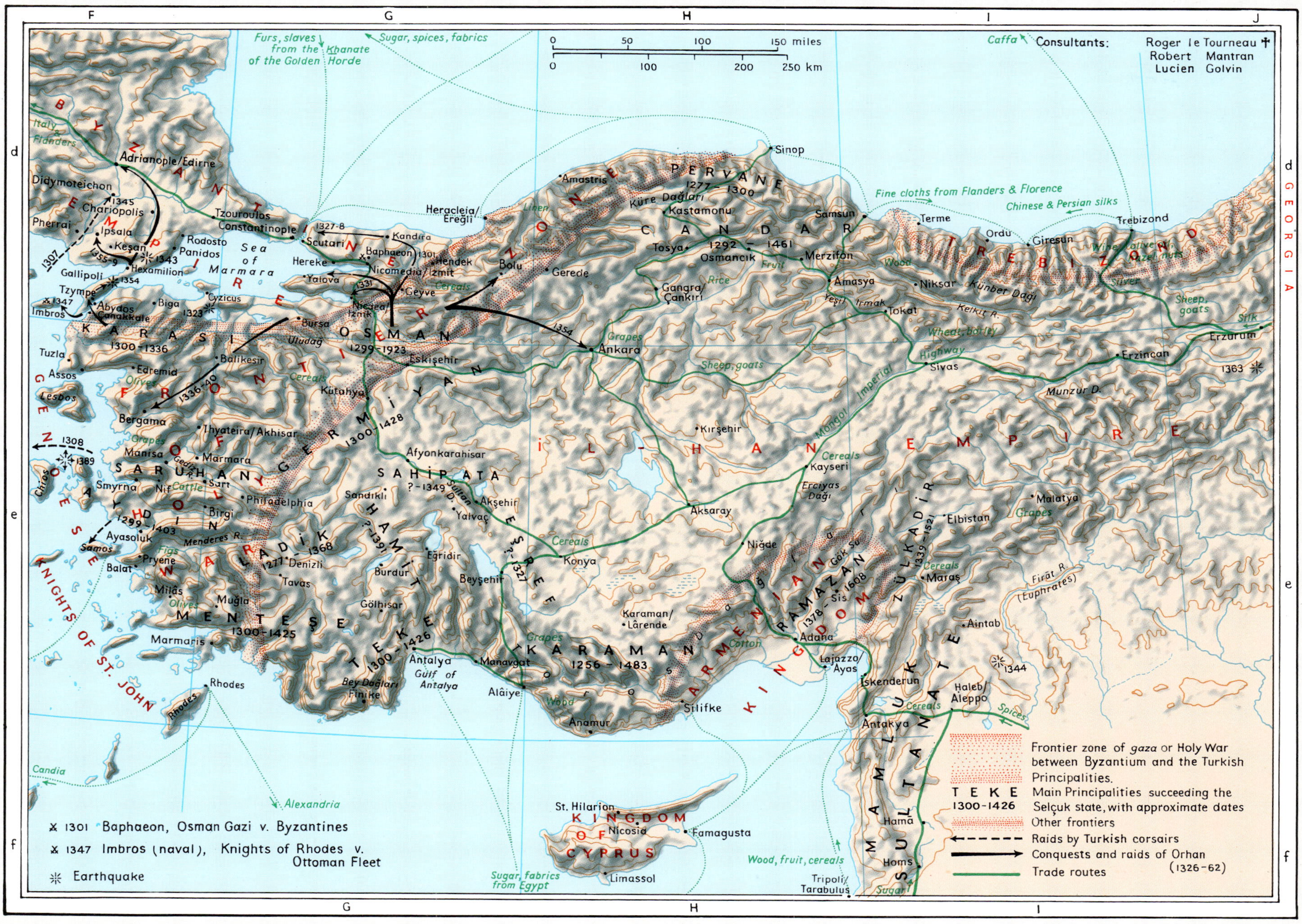

OTTOMAN EXPANSION A.D. 1362-1402. THE FIRST CONQUEST OF RUMELIA AND ANATOLIA

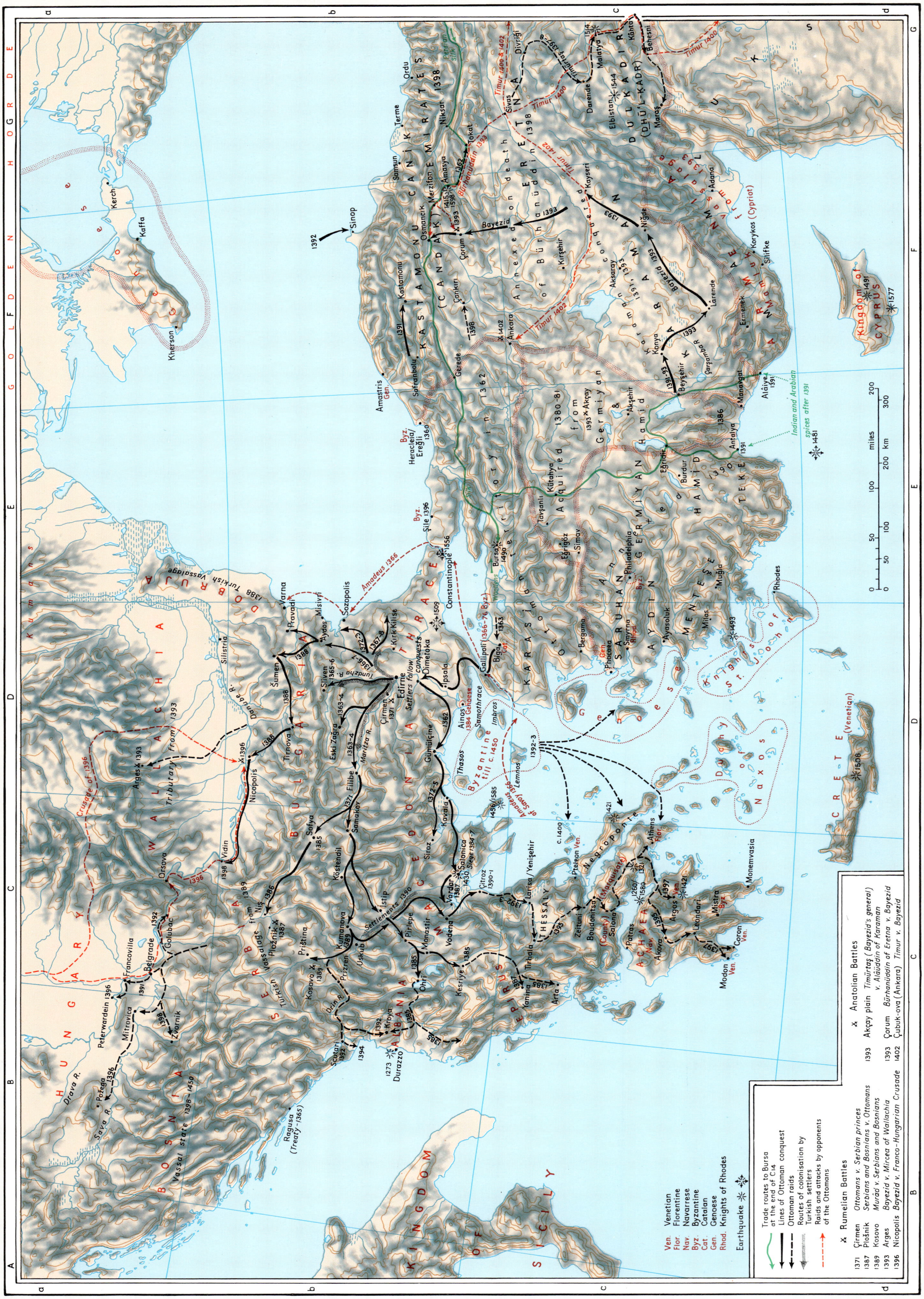
Ven. Venetian
Flor. Florentine
Nav. Navarrese
Byz. Byzantine
Cat. Catalan
Gen. Genoese
Rhod. Knights of Rhodes
Earthquake
Trade routes to Bursa at the end of C14
Lines of Ottoman conquest
Ottoman raids
Routes of colonisation by Turkish settlers
Raids and attacks by opponents of the Ottomans
Rumelian Battles
1371 Çirmen Ottomans v. Serbian princes
1387 Plošnik Serbians and Bosnians v. Ottomans
1389 Kosovo Murâd v. Serbians and Bosnians
1393 Arges Bayezid v. Mircea of Wallachia
1396 Nicopolis Bayezid v. Franco-Hungarian Crusade
Anatolian Battles
1393 Akçay plain Timürtaş (Bayezid's general) v. Alâüddin of Karaman
1393 Çorum Bürhanüddin of Eretna v. Bayezid
1402 Çubuk-ova (Ankara) Timur v. Bayezid
miles 0 50 100 200 300
km 0 50 100 200

ANADOLU AND RUMELI IN THE LATER C17

OTTOMAN NAVAL POWER IN THE 16TH CENTURY

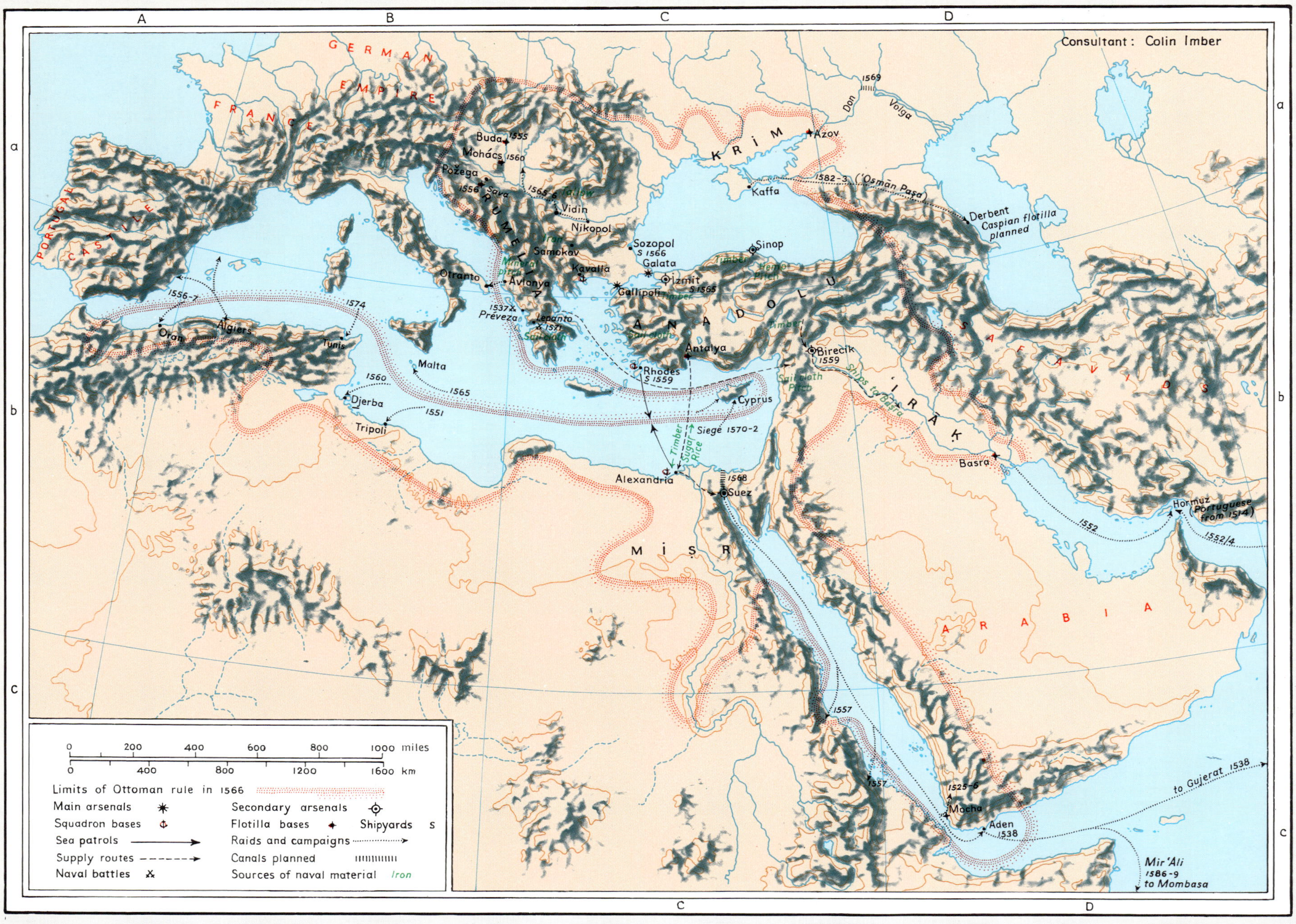

İSTANBUL

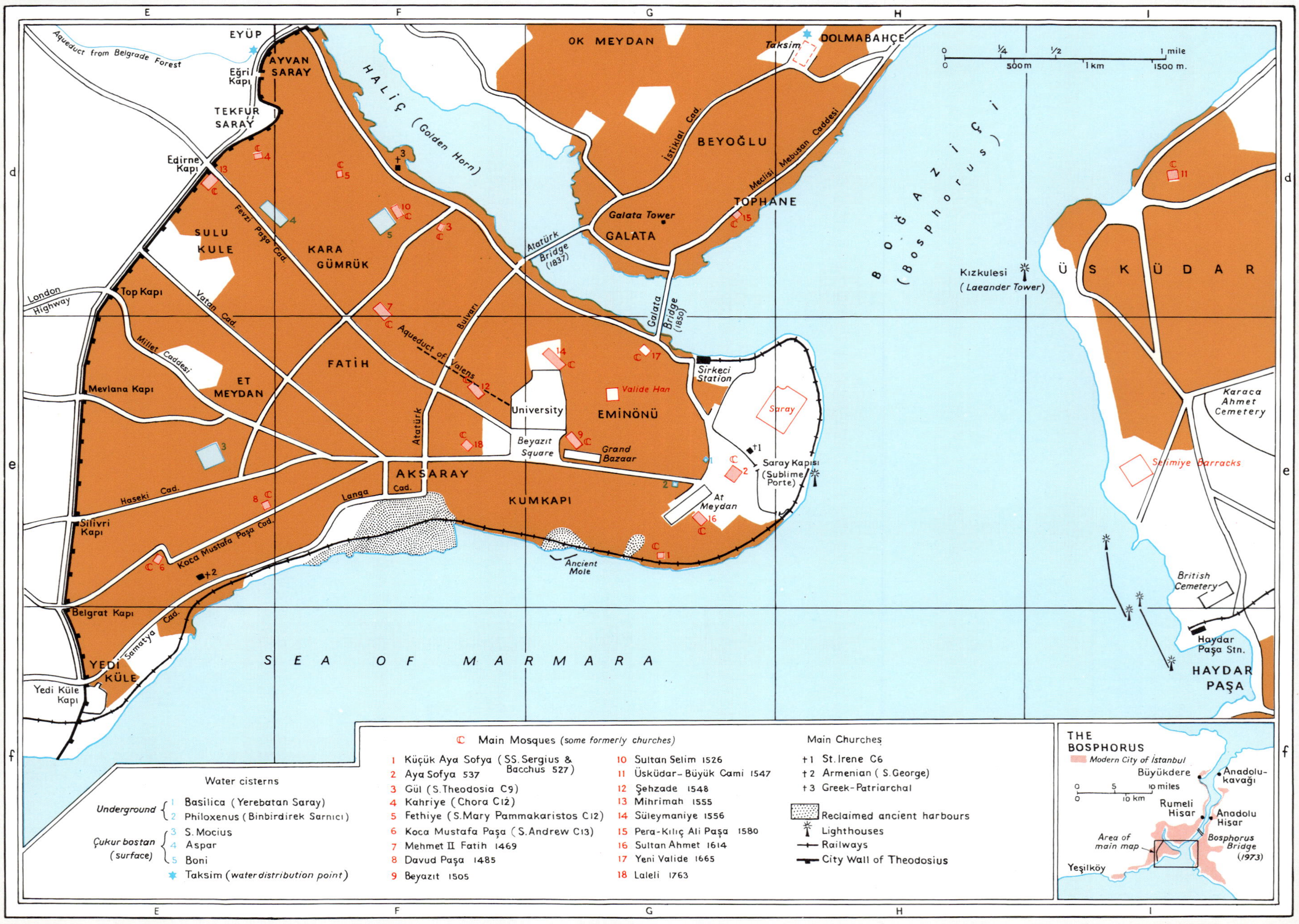

SECTARIES IN ANATOLIA CC13-16

THE SPREAD OF THE ANATOLIAN SECTARIES CC15-17

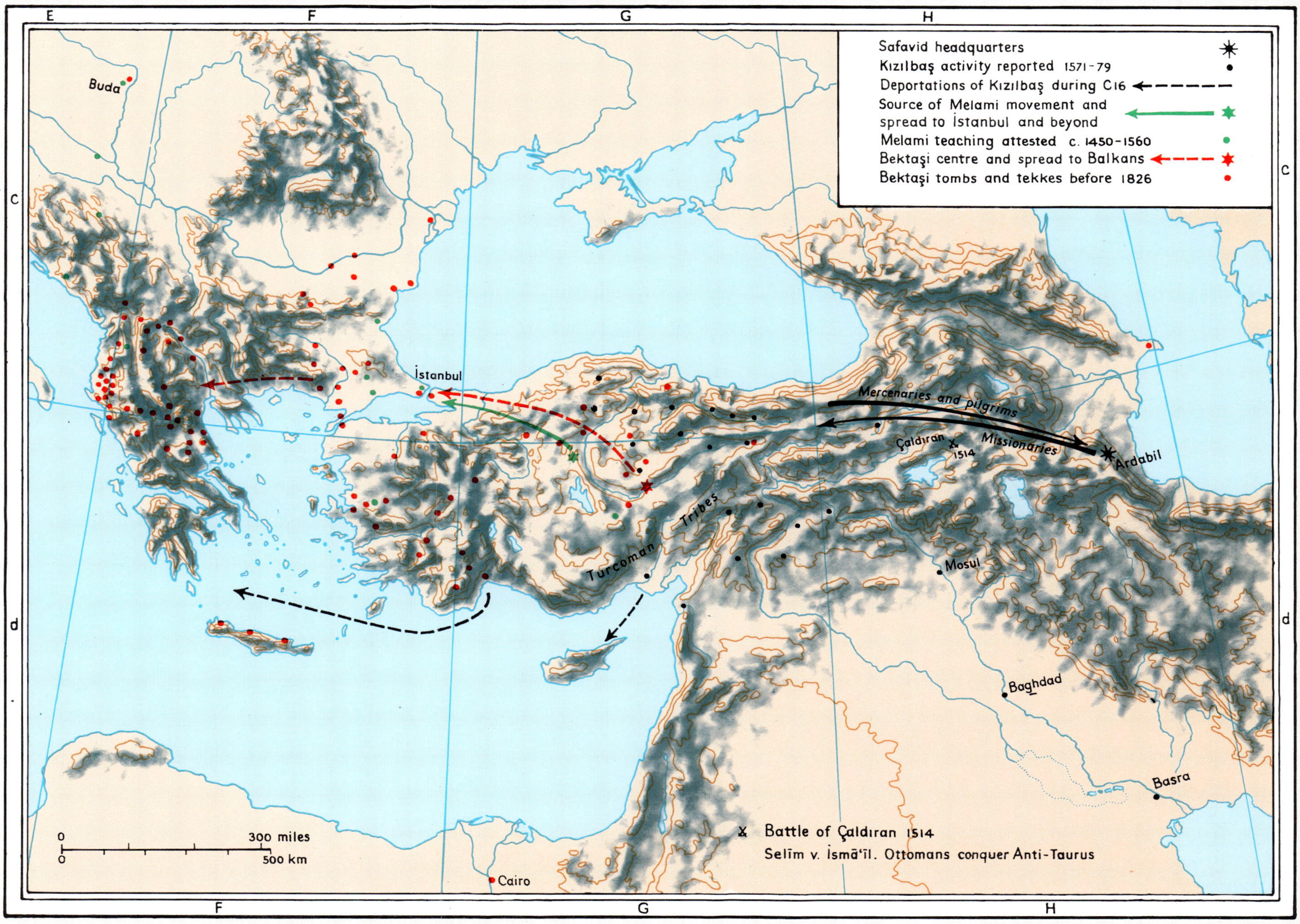

ANADOLU AND RUMELI IN THE LATER C19

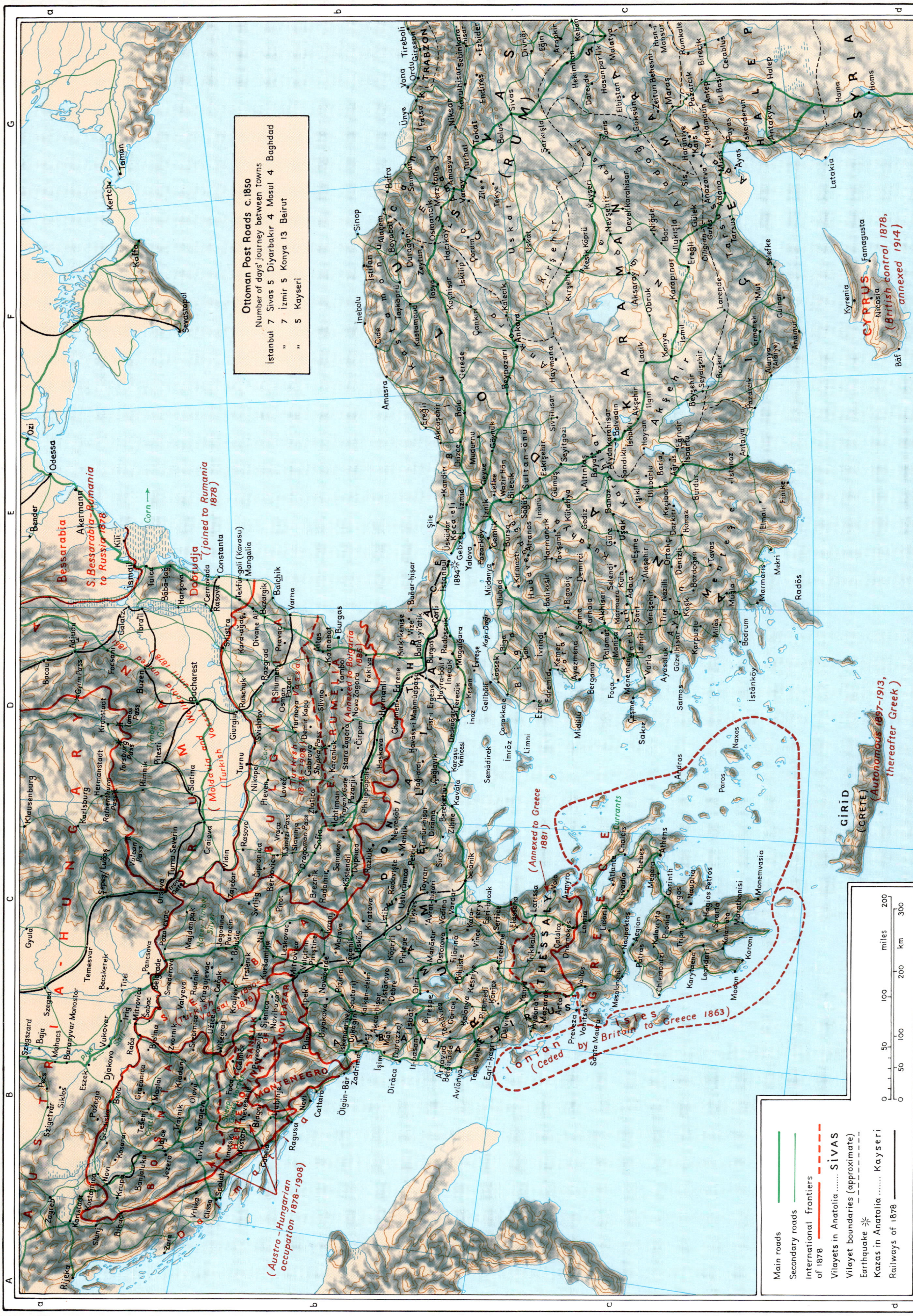

SPAIN AND THE MAGHRIB CC 7-8
THE ARAB CONQUEST (with dates)

WESTERN MEDITERRANEAN IN THE 9TH CENTURY

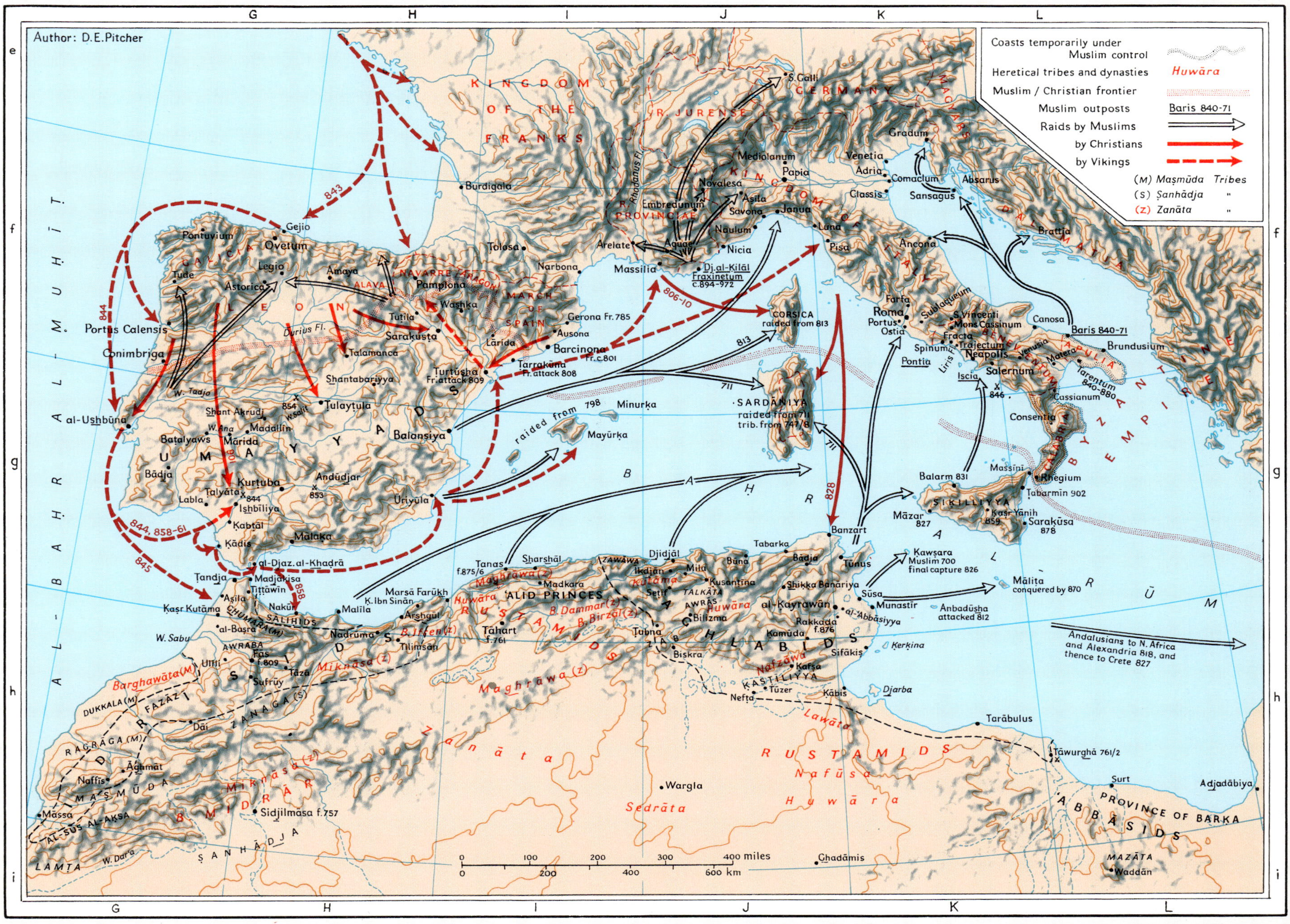

THE MUSLIM CONQUEST OF SPAIN - EARLY C8

SPAIN UNDER THE UMAYYADS c.890

KINGDOM OF THE FRANKS
AL-ANDALUS
AL-THAGHR AL-AʿLĀ
AL-THAGHR AL-AWSAṬ
AL-THAGHR AL-ADNĀ
AL-DJAZ. AL-SHARKIYYA
Reconquered by al-Khawlānī AK 903
AL-BAḤR AL-MUḤĪṬ
Depopulated Area
KINGDOM OF LEON
CALIPHATE OF CORDOBA
NAVARRA
ARAGON
The principal campaigns of al-Mansur
981 A.D.
985
997
1002
Limit of Muslim territory
B. BAKR Autonomous or Rebel Lordships etc.
Domain of Ibn Ḥafṣūn c.890
AK 918 Date of submission to the Amīr of Ḳurṭuba
Christian territory
0 50 100 150 miles
0 100 200 km
0 100 200 miles
0 100 200 300 km
To Morocco
Author: D.E. Pitcher
Consultant: J.F.P. Hopkins

SPAIN c.A.D. 1035 THE PARTY (*TAIFA*) KINGS

SPAIN, THE CHRISTIAN RECONQUEST (A.D. 1035-1482)

NORTH AFRICA - C14

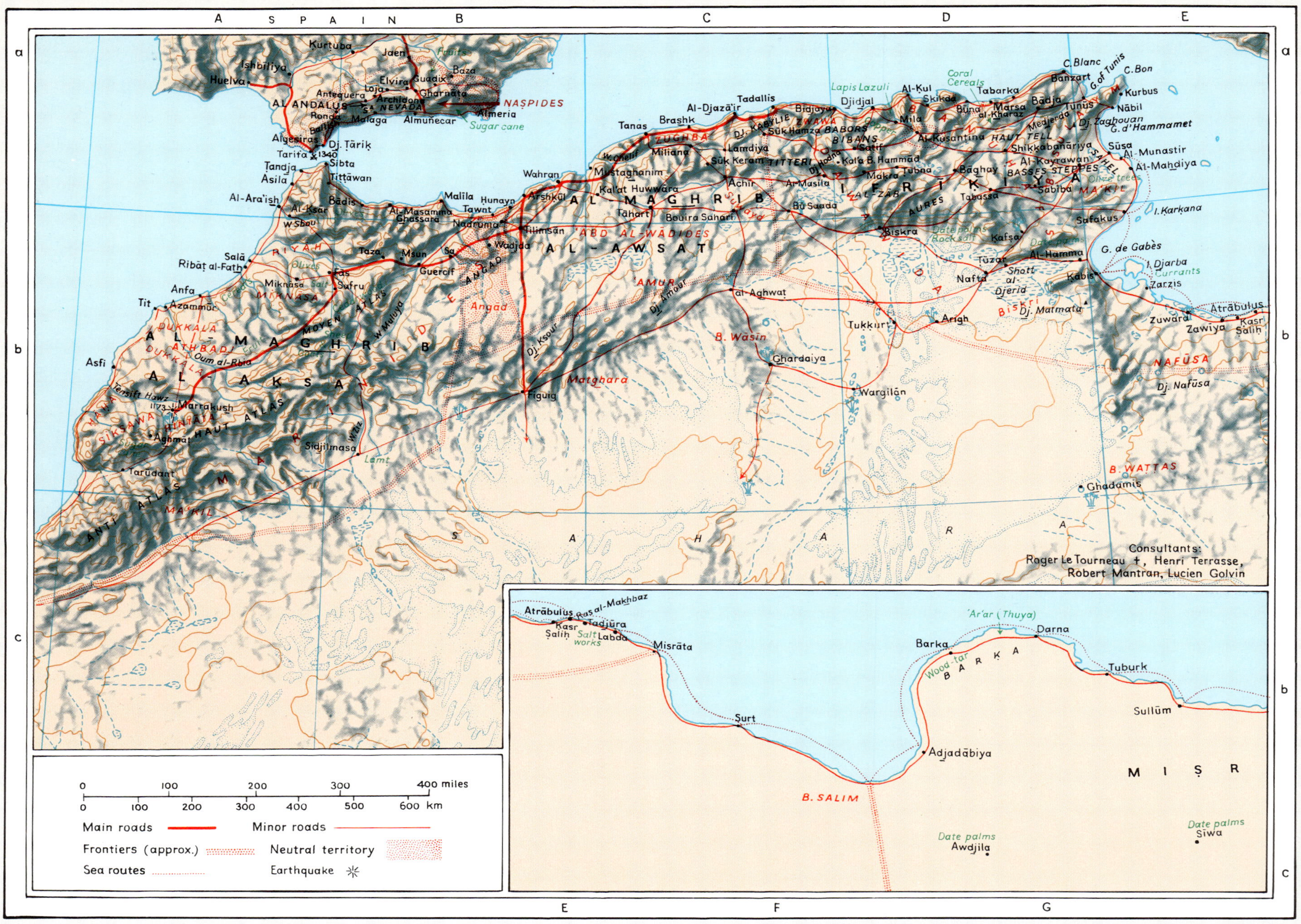

THE BARBARY STATES - C 17

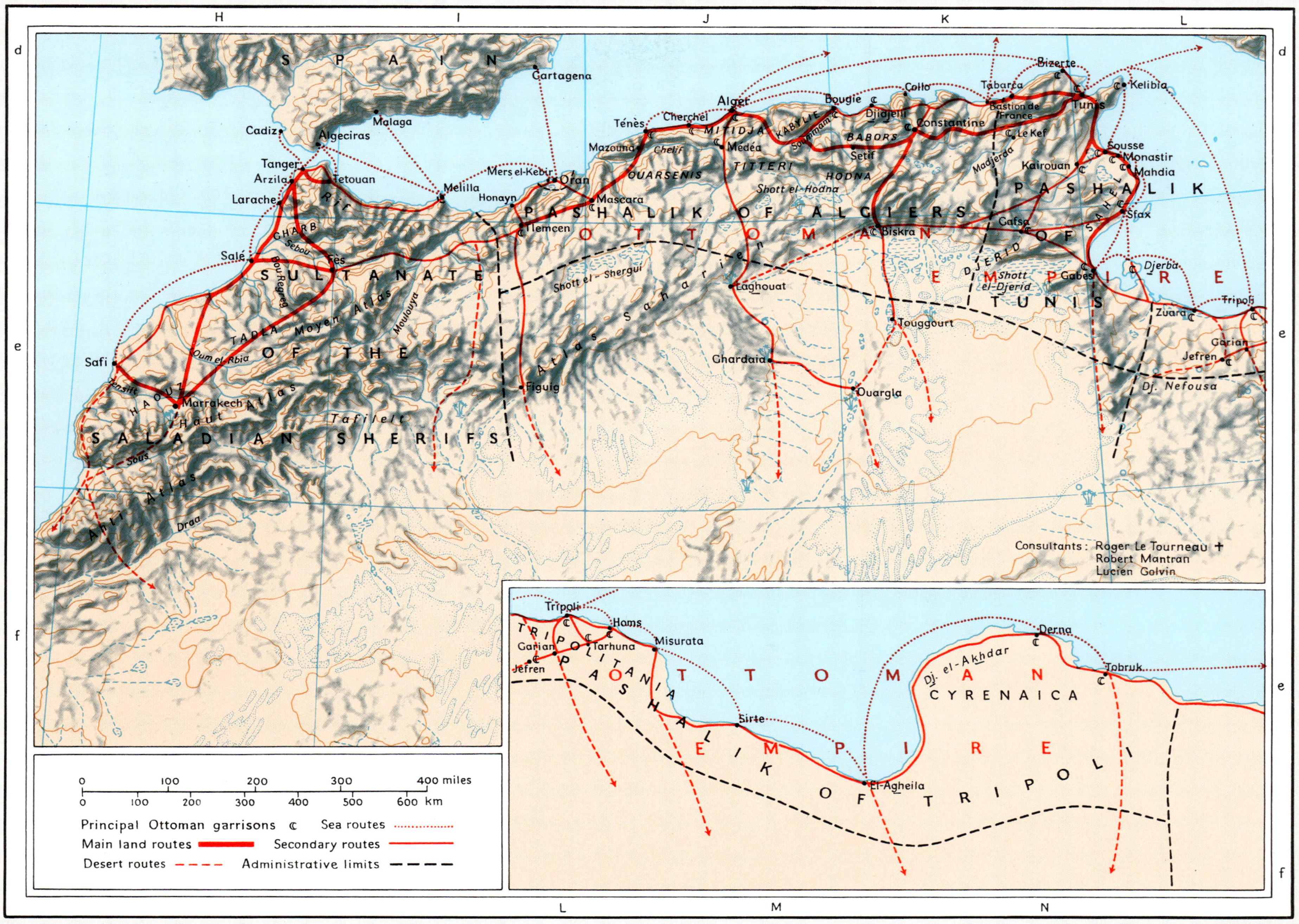

NORTH AFRICA AND THE SUDAN c.1610

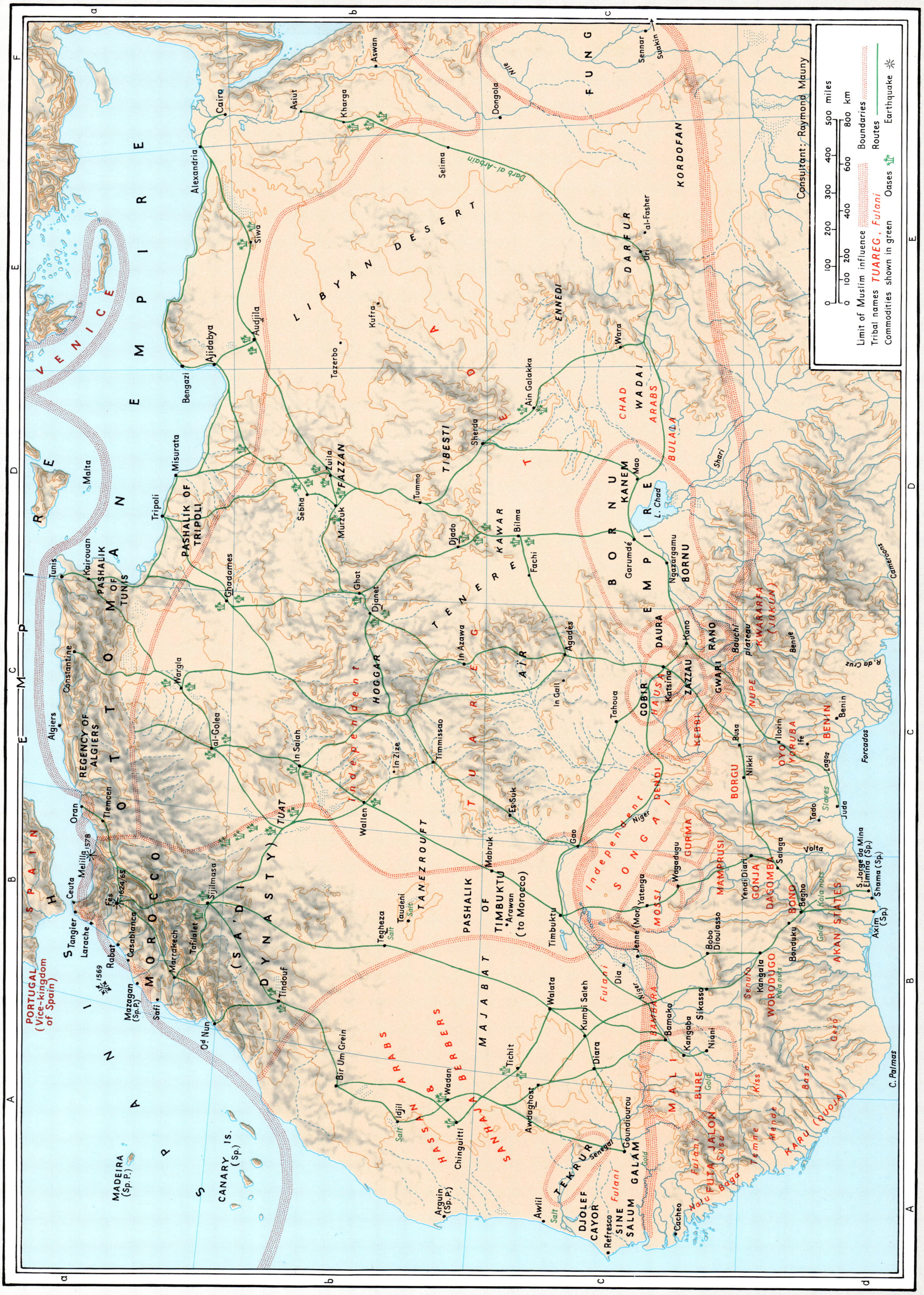

NORTH AFRICA 1700-1830

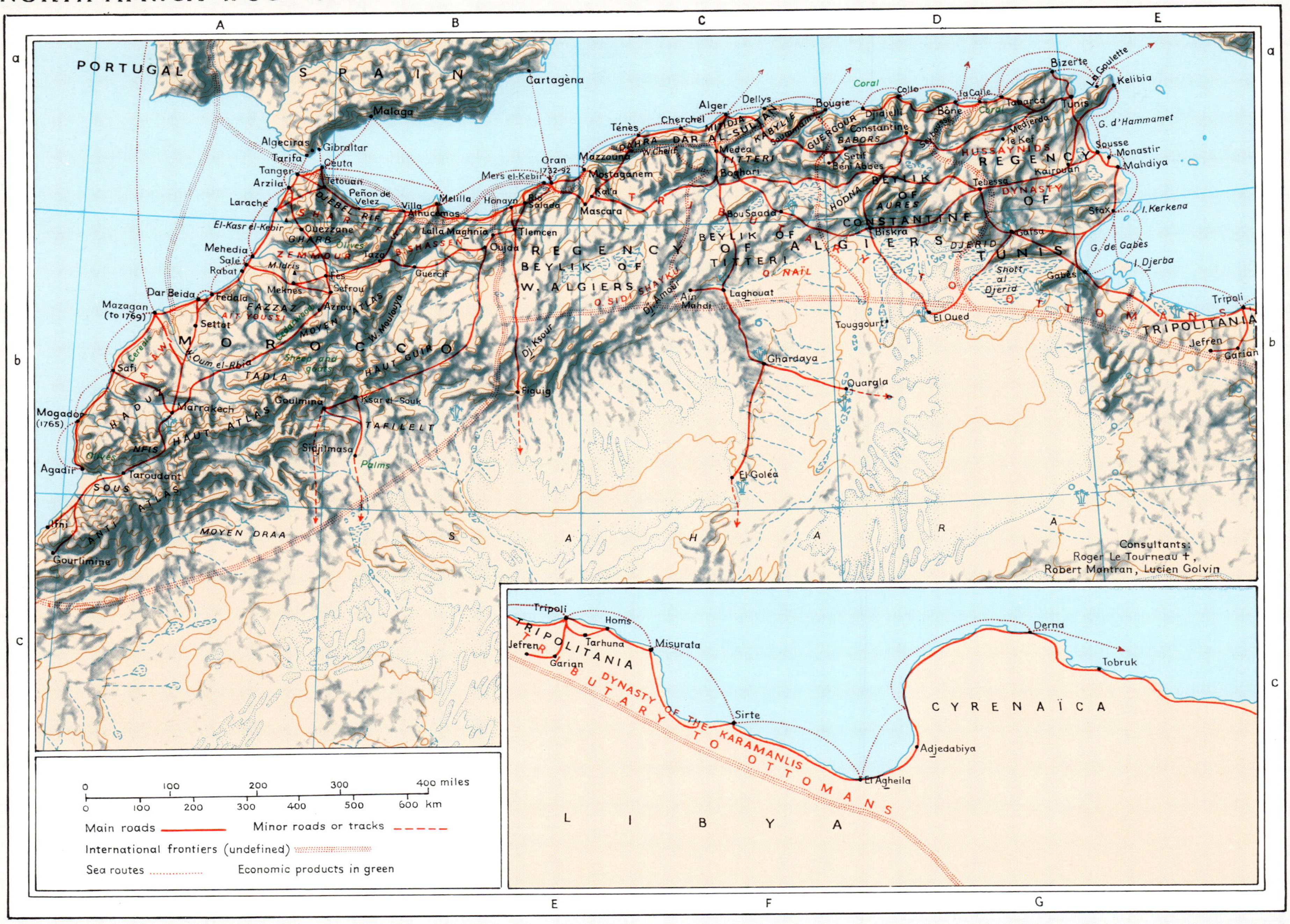

NORTH AFRICA 1830-1912

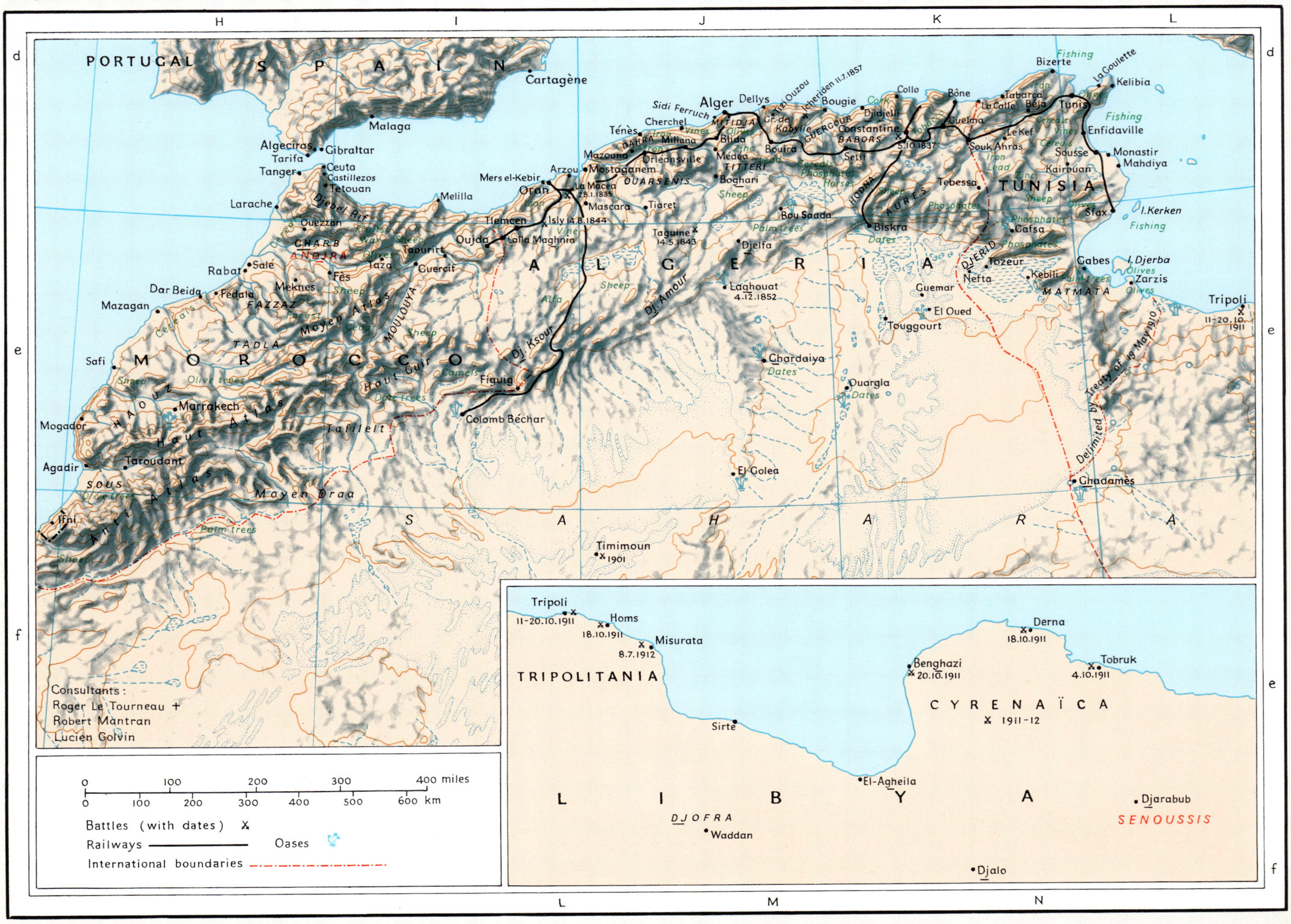

NORTH AFRICA SINCE 1912

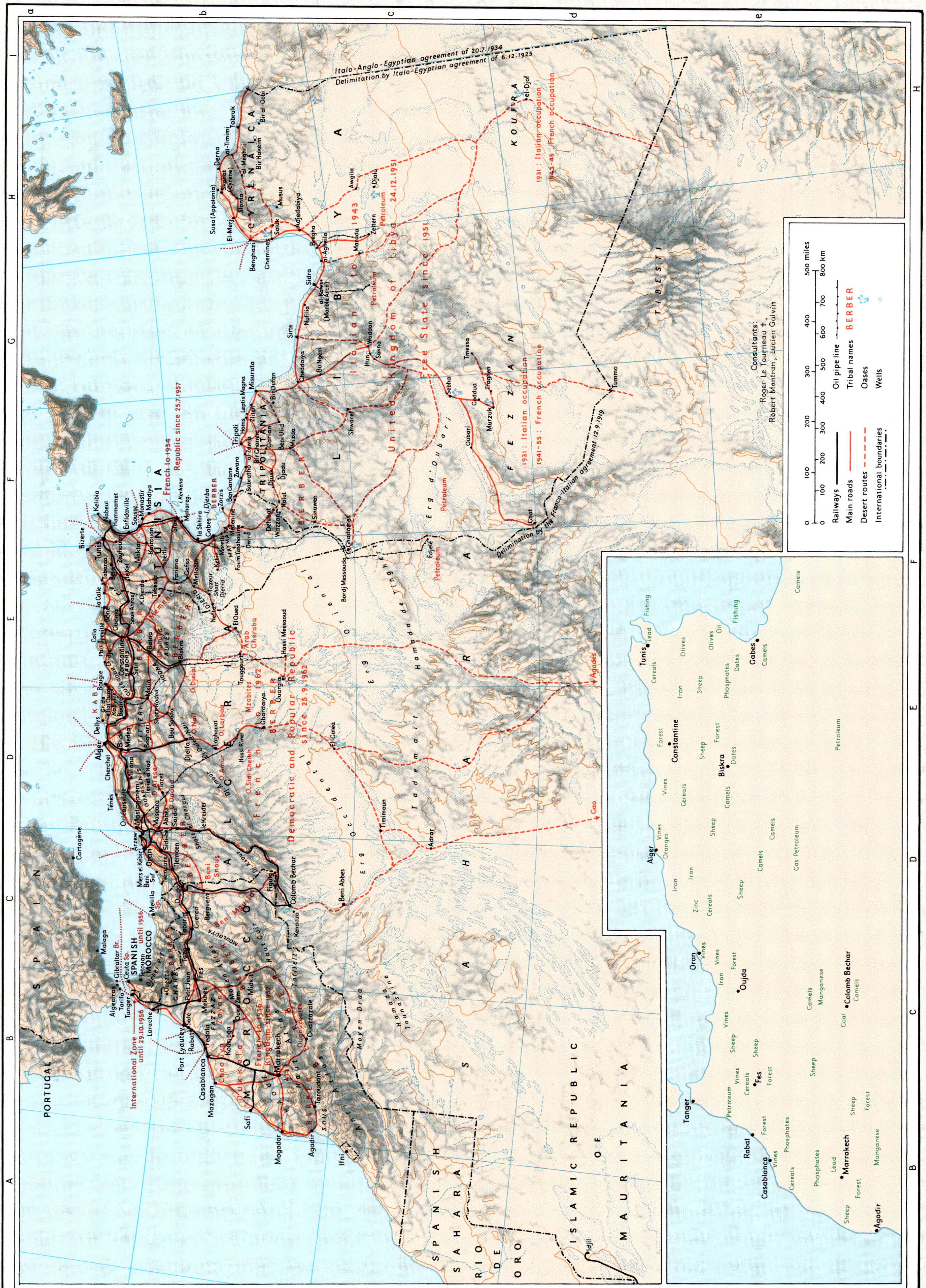

THE INDIAN OCEAN c.A.D. 1000

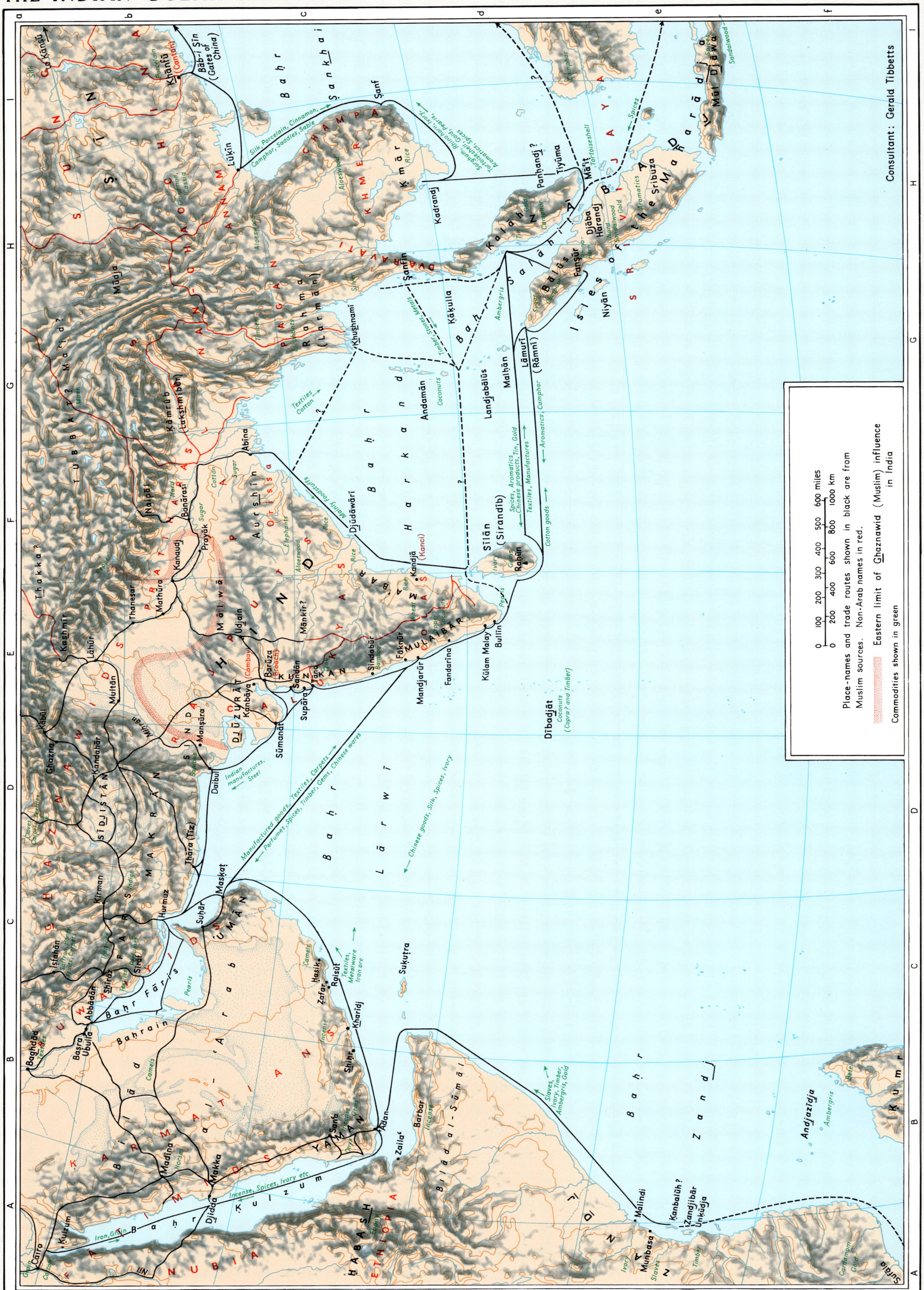
0 100 200 300 400 500 600 miles
0 200 400 600 800 1000 km
Place-names and trade routes shown in black are from Muslim sources. Non-Arab names in red.
Eastern limit of Ghaznawid (Muslim) influence in India
Commodities shown in green
Consultant: Gerald Tibbetts

THE INDIAN OCEAN IN THE 15TH CENTURY

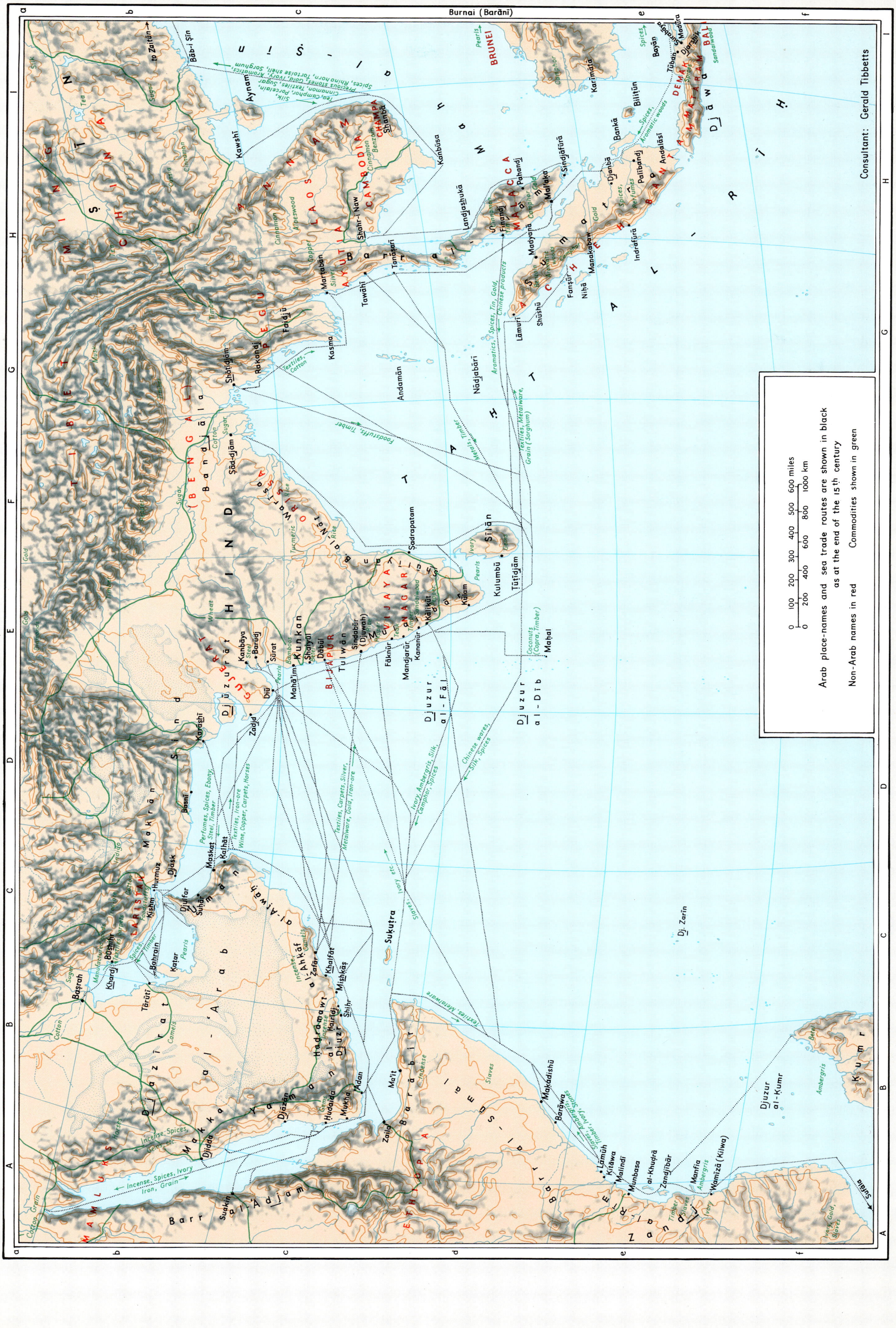

THE TURKS AND PORTUGUESE IN THE INDIAN OCEAN

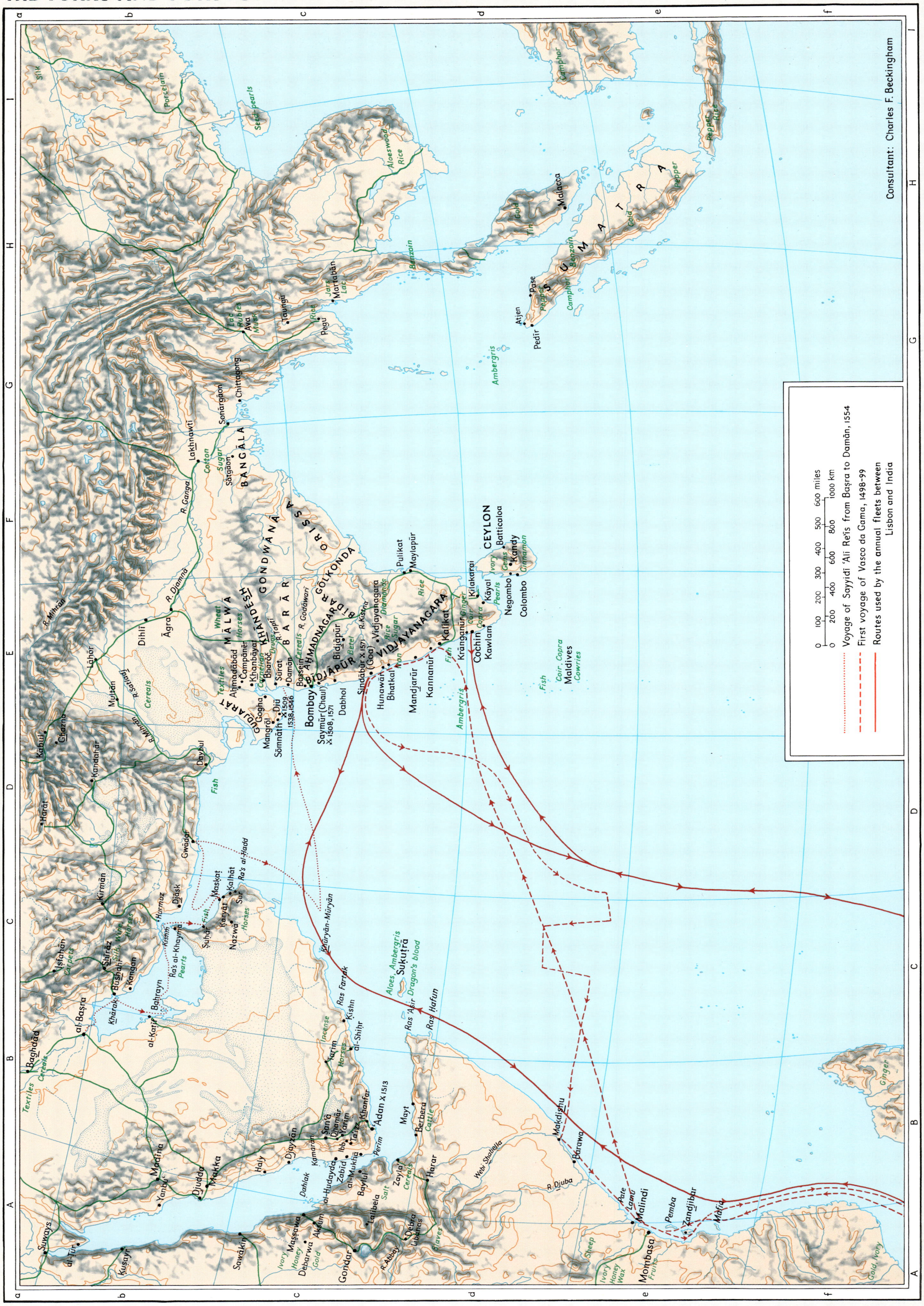

EARLY MUSLIM PENETRATION OF INDIA C.8 – C.13

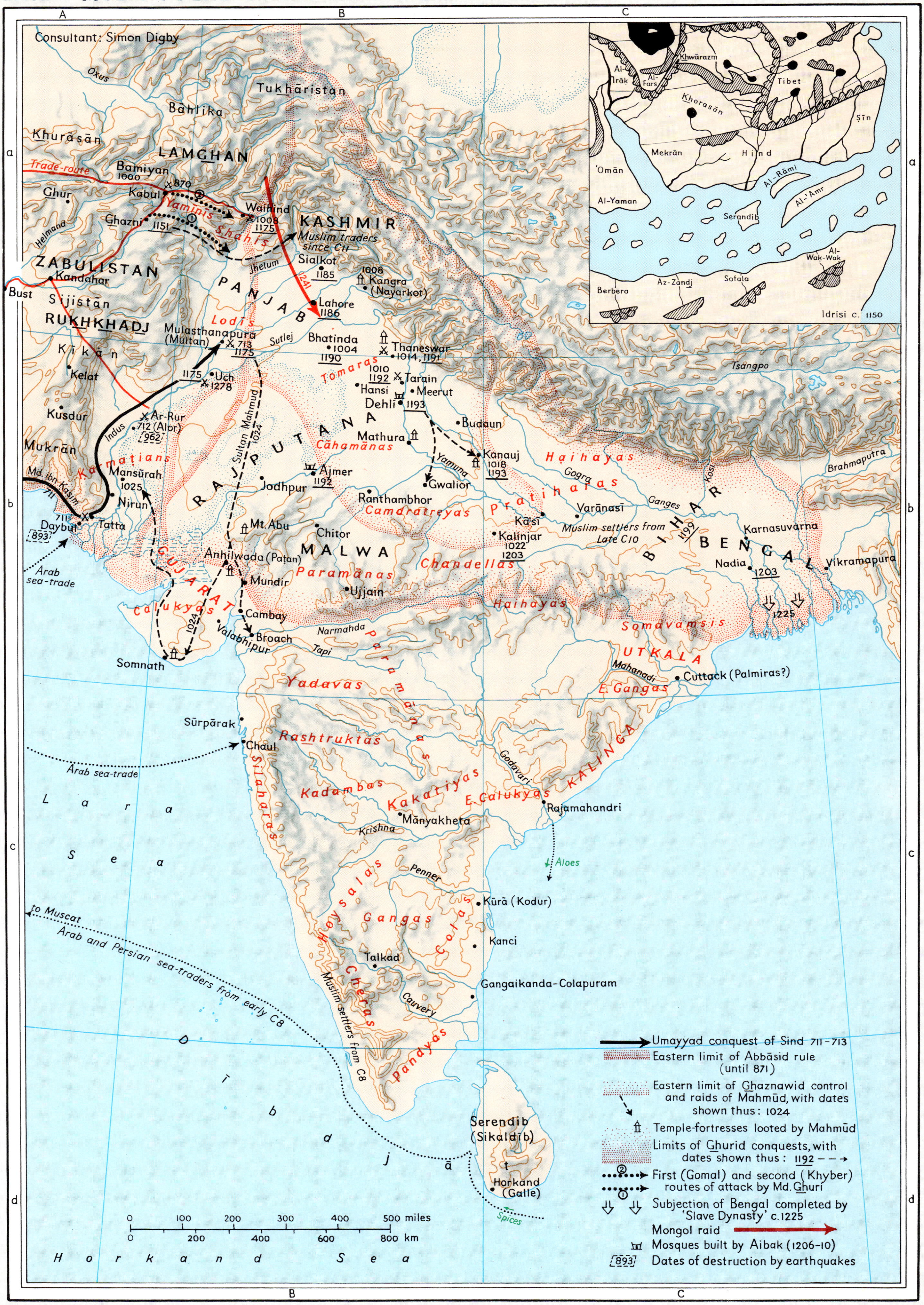

THE GREATER DELHI SULTANATE (KHALJI AND EARLY TUGHLUK) A.D.1290-1335 (first Muslim conquest of the Deccan)

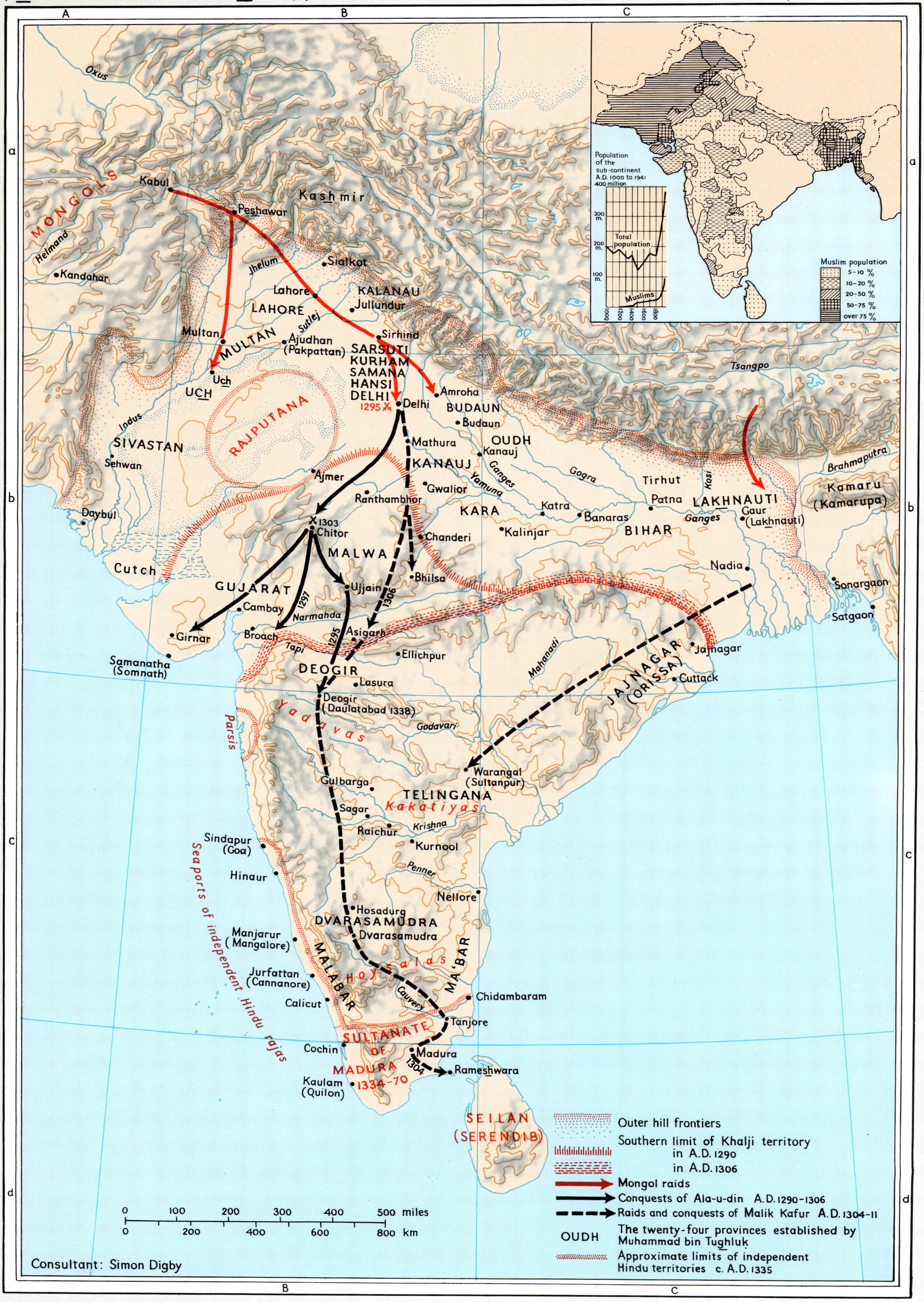

MONGOLS
Kabul
Peshawar
Kashmir
Helmand
Kandahar
Oxus
Jhelum
Sialkot
Lahore
LAHORE
KALANAU
Jullundur
Sutlej
Multan
MULTAN
Ajudhan (Pakpattan)
Sirhind
SARSUTI
KURHAM
SAMANA
HANSI
DELHI
Uch
UCH
Delhi
1295
Amroha
BUDAUN
Budaun
RAJPUTANA
Indus
SIVASTAN
Sehwan
Mathura
OUDH
Kanauj
KANAUJ
Ganges
Yamuna
Gogra
Ajmer
Gwalior
Ranthambhor
Daybul
1303
Chitor
Chanderi
KARA
Katra
Kalinjar
Banaras
Tirhut
Patna
Kosi
LAKHNAUTI
Gaur (Lakhnauti)
BIHAR
Tsangpo
Brahmaputra
Kamaru (Kamarupa)
MALWA
Cutch
GUJARAT
Ujjain
Bhilsa
Nadia
Sonargaon
Satgaon
Cambay
1297
1306
Narmada
Girnar
Broach
Tapi
1295
Asigarh
Ellichpur
Jajnagar
Samanatha (Somnath)
DEOGIR
Lasura
Mahanadi
JAJNAGAR (ORISSA)
Cuttack
Deogir (Daulatabad 1338)
Parsis
Yadavas
Godavari
Warangal (Sultanpur)
Gulbarga
TELINGANA
Kakatiyas
Sagar
Raichur
Krishna
Kurnool
Sindapur (Goa)
Seaports of independent Hindu rajas
Hinaur
Penner
Nellore
Hosadurg
DVARASAMUDRA
Dvarasamudra
Manjarur (Mangalore)
MALABAR
Hoysalas
MA'BAR
Jurfattan (Cannanore)
Calicut
Cauvery
Chidambaram
Tanjore
SULTANATE OF MADURA 1334-70
Cochin
Madura
1304
Rameshwara
Kaulam (Quilon)
SEILAN (SERENDIB)
Population of the sub-continent A.D. 1000 to 1941
400 million
300 m.
200 m.
100 m.
Total population
Muslims
1000
1200
1400
1600
1800
Muslim population
5-10 %
10-20 %
20-50 %
50-75 %
over 75 %
Outer hill frontiers
Southern limit of Khalji territory
in A.D. 1290
in A.D. 1306
Mongol raids
Conquests of Ala-u-din A.D. 1290-1306
Raids and conquests of Malik Kafur A.D. 1304-11
OUDH
The twenty-four provinces established by Muhammad bin Tughluk
Approximate limits of independent Hindu territories c. A.D. 1335
0
100
200
300
400
500 miles
0
200
400
600
800 km
Consultant: Simon Digby
A
B
C
a
b
c
d

1335-1415 CONTRACTION OF MUSLIM RULE UNDER THE TUGHLUK AND SAYYID DYNASTIES

INCIDENCE OF FAMINES
Showing dates and whereabouts of some more severe instances.
The belt of low and intermediate rainfall is particularly liable to suffer, and so are the zones over which the convergence of air-currents may shift from year to year.
FAMINE PRONE
1658 - 60
1769-71
1943
1630 - 39
1799 - 1801
1877 - 78
Inter-Tropical Convergence Zone
Convergence Zone of Monsoon Currents
MONGOL EMPIRE OF SHAHRUKH
Oxus
Helmand
Kandahar
Kabul
Peshawar
Srinagar
KASHMIR 1334 (-1586)
Jhelum
Khokars
Sialkot
Lahore
Suket
Sutlej
Sirhind
Talamba
Dipalpur
Multan
Batinda
Samana
Bhatnair
Saharanpur 1340
Hardwar
Tsangpo
Hisar
Meerut
Delhi (Indarpat) 1398
Rewari
Sargadwari
Koti
Sukkur
Indus
Bikaner
RAJPUT CONFEDERACY
Jaisalmer
Ajmer
Mainpuri
Agra
Yamuna
Kanauj
Etawah
JAUNPUR
Gogra
1394 (-1478)
Sharjis
Jaunpur
1434-78
Prayag
Banaras
Kalpi
Gwalior
R. Chambal
Ranthambhor
LAKHNAUTI
Kosi
Brahmaputra
KAMARU
Patna
Ganges
Gaur (Lakhnauti)
BIHAR
BENGAL
Satgaon
1340 (-1576)
Sanargaon
Satgaon (Chittagong)
Kalinjar
Sonda
Tatta
1396
GUJARAT
(-1573)
Abu
Chitor
Mandura
MALWA
1392 (-1531)
Ujjain
Patan
Asaval
(Ahmadabad 1411)
1424
Cambay
Dhar
Narmada
Broach
Junagadh
Girnar
Verawal
Somnath
Pilgrimage to Makka
KHANDESH 1400
Burhanpur
Tapi
Surat
GONDWANA c. 1350
JAJNAGAR (ORISSA) 1344
Cuttack
Puri
Deogiri (Daulatabad 1338)
Cotton cloths brocades
Thana (Bombay)
Chaul
BAHMANI KINGDOM
Dharur
Godavari
Poona
1347 (-1526)
Dabul
Bidar
Gulbarga
TELINGANA 1343 (to Vijayanagar 1346)
Warangal
Rajahmundri
Cotton-silk fabrics, jute, caps, guns, knives
Mudgal
Krishna
Belgaon
Sindabur (Panjim) (Goa)
Vijayanagar
VIJAYANAGAR 1336 (-1565)
Penner
Hinaur
Hosadurga
Horses, bullion
To Persian Gulf
Pearls, perfumery, jewels, ivory, ebony, sandalwood, camphor, cloves, nutmeg, pepper and coconuts
Mangalore
Dvarasamudra
Conjeeveram
Gingi
Cannanore
Ship-building
Calicut
Cauvery
Persian traders in the Maldives and Laccadives
SULTANATE OF MADURA 1340-70
Madura
Quilon
Ship-building & pearls
Palace
Mosque
Fort
Royal Tombs
Bridge
Outer hill frontiers
Sultanate of Delhi - in late Tughluk times (c.A.D. 1405)
under the early Sayyid Dynasty c.A.D. 1414
c. 1440
Mongol raids c. A.D. 1325-50
Muhammad Shah Tughluk A.D. 1345-50
Taghir in Kathiawar-Sind A.D. 1349-50
Timur's line of conquest A.D. 1398-99
Approximate limits of independent MUSLIM and HINDU territories of the Deccan with dates of separation
0 100 200 300 400 500 miles
0 200 400 600 800 km
Consultant: Simon Digby

INDIA c. A.D. 1530 (The death of Babur)
THE FIRST MUGHUL CONQUEST

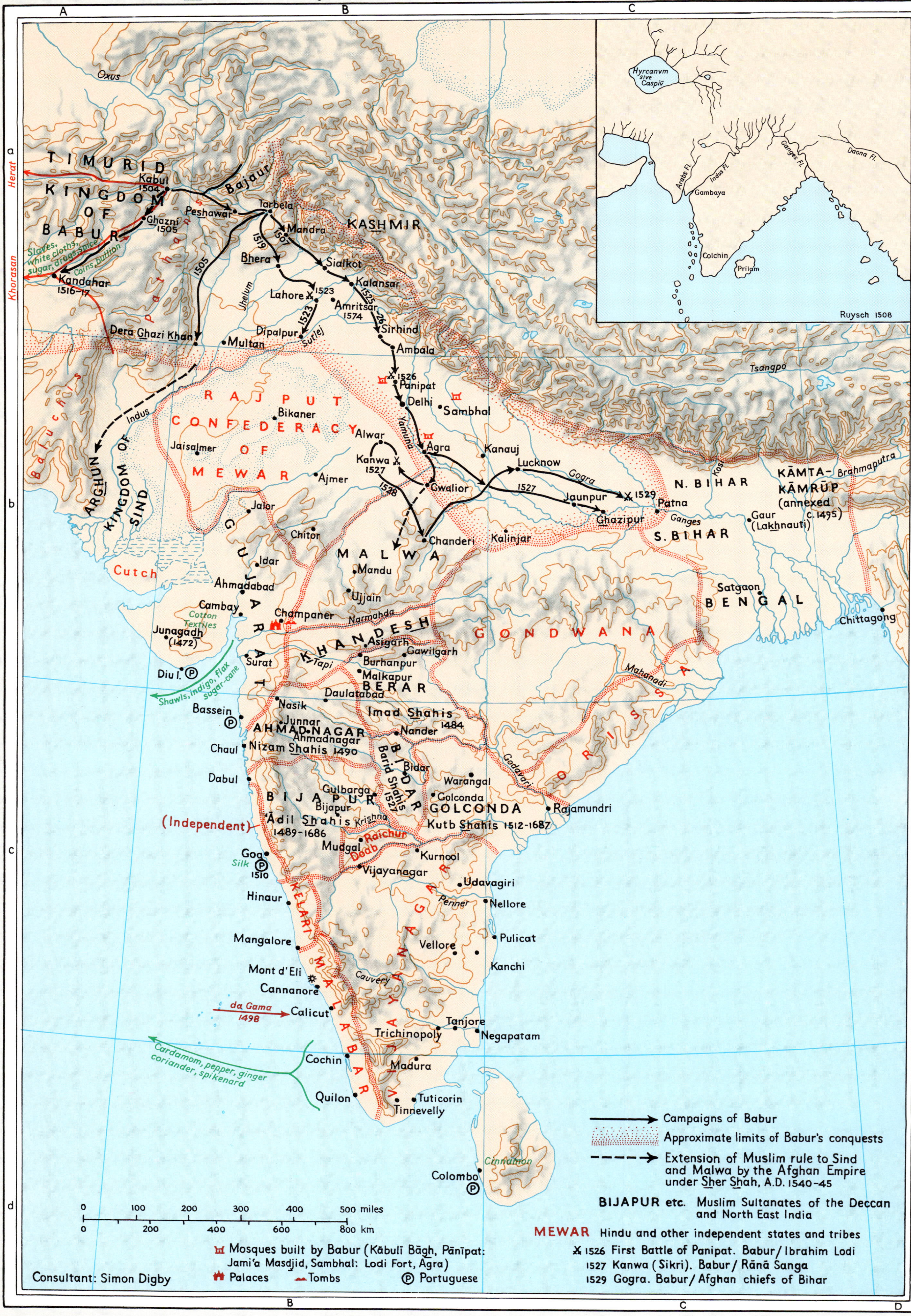

INDIA c.A.D. 1605 (End of reign of Sultan Akbar)

INDIA c. A.D. 1690 Maximum extent of the Mughul Empire under Aurangzeb (Second conquest of the Deccan)

INDIA c.A.D 1770 Maratha expansion and beginning of British administration

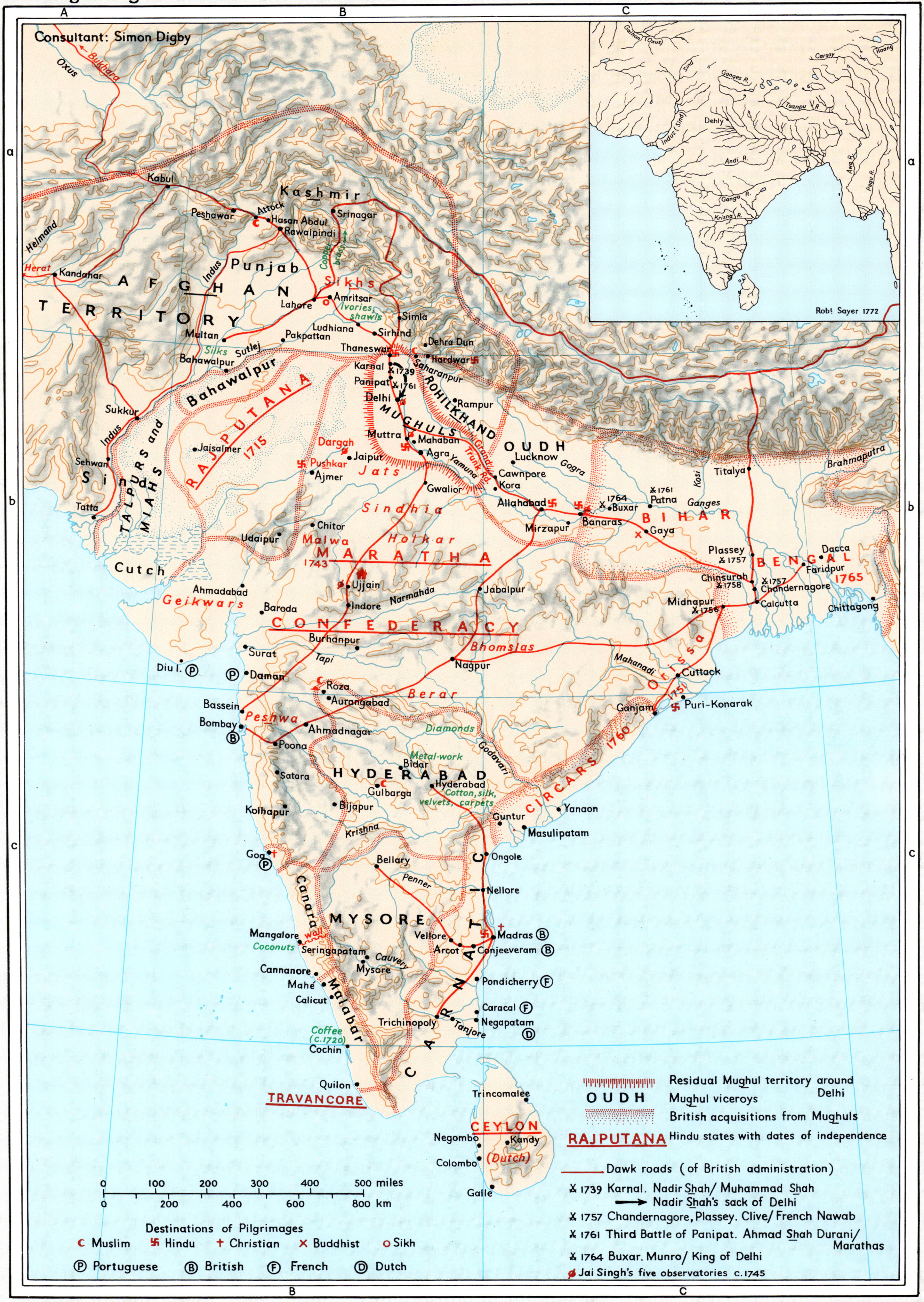

CRADLE OF JAVANESE ISLAM

MADURA — Aroseboya · Bangkalan · Sampang · Terung · Pasuruhan
Sidayu · Leran · Gresik · Ampel · Denta · Surabaya
Grave of Malik Ibrahim died 1419
Giri · Bantas · Penanggungan
Majapahit
Berbek · Solo

**INDONESIA AND MALAYA
THE COMING OF ISLAM AND
THE FIRST MUSLIM EMPIRES**

0 100 200 300 400 500 miles
0 200 400 600 800 km

Approximate extent of the Demak Empire in 1515 .... " 1545
Javanese/Sundanese language boundary
1527 — Date of Demak conquest
Non-Muslim empires or kingdoms with dates
     of period of flourishment
Non-Muslim peoples
Graves of holy men or princes

- - - - - -
1527
MAJAPAHIT
1292–1527
Sundanese
+

Consultant: H. J. de Graaf

MINDANAO · Jolo · Sibutu
Brunei · BORNEO · Dyak · Sukadana · Banjarmasin · Martapura
CELEBES · Toraja · Macassar · Gowa
SERAM · Buru · Ambon
Ternate 1475 Cloves · Tidore · Afu 1475 Cloves 1525 · Nutmegs · Banda 1475 · ALFURS
TIMOR · FLORES · SUMBA · SUMBAWA · LOMBOK · BALI
Celebes · Edible birds' nests · Rice · Gresik · DEMAK 1475–1588 · Pajang · Majapahit · Japara
Sunda Kalapa · Bantam · Pajajaran · Sundanese
Palembang · Jambi · Minangkabau · Bangkahulu · Pepper · Batak
Samudra Pasei 1275 · Perlak · Pedir · Kutaraja · Atjeh · Pidie · Pasei · Aru · Siak · Indragiri · Kampar · Pagerrujung 1500 · Paridnan
MALAYA · MALACCA c.1400–1511 · Johore · Pahang · Trengganu · Kelantan · Selangor · Kedah · Singkel · Batus · Tapanuli · Piru · Paridnan
Tumasik · 1540 · Pepper

Imperial frontiers of Malacca
   and Demak
Approximate date of Islamisation
   or Muslim conquest
Non-Muslim empires or kingdoms
Non-Muslim peoples
Commercial routes to the Spice Islands
1540 — Majapahit
Dyak

THE EMPIRE OF DEMAK (c.1475–1588)

BALI · Gèlgèl 1690
Panarukan · Bolimbangan
MADURA · Sumenep · Pamekasan · Sampang
Aroseboya · Surabaya 1528 · Pasuruhan 1535 · Trengguruh 1545 · Malang
Tuban 1527 · Gresik · Giri + · Jipang · MAJAPAHIT 1292–1527 · Kadiri · Blitar
Japara 1475 · Pati · Kudus · Adilangu · PAJANG c.1550–88 · Demak 1475–1588 · Semarang · Pengging + · Tembayat · Banyumas
Tegal · Banjumas
Gunung Jati + 1475 · Cheribon 1475
Sunda Kalapa (Jakarta) 1526 · Banten 1526 · PAJAJARAN 1333–1579
Sundanese · Indonesia
(Area of inset)

0 50 100 150 200 miles
0 100 200 300 km

JAVA

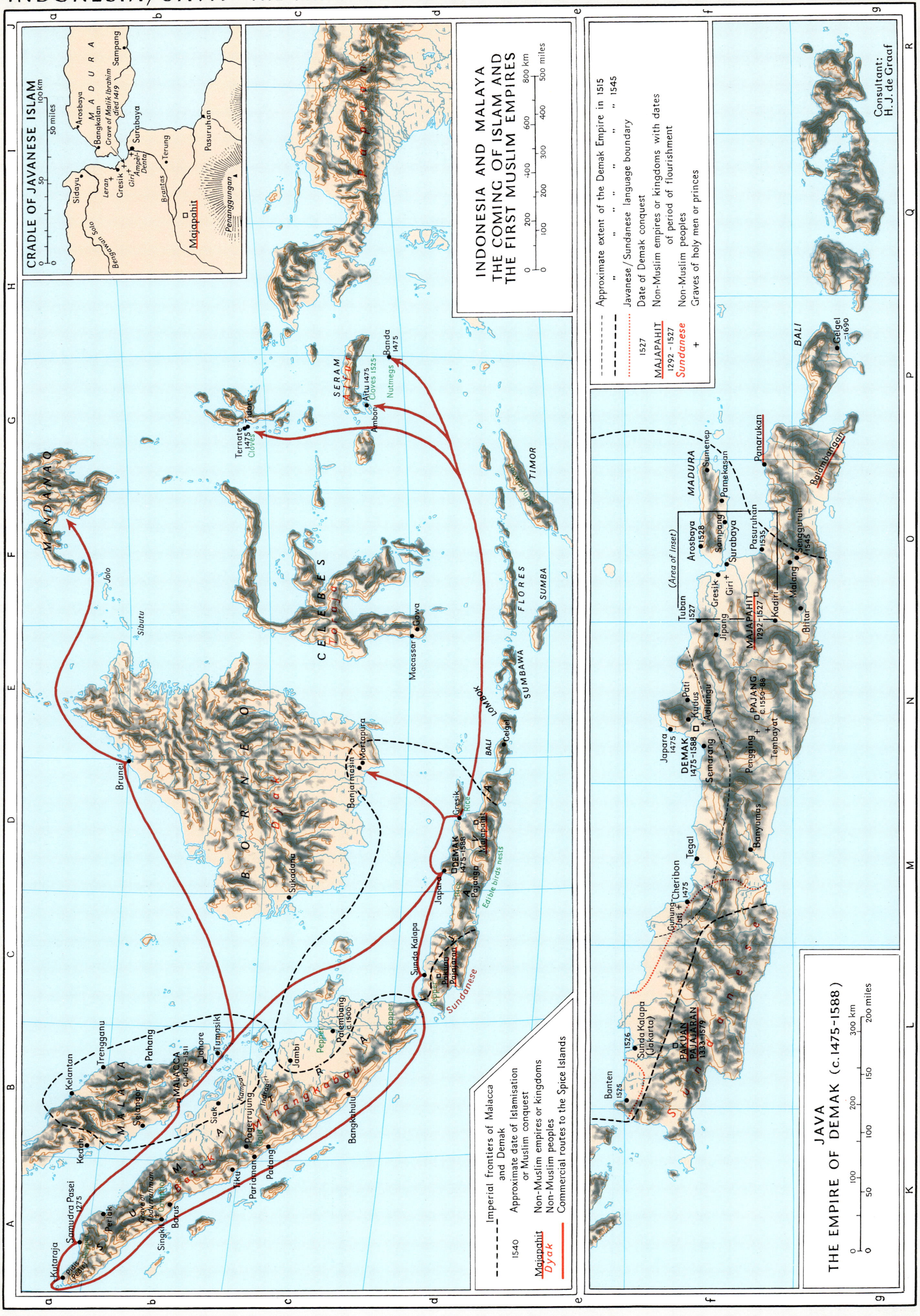

INDONESIA/JAVA A.D. 1500-1750

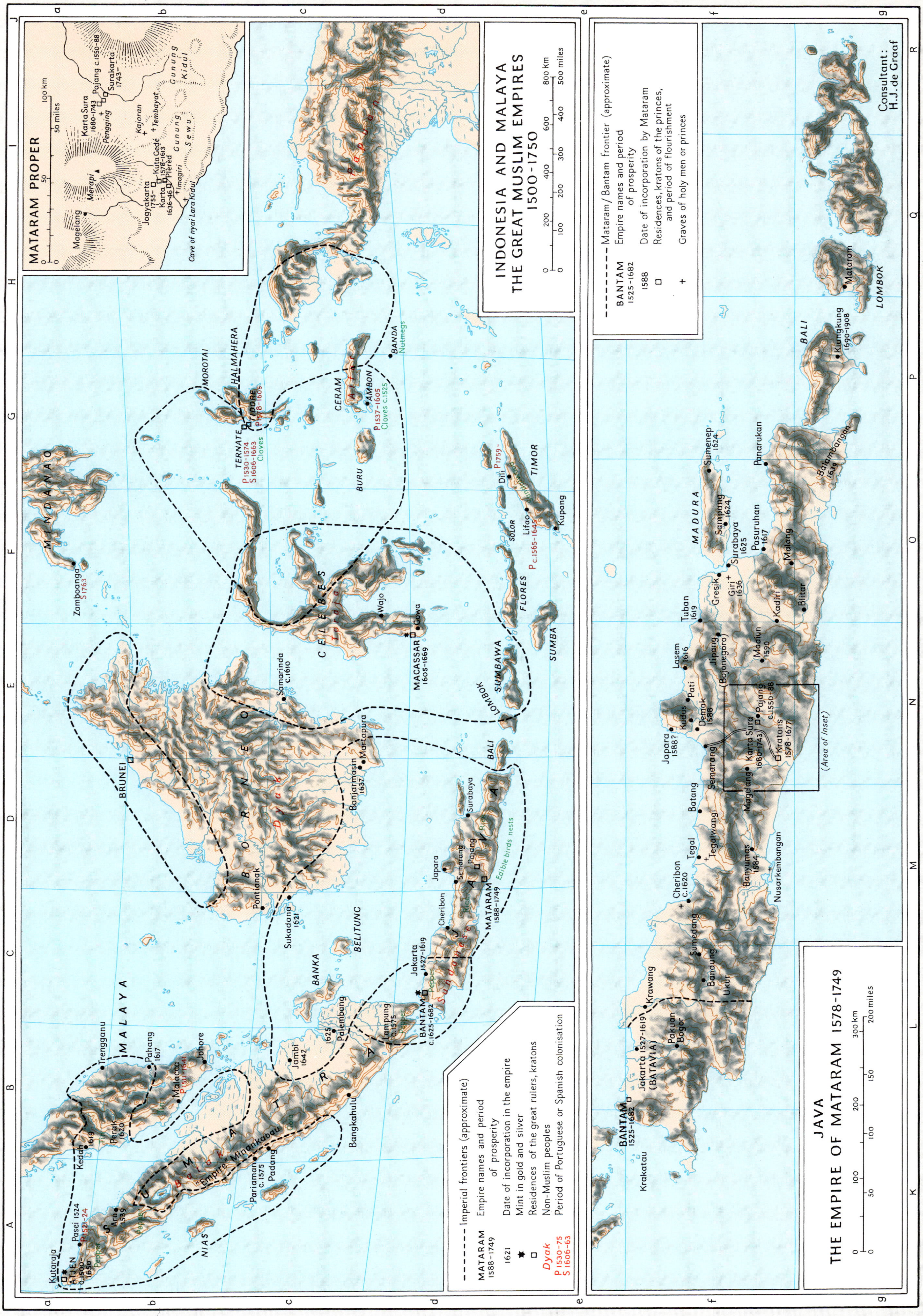

INDONESIA/JAVA EUROPEAN COLONISATION

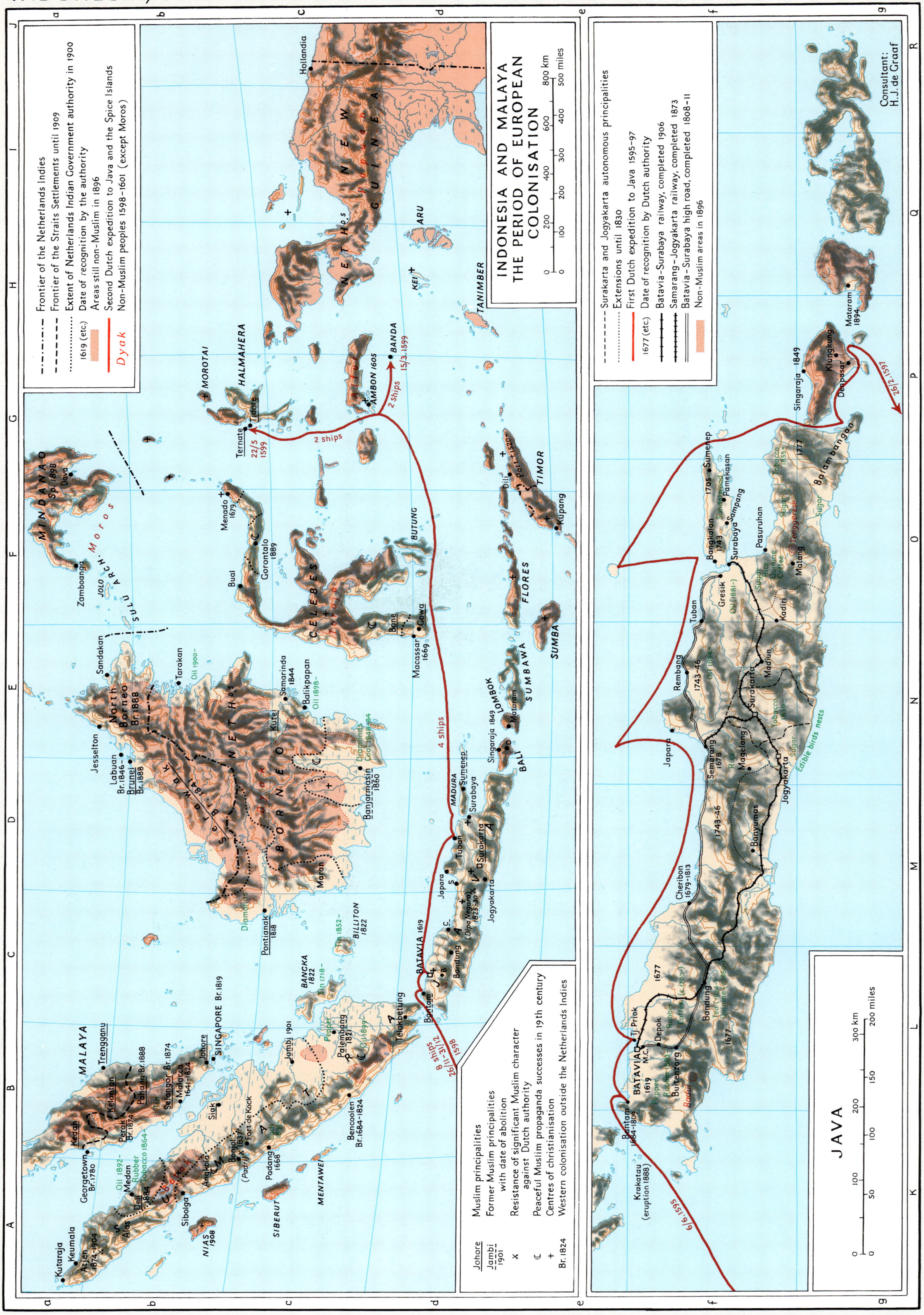
INDONESIA AND MALAYA
THE PERIOD OF EUROPEAN COLONISATION
Frontier of the Netherlands Indies
Frontier of the Straits Settlements until 1909
Extent of Netherlands Indian Government authority in 1900
1619 (etc.) Date of recognition by the authority
Areas still non-Muslim in 1896
Second Dutch expedition to Java and the Spice Islands
Dyak Non-Muslim peoples 1598-1601 (except Moros)
Johore Muslim principalities
Jambi 1901 Former Muslim principalities with date of abolition
Resistance of significant Muslim character against Dutch authority
Peaceful Muslim propaganda successes in 19th century
Centres of christianisation
Br. 1824 Western colonisation outside the Netherlands Indies
Surakarta and Jogyakarta autonomous principalities
Extensions until 1830
First Dutch expedition to Java 1595-97
1677 (etc.) Date of recognition by Dutch authority
Batavia-Surabaya railway, completed 1906
Samarang-Jogyakarta railway, completed 1873
Batavia-Surabaya high road, completed 1808-11
Non-Muslim areas in 1896
JAVA
Consultant: H.J. de Graaf

ISLAM IN CHINA

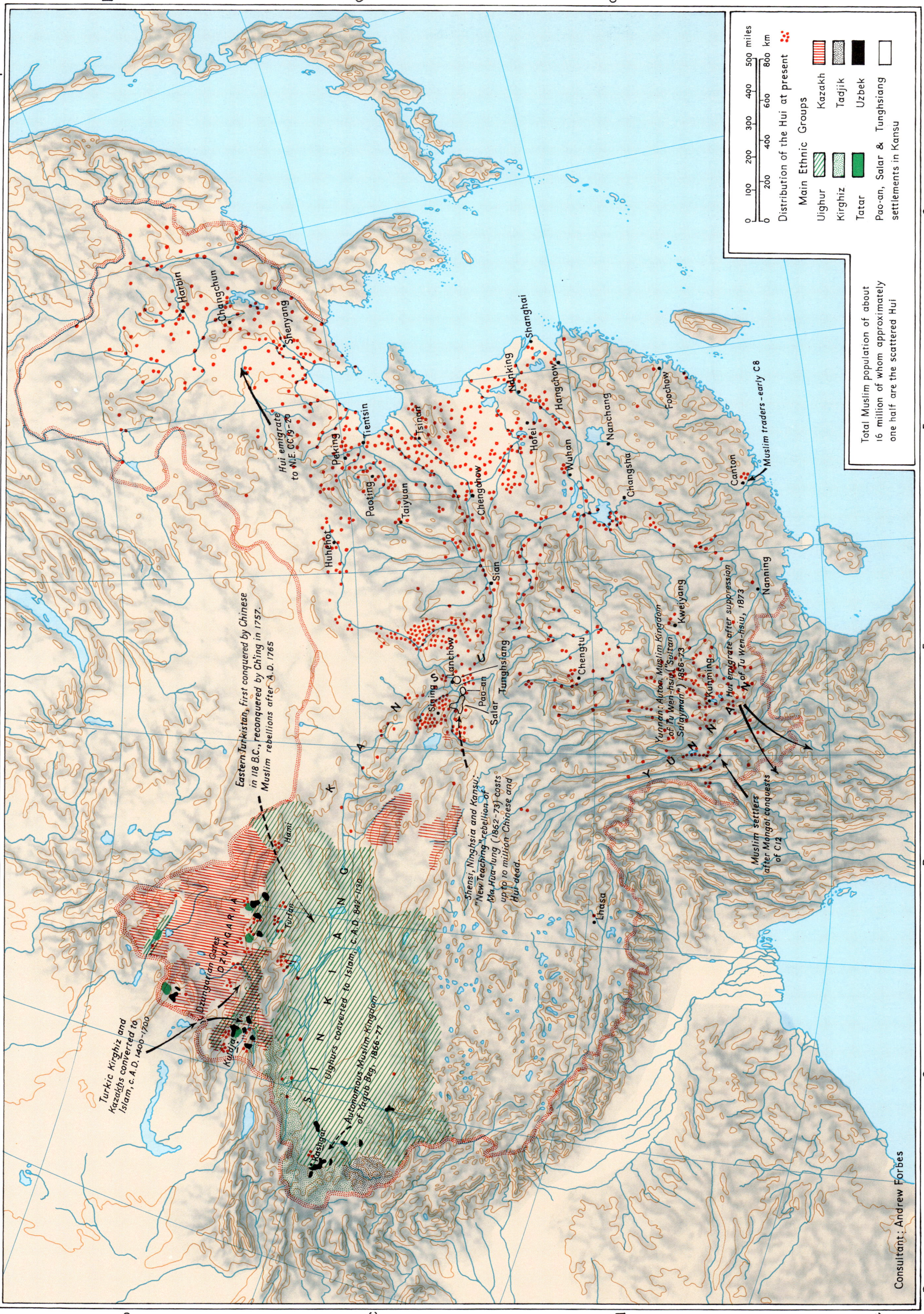
Main Ethnic Groups
Uighur
Kirghiz
Tatar
Kazakh
Tadjik
Uzbek
Pao-an, Salar & Tunghsiang settlements in Kansu
Distribution of the Hui at present
0 100 200 300 400 500 miles
0 200 400 600 800 km
Total Muslim population of about 16 million of whom approximately one half are the scattered Hui
Muslim traders - early C8
Hui emigrate after suppression of Tu Wen-hsiu, 1873
Yunnan: Autonomous Muslim Kingdom of Tu Wen-hsiu, 'Sultan Sulayman', 1856-73
Muslim settlers after Mongol conquests of C12
Shensi, Ninghsia and Kansu: 'New Teaching' rebellion of Ma Hua-lung (1862-73) costs up to 10 million Chinese and Hui dead.
Eastern Turkistan, first conquered by Chinese in 118 B.C., reconquered by Ch'ing in 1757. Muslim rebellions after A.D. 1765
Hui emigrate to N.E. CC.19-20
Turkic Kirghiz and Kazakhs converted to Islam, c. A.D. 1400-1700
Uighurs converted to Islam, c. A.D. 842-1130
Autonomous Muslim Kingdom of Yaqub Beg, 1866-77
Dzungarian Gates
DZUNGARIA
SINKIANG
KANSU
YUNNAN
Harbin
Changchun
Shenyang
Peking
Tientsin
Tsinan
Nanking
Shanghai
Hangchow
Hofei
Wuhan
Nanchang
Foochow
Changsha
Canton
Nanning
Kweiyang
Kunming
Chengtu
Sian
Chengchow
Taiyuan
Paoting
Huhehot
Lanchow
Sining
Pao-an
Salar
Tunghsiang
Lhasa
Hami
Turfan
Kuldja
Kashgar
Consultant: Andrew Forbes

INDEX OF PLACE-NAMES AND ETHNICS

(*Ethnics* and *personal names* in italics)

Āba 16 Ab
Abāda 16 Bc
Abāda (Ḳaryat ʿAbd al-Raḥmān) 16 Bd
ʿAbadān, Abbādān 1.6.iii 22 Db 44 Ba
Abadiya 1.6.i 36 Db
Abariz (Paris) 1.2.vi
Abarḳūh 16 Bc
Abasgi 19 Ca
Abasgia 8 Cb
Abaskūr 16 Cb
Beni Abbad 38 Cd
Abbādān 44 Ba
Shah Abbas Causeway 26 Db
Abbasids 8 Cc 21 24
Abbay R. 46 Ac
ʿAbd Kays 15 He 19
ʿAbda (Eboda) 14 Jf
ʿAbd al-Wādides 40 Cb
Abdal Morad et al. 33 Ba
Abdurrahman, grave of 54 Ab
Abesehr 9 Bd 10
Abhar 16 Ab
Abi Zār al-Ghafārī St. 23 Gef
Abīna 44 Fb
Abisama opp. 14 Ee
Abīward 16 Db 19
Abkhazi 26 Ca
Abr 15 Ca 22 Hg
Abradj 16 Bc
Abrūn I. 16 Bd
ʿAbs 19 Dc
Abu Mt. 47 Bb 49
Abu Dāʾūdids 24 Cc
Abucaei 14 Db Mg
Abyar ʿAlī 22 Ff
Abydos (Ābidus) 1.4.v 19 Ba 28 29
Abyssinia (Ethiopia) 13 Cd
academies 5 8–10
Accipitram vic. 14 Ec
Accipitum 14 Bd
Accra 12 Ad
Achaea, Achaia 30Cc 10 Bc
Achchitae 14 Cd Mj
Acheh 45 Gd
Achīr (Boghari) 40 Ca 43
Achrua 14 Bb
Achyraus 28 Ab
Acme opp. 14 Cd
Acroenum 28 Ge
Adala 31 Ec 34
ʿAdan (Aden, Arabia metrop.) 5 Cd 6–15 19 22 44 45
Adana 22 Bb 26–31 33 34
Adara opp. 14 Db
Adhana, W. 15 Bb
Adharbaydjan (Azerbaijan) 19 Db 20 24
Adil Shahis of Bijapur 50 Bc
Adilangu 54 Nf
Adjā, Dj. 19 Dc
Adjadābiya, Ajidabya 40 Gb 41 Ea 42 43
al-Adjam 11 Cd
Adjmēr, *see* Ajmer
Adjudu 34 Da
Adra 14 Ba
Adramyttium (Edremid) 28 Ab 29
Adrar 13 Ac
Adrassus 28 Cb
Adrianople (Edirne) 7 Bb 19 22 27 29
Adulis 5 Cd 6 14 19
Aegion (Vōstîce) 34 Cc
Aegyptus (Egypt) 14 Aa–c
Aenus 28 Aa
Aethiopia 14 Ad–e
Afghānistān 13 Dc 24
Afif 22 Gf 26
al-Afladj 15 Hf
Aflandris (Flanders) 1.2.vi
al-Afrandj 1.2.vi
Africa 22 Eg
Afrīdhān 17 Fa
Afrighids 24 Ab
Afrizia 1.2.vi
Afşar 33 Cb
B. al-Aftas 38 Cc
Afyonkarahisar 25 Bb 26 27 29 31 33 34
Agadès 8 Bd 9–12 41 43
Agadir 42 Ab He
Agathoclis 14 Ee
al-Agheila 40 Me 42 43
Aghlabids 8 Bc
Aghmāt 35 Ad 40
Aghrims 1.2.vii
al-Aghwat (Madīna) 23 Gf
al-Aghwat (Laghouat) 40 Cb
Agiu 6 Db
Agni 12 Ad
Agra 46 Eb 49–53
Ağras 31 Ec 34
Ağrîbōz (Chalcis) 31 Cc
Āhangaran 17 Eb
Ahar 22 Da
al-Ahḳāf 19 Dd 45
Aḥmadābād (Asaval) 49 Bb 53
Aḥmadnagar 46 Ec 50–53
Ahuwān 16 Bb
Aḥwar, W. 15 Cc
Ahwāz 6 Cc 7 16 20 22 25–27, see Hormuzd, Hurmuzshahr
Aḥyolı 31 Db
ʿAidāb 1.5.ii
Aigun 12 Fb
Aila 5 Cc 6 7, see Ayla, Akaba
Ain Galakka 41 Dc
Aīn Mahdi 42 Cb
Aīna 14 Db
Ainos 30 Db, see İnöz
Aintab (Gaziantep) 25 Bb 26 29 33
Ainuna 22 Fe
Aïr 6 Bd 7 9–12 41
Aissa, O. 43 Da
Aït Voussi 42 Ab
Aitu 54 Gc
Ajmer 24 Kh 47–53
Ajudhan (Pakpattan) 48 Ba
Aḳaba (Aila, Ayla, Elana) 14 Jg 15 25 27
Akaba (Hamad) 22 Gd
Akan States 41 Bd
Aḳca-ḥiṣār 31 Bb
Akça-kızanluk (Kazanluk) 31 Db
Akcaşehir 31 Eb
Akçay 30 Ec
Ākent 1.5.i
Dj. al-Akhdar 19 Ec 40 Ne
Aḳhiṣār (Thyatira) 29 Fe 31 34
Aḳhiṣār (Balkans) 31 Ba
Akhlāt 22 Ca 24
Akhor 25 Db
Akhrida (Ochrid) 1.4.v
Akhsīkak 17 Eb
Akhsīkath 24 Db
Aḳīḳ, W. 15 Gf
ʿAkk 19 Dd
ʿAkkā (Acre) 22 Bb
Aḳ-kermān (Akermann) 31 Ea 34
Akovo 30 Cc
Djaz. Aḳritash (Crete) 1.4.iv
al-Aksa 7 Ac
Aḳsarāy (Archelais) 26 Bb 29–31 33 34
Aksaray (Istanbul) 32 Fe
Akşehir 29 Ge 30 31 33 34
Aksum 15 Fh 19 46, see Axum
Alaca (Hüseynabad) 33 Ca
Alaca-ḥiṣar 31 Cb, see Kraljevo
Alaçem 31 Fb 34
Alai mts 24 Dc
Alāiye (Alanya, ʿAlāya) 29 Cb 30 31 33 34
Ala-kenīse (Osman Pazar) 31 Db
Alamanīn 1.2.vi
Alamūt 16 Bb
Alans 5 Cb 9 19
Alas 56 Ab
Alaşehir 29 Bb 31 34
Alāşōnya (Elassona) 31 Cc
Alava 37 Ea
Alāwi 42 Ab
Alaya 29 Cb, see Alāiye
Albacete 36 Fc 38 39
Albania 30 BCb
Albarracín 36 Fb 38
Albazin 12 Fb
Albus Portus 14 Ab
Alcalá (Castile) 36 Eb
Alcalá de Guadaira (Andalusia) 36 Dd
Alcántara 36 Cc 39
Alemanni 7 Bb
Aleppo (Haleb) 7 Cc 8 20 22 25–27 29 33, see Chalybon
Alexandretta (İskenderūn) 13 Cc 27 31
Alexandri 14 Gb
Alexandria (in Egypt) 5 Bc 6 9–11 14 15 22 25–27
Alexandria Troas 28 Ab
Alfur 54–56 Gc
Algeciras (al-Djazīrat al-Khadrā) 38 Dd 40 42 43
Algeria 13 Bc 40 42 43 45
Algers (al-Djazāʾir, Algiers) 7 Bc 9 12 32 40–43
Alguaire 37 Gb
Alhama 39 Hc
Alhum (ʿAyn al-Humm) 16 Bb
Ali Rajas 51 Bc
Alicante 36 Fc 38 39
ʿAlidj, Raml 15 Ae
Alids 8 Cc 21
ʿAlilü 33 Db
Allahabad 51 Cb 52 53
Almadén 38 Dc 39
Almansa 36 Fc
Almazán 39 Eb
Almeria 36 Ed 38–40
Almodóvar 36 Dc 38
Almoravids 9 Ac 38 Hd
Almunécar 36 Ed 40, see al-Munakkab
Alor (al-Rur) 6 Dc 8 47
Alora 39 Gd
Alpuente 38 Fc
Altın Taş 31 Ec 33 34
Aluana 14 Cc
Alwa 5 Cd 6–10
Alwar 50 Bb
Āma 19 Db
Amara 14 Dd
Amarkot 51 Ab 52
Am-ʿAṣalah 15 Bc
Amastris, Amasra 19 Ca 28–30 34
Amasya (Amaseia) 19 Ca 22 26 28–30 33 34
Amaya 35 Bb 36 37
Ambala 50 Ba
Ambār (Anbar) 15 Gd 19 22
Amber Palace (nr. Jaipur) 51 Bb
Ambilobe 9 Ce
Ambon 54 Gc 55 56
Āmid (Amida, Diyarbakır) 6 Cc 19 20
ʿAmīk plain 33 Db
Amirids 38 Fc
Amisus (Samsun) 19 Ca 28
Ammaca 14 Da
Amman 25 Bb 27
Amol (Amul in Tabaristān) 1.7.iv 20 Db
Amorium 19 Cb 20 28
Dj. Amour 40 Cb 43 43
Amoy 13 Ec
Ampèl-Denta 54 Ib
Ampurdan 38 Ha
Ampurias 37 Ha
al-ʿAmr 47 Ca
ʿAmrān 15 Ab
Amritsar 50 Ba 51
Amroha 48 Bb
Amsterdam 11 Bb
Amu Daryā (Djayhūn, Oxus R.) 17 Ea 24 25
Āmul (Tabaristān) 1.7.iv 16 Bb 19 Eb 20
Āmul (Transoxiana), Amul-i Shaṭṭ 17 Ea 19 24
ʿAmur, O. 40 Cb 43
Āna, W. 37 Dc
Anābolī (Nauplia) 31 Cc
Anadolu Hiṣār 32 If
Anadolukavağı 32 If
Anamur (Anemurium) 28 Cb 31 34
Anar 16 Cc
Anaradhapura 8 Dd
Anarak 26 Db
Anatolian seismic zone 18 Ba
Anatolikon 28 Bb
Anazarva, Anazarbus 28 He 31 Fc 34
Anbār 17 Eb
al-ʿAnbarīya 23 Eg
Ancyra (Angora, Ankara) 19 Cb
Andabalis 28 Cb
Andahar Tekkesi 33 Db
Andalāsī 45 He
al-Andalus 7 Ab 37
Andamān Isls. 44 Gc 45
Andarab 20 Eb
Andarāha 17 Fb
Andhra 5 Dd
Andičārāgh 17 Fb
Andidjan 24 Db 26 27
Andıra (Andros) 31 Dc 34
Andjazīdja 44 Bf
Andjīra 16 Cc
Andjra 42 He
Andkhūd, Andkhūy 24 Cc Jf
Andūdjar, Andūja 36 Dc 37 Dc
Andūrūa 31 Cc
Anfa (Dar Beida) 40 Ab 42
Angād 40 Bb
Ange vic. 14 Fd
Angelī-ḳaṣri 31 Cc
Angkola 56 Ab
Angkor 10 Ed 11
Anglo-Saxons 5 Ab
Angola 13 Be
Angora, see Ankara
Angren R. (N. Ilāk) 24 Db
Anhilwāda (Paṭan) 24 Ki 47
Ānī 19 Da
Ankara (Ancyra, Angora) 7 Cb 11 13 20 22 25–28 30 31 33 34
Anklitara, Djaz. 1.2.vii, Kingdom of England 9Ab 10–12
Ankole 12 Be
Ankuna (Ancona) 1.2.v
Annam 7 Ec 8 9 12 44 45
Anṭākya, see Antioch
Antalaots 9 Ce
Anṭāliya (Attaleia) 25 Bb 26 27 28–34
Antep (Aintab, Gaziantep) 31 Gc 34
Antequera 36 Dd 38–40
Anti-Atlas mts. 40 Ac 42 43
Antioch (in Pamphylia) 28 He
Antioch (in Phrygia) 28 Ge
Antioch (in Pisidia) 22 Ba 28
Antioch (in Syria; Anṭākya) 1.5.iv 19 Cb 20 25 26 28 29 31 33 34
Antiochi Canalis 14 Ce
Anti-Taurus mts. 28 Db
Anuradhapura 5 Dd 7
Apamea (Dinar) 28 Bb
Apamea (Hama) 28 Dc
Apamea (Zeugma) 28 Db
Apologus 5 Cc, see al-Ubulla
Apphana 14 Eb
Appolonia (Susa) 43 Hb
Aquae Sarvenae 28 Cb
aqueduct (İstanbul) 32 Ed
Aquitaine 10 Bb
Aqyān (Shibām) 15 Ab
Arab Gheraba 43 Eb
Arabia 32 Db
Arabia Emporium, see ʿAdan
Arabia Deserta 14 Da
Arabia Felix 14 Mh
Arabia Petraea 14 Ba
Arabian Sea 19 Fd
Arabic language 4 Cc
Arabissos (Arabissus) 19 Cb 28
Arabkir, see Arapkir
Arabs (*Arabanitae*) 9 Bc 14 Dd 17 Eb 21 Aa
Aradus (Muharrak) 14 Gc Ng
Arae Alexandri (Portus Macedonum) 14 Og
ʿArafa 23 Db
Aragon 9 Ab 10
al-Araʾish (Larache) 40 Aa 42
Arakan 12 Ec 52
Aral Sea 19 Ea 24
Arama 15 He
Aramaya 14 Bb
Arapkir (Arabkir) 26 Bb 31 33 34
Ararat, Mt. 26 Cb
Arawan 41 Bc
Araxes R. 19 Db
ʿArban 19 Db
Archelais Colonia (Aksaray) 28 Cb He
Archidona 40 Ba
Arcla 28 Gd
Arcos 38 Dd
Arcot 53 Bc
Ardabīl (Ardebil) 1.6.v 6 Cc 7 16 20 22 25 26 33
Ardakhushmithan 24 Bb
Ardestān (Ardistān) 16 Bc 25
Are ins. 14 Cd
Are regia 14 Ee
Arévalo 39 Db
Arga vic. 14 Bc
Arganzon 37 Ea
Arghiyān 16 Db
Arghun kingdom 50 Ab
Arguin 12 Ad 41
Arhöz (Argos) 30 Cc 31 34
Arīgh 40 Db
Aris R. (Isfīdjāb) 24 Cb
Arkadīyya 1.4.iv
Armābil (Las Bela) 17 Fd 20 25
Armaxa 28 Db
Armenia 6 Cc 8–10 20 22 25 29
Armeniakon 28 CDa
Armyro (İrmiye) 34 Cc
Arnavud (Belğirāde) 31 Bb 34
Arosbaya 54 Ia Of
Arra vic. (Haīl) 14 Lg 14 Db
Arradjān 16 Bc 20 26
Arrān 16 Aa 20 22 24
Arsae 14 Bc Kh
Arṣāh 1.8.vi
Arshḳūl 40 Ba
Arsinoë (N.) 14 Jg
Arsinoë (S.) 14 Ce Lj
Arsuz 33 Cb
Arta 30 Cc, see Narda
Artaxata 5 Cb
Artemita 14 Cb
Aru 55 Ab
Aru Isl. 56 Hd
ʿAryab 22 Hh
Arzila (Asila) 40 Aa 42
Arzindjan (Arzandjan, Erzincan) 22 Ca 25
Arzou 42 Id 43
Asabon prom. et mons 14 Gc Ogh
Asadābād (W) 16 Ab
Asadābād (E) 16 Cb 20
Asak 16 Ac
Asateni 14 Db Mg
Asaval (Ahmadabad) 49 Bb
Asawad 13 Ad
Asbanṭu 1.3.v
Ascalon 19 Cb
Ascension Isl. 13 Ae
Ascitae 14 Fe Mi
Asfandjay 17 Fc
Asfi (Safi) 40 Ab He
Dj. Asgarun 1.8.v
Ashanti 10 Ad 11
Ashar 15 Hg
Ashkabad 27 Db
Dj. Ashlūth 1.9.iv
Ashraf 21 Bb
Asigarh 48 Bb 50 51
Asila, see Arzila
Asir 12 Cd
Asiut, see Asyut
ʿAskar Mukram 16 Ac
Āskisīyya 1.6.vi
Aslam 15 Hf
al-Aslāmī 37 Fc
Aspa 14 Gc
Aspar Cistern 32 Fd
Aspendus 28 Bb

Assos 29 Fe
Astaboras (Atbara) R. 19 Cd
Astara 26 Cb 27
Astarābād (Asterabad) 16 Cb 26
Astoa vic. 14 Fd
Astorga (Asturica) 35 Ab 36–38
Astrakhan 10 Cb 11 13 26
Asturia (Asturias) 7 Ab 35 37 39
Asturica (Astorga) 39 Ca
Aswan (Assuan) 7 Cc 25 27 41
Asyut (Asiut, Assiuṭ) 1.4.ii 27 Bc 41
At Meydan 32 Ge
Atabegs 21 Cb
al-Atam 15 Bb
Atansiyya 37 Eb
Atatürk Bridge 32 Gd
Atatürk Bulvarı 32 Fe
Atbara 27 Bd
Atbara R., see Astaboras
Atchin 12 Ed, see Atjen
Athbadi 40 Ab
Athens (Atina) 19 Bb 30 31 34
N. Āthil 1.6.vi
Athroetai 14 Kg
Atia 14 Ec
Atina, see Athens
Atjen 46 Gd 55 Aa 56, see Atchin
Atlante (Talande) 34 Cc
Atlas, Haut 40 Ab 42 43
Atlas, Moyen 40 Bb 42 43
Atlas Saharien 40 Je
Aṭrābezūnda 1.6.v, see Trabzōn
Atrāblus, see Tripoli
Atramitae (*Hadhrami*) 14 Ee Mj
Atranos 31 Ec 34
Atrek R. 16 Cb
Atta vic. (Attene, Chattenia) 14 Ec Ng
Attaei 14 Ec Nh
Attaleia (Anṭālya) 28 Bb Ge
Attock 53 Ba
al-Aṭwāḥ 45 Cbc
Audjila (Awgila, Awdjila) 5 Bc 7 9–12 40 41 43
Aurangabad (Khirki) 51 Bc 52 53
Aurariola 36 Hc
Aurès mts. 40 Da 42 43
Aurshin (Orissa) 44 Fb
Djaz. Aurshin 1.8.ii
Ausara vic. 14 Fd
Austria-Hungary 13 Bb
Autrigonia 36 Hc
Autun 7 Bb
Ava 11 Ec 12 46
Avars 5 Bb 6 7 19 Ba
Avignon 7 Bb 35
Avila 38 Db 39
Avlōnya 31 Bb 32 34
'Avrat-ḥiṣāri 31 Cb 34
Awadh 24 Mh
al-Awāli 23 Ggh
Awārik 16 Cd
Awasim 20 Bb
Awdaghost 41 Ac
Awgila, see Audjila
Awlil 41 Ac
al-Awsat 40 Cb
Axim 12 Ad 41
Axum 5 Cd 6 10 see Aksum
Āyā Sōfya Mosque 32 Ge
Āyā-mavra (Sta. Maura) 31 Cc
Āyā-petrī (Hagios Petros) 31 Cc
Ayas 31 Fc 34, see Lajazzo
Ayasoluk 29 Fe 30 31 33 34
Ayazmend 31 Dc 34
'Aydhab (Aydhub) 7 Cc 22 26
Aydın 27 Ab 30 31 34
Awdjila, see Audjila
Aydōnāt 31 Cc 34
Aydos (Aitos) 30 Db 31 34
Ayla (Akaba) 15 Ee
'Ayn Djalut 10 Cc
'Ayn al-Humm (Alhum) 16 Bb
Aynam 45 Ic
al-'Aynīya 23 Fg
Ayutia 45 Gc
Ayvansaray 32 Fd
Ayyubids 21 Bb
Azad 15 He
Āzādwār 16 Cb
Azammur 40 Ab
Azande 7 Bd 8 9 12
Azar 26 Cb
Azd 15 Hg
Azd Sarāt 19 Dd
Azd 'Umān 19 Ec
Azov 32 Ca

Bāb al-Abwāb 22 Da, see Darband
Bāb al-'Anbarīya 23 Eh
Bāb al-Awāli 23 Gg
Bāb al-Basri 23 Ff
Bāb al-Djum'a 23 Gf
Bāb al-Hammām 23 Gg
Bāb al-Kuba 23 Fg
Bāb al-Kufa 23 Ef
Bāb al-Madjidi 23 Gf
Bāb al-Mandab 1.5.i 19 Dd
Bāb al-Masrī 23 Fg
al-Bāb al-saghir 23 Ff
Bāb al-Shāmī 23 Ff
Bāb al-Shūna 23 Fg
Bāb al-Seil 23 Eg
Bāb-i Ṣīn 44 Ib 45
Bābā-ṭağ 31 Ea 34
Bābā-yi atiḳ 31 Db 34
Babors 40 Da Kd 42 43
Baburi Kingdom 50 Aa
Babylon 14 Da Lf
Bac 31 Ba
Bacau 34 Da
Badakhshān 7 Dc 12 17 20 24 26 52
Bakakhshān Ford 17 Fb
Badajoz 36 Cc 38 39, see Baṭalyaws
Badeo regia 14 Cc
Bādghīs 17 Db
Badhash 16 Cb
Badi 10 Cd
Bādis (Peñon de Velez) 40 Ba
Bādja 1.10.ii: 37 Cc: 40 Da, see Beja
Badjarwan (Badjavan) 16 Aa 22 Da
Badjdjāna 37 Ed
Badjila 15 Hg 19
Badlis (Bitlis) 19 Db 22
Badr 15 Ff 23 Gh
Badui 56 Lf
Baduspānids 16 Bb
Baetius fl. 14 Bc Kg
Baeza 38 Ed, see Bayyāsa
Bāf 31 Fd
Bafḳ 16 Cc 25
Bafra 31 Fb 34, see Paurae
Bāft 16 Cd
Baghān 16 Cc
Bāghay 40 Da
Baghdād 1.6.iv 7 Cc 8–10 20 22 24–26 33
Baghlān 17 Fb
Baghnin 17 Ec
Baghshūr 17 Eb
Baguirmi 11 Bd 12
Bahār 16 Ab
Bahawalpur 53 Bb
Bahila 19 Dc
Bāhlika 47 Aa
Bahmani Kingdom 11 Dd 49
al-Bahnasā 19 Cc
Baḥr Abaskūn 16 Ba
Baḥr Fāris 44 Cb
Baḥr Harkand 44 Fc
Baḥr al-Khazar 16 Ba
Baḥr Ḳulzum 44 Ab-Bc
Baḥr Lārwī 44 Dc
Baḥr al-Muḥīṭ 37 Aa-d
Baḥr al-Mutawassiṭ 37 Fd-Ib
al-Baḥr al-safī 15 If 20
Baḥr Salāhiṭ 44 Gd
Baḥr Ṣankhai 44 Ic
Baḥr Zandj 44 Be
Baḥrain (al-Baḥrayn) 15 He 19 20 44
Baḥrain Isl. 26 27 45 46, see Tylus
Bahris 38 Cd
Baiae 28 Db, see Payas
Baiba 14 Cc
Baiburt, Bayburt 28 Jd 29
Baighal L. 10 Eb
Baja 34 Ba, see Bāya
Bajaur 50 Ba
Bākharz 17 Db
Bakhtagān L. 16 Bd
al-Baḳī'a cemetry 23 Gf
Bakongo 9 Be
B. Bakr (*Arabia-Bakr b. Wā'il*) 15 He 19 Db; (Spain) 37 Bd
Bakrābād 17 Fc
Bākū 7 Cb 20 22 25–27
Bakuba 7 Be 8 9 11
Balambangan 54 OPg 55 56
Balansiya (Valencia) 37 Fc,
Balāsāghūn 24 Db Ke
Balat 29 Fe
Bali 45 Ie 54–56
Balikesir 26 Ab 31 36 37
Balikpapan 56 Ec
Balīn (Kanbalī) 17 Fe
Bālish (Wālishtān) 17 Fd
Balkh 5 Dc 6–11 17 19 20 24 26 52
Balkhān Kūh 16 Ca
Balkhash L. 24 Da Ld
Ballish 40 Aa
Balts 6 Bb 7 8
Baluchis (*Balūč*) 16 Dd 50 Ab
Baluchistan 13 Dc 26
Balunda 7 Be 8 9 11
Balūniyya (Poland) 1.3.vi
Bālūs 7 Ed 44
Bālya-bādra (Patras) 31 Cc
Bam 16 Dd 20 25
Bamaka 41 Bc
Bamārāmān (Brahmanābād, Mansūra) 17 Fd
Bambara 41 Bc
Bambuk 9 Ad 10
Bambyce 28 Db
Bāmīyān 17 Fb 19 20 24 26 47
Bampūr 17 Dd 20 25
Bampūr R. 17 Dd
Bana 14 Ee
Banā, W. 15 Bc
Banadika, Khalidj al-(Adriatic) 1.3.v
Banākath 24 Cb
Banā-lukā (Banjaluka) 31 Ba 34
Banana 13 Be
Banāras (Benares, Varanasi) 8 Dc 10 24 44 47–49 51–53
Banaz 31 Ec 34
Dj. Banbūān 1.1.ii
Banda 10 Fe 54–56
Bandar Abbas (Gombroon) 12 Cc 26 27
Band-i Amīr, Band-i 'Aḍudī 14 Bd
Bandırma 27 Aa
Bandjala (Bangala, Bengal) 45 Fb
Bandung 55 Lf 56
Bangala, see Bandjala
Bangalore 52 Bc
Bangka (Bankā) 45 He 55 56
Bangkahulu (Bencoolen) 54 Bc 55 56
Bangkalan 54 Ia
Bangkok 13 Ed
Ban-i Afrīdūn 16 Cb
Bāniya 17 Fe
Banjarmasin 54 Dc 55 56
Bantám, Banten 12 Ee 54 45 He 55 56
Bantayan 10 Fe
Bantu 4 5 Bde 6–9
Banubari 14 Bc Kh
Banyumas 54 Mf 55 56
Banzart, see Bizerte
Baphaeon 29 Gd
Barābir (Barbar) 44 Bc 45
Barakdiz (Karīnayn) 17 Eb
Baranyvar Monostor 34 Ba
Barār (Berar) 46 Eb 50 51
Barātigin 24 Ab
Barāwa 8 Cd 11 45 46
Barbar, Barbaria 19 Dd, see Barābir
Barbashtar 37 Ga
Barcelona (Barcinona) 7 Bb 8 35–38
Bardā'a (Bardhā'a) 19 Da 22
Bardashīr, Bardasir (Khābis) 16 Cc 19 Eb
Bārdōnya 31 Cc
Barūdj 45 Eb, see Broach
Bāre (Paros) 31 Dc
Barhinadvipa (Borneo) 10 Ede
Barid Shahis 50 Bc
al-Barīrah 15 Cb
Baris 28 Bb, see İsparta
Barḳa 1.3.iii 6 Bc 7–12 40
Barla 31 Ec 34
Baroda 53 Bb
Barracks, Turkish 23 Aa Eh
Barr al-Adjam 45 Abc
Barr al-Nāt 45 Fc
Barr al-Siām 45 Gc–Hd
Barr al-Sūmāl 44 Bd 45, see Somaliland
Barsāna 1.3.iv
Barskhān 24 Db
Barugunde 33 Da
Barus 54 Ab
Baruza, see Broach, Barūdj
Barzah 22 Db
Barzand 16 Aa
Basa 41 Bd
Bāsand 17 Fa
Basdjirt al-Dākhila 1.7.vi
Bashgirts 7 Cb 8
Bashin 17 Eb
Bāsht 16 Bc
Basilica (Yerebatan Saray) Cistern 32 Ge
Basima 15 He
Basni (Pasni) 45 Db
Basques 5 Ab 6 8
Baṣra 7 Cc 8 9 12 13 15 20 22 24–27 32 33 44 46
Bassein 46 Ec 50–53
Bastion de France (Mersa al-Kharaz) 40 Da Kd
Baṣunnā 16 Ac
Batak 54 Ab 55 56
Baṭalyaws 37 Cc see Badajoz
Batang 55 Mf
Batavia (Jakarta) 13 Ee 56
Bathurst 13 Ad
Bathys (Arabia) 14 Ac
Bathys (Rhyax) 28 Db
al-Bāṭina 19 Ec
Batinda (Bhatinda) 47 Ba 49
Batn Ardashir 14 Ng
Batn Faldj 15 He
Batna (Ṭubna) 40 Da 43
Batrasavave 14 Og
Batticaloa 46 Fd
Batum 13 Cb 25–27
Bauchi Plat. 41 Ccd
Baule 12 Ad
Bawandids 16 Bb
Bāya 31 Ba, see Baja
Bayādh 15 Hf
Bayān 45 Ie
Bayat 31 Ec 34
Bayḍā 16 Bc
al-Bayḍā' 15 Bc 16
Baydjan 26 Cb
Bayhaḳ (Sabzawar) 16 Cb 19 24
Bayhān, W. 15 Bb
Bayirku 5 Eb
Baykand 17 Ea 24
Baylakān 22 Da
Baylul 46 Bc
Bayyāna 37 Dd
Bayyāsa 37 Ed, see Baeza
Baza 36 Ed 38 40
Bazaar, Grand 32 Ge
Bazargik (Ḥacioğli-bāzārī) 34 Db
Bazda 17 Ea
Bazwān, Buḥaīre 1.9.iii
Beckerek (Becskerek) 31 Ca 34
Bedja, Bega 8 Cc 19 Cc
Begho 41 Bd
Behesni 30 Gc
Behroosh 26 Db
Beinam 29 Cb, see Gorbeous
Beirut (Berytus) 13 Cc 15 19 25 27
Beja (Spain) 36 Cc 38 39, see Bādja
Beja (Tunisia) 42 Kd 43
Bejar 39 Db
Bektaş, see Hacci Bektaş
Belalcázar 36 Dc
Belgaon 49 Bc
Belğirāde 31 Bb
Belgium 13 Bb
Belgrade 30 Ca 31 34
Belgrade Forest 32 Ed
Belgrat Kapı 32 Ef
Belitung 55 Cc 56, see Billiton
Bellary 52 Bc 53
Belmez 36 Dc
Belmonte 39 Ec
Belocome 28 Ba
Belušic (Pilaşce) 34 Cb
Bemba 11 Ce
Ben Gardane 43 Fb
Benavente 36 Da 39
Bencoolin, see Bangkahulu
Bender 31 Ea 34
Benefşe (Monemvasia) 31 Cc
Bengal (Bandjala, Bangala) 11 Dc 12 13 45 46 49–52
Bengawan (Solo) R. 54 Ha
Benghazi (Bengazi) 41 Ea 42 43
Benguela 12 Be 13
Beni Abbès (Ḳalé B. Hammād) 40 Da 42
Beni Saf (Hunayn) 43 Ca
Beni Ulid 43 Fb
Benin 11 Bd 12 41
Benue R. 41 Cd
Berar, see Barār
Berara 22 Gf
Berbers 5 Acd 6
Bere 14 Db
Bereketlü 31 Db 34
Berenice 14 Ac Kh 5 6
Berenvar 31 Ba
Bergama (Pergamum) 26 Ab 29 30 31 34
Berguent 43 Cb
Berkōfça (Berkovica) 31 Cb 34
Berlin 13 Bb
Berlin-Baghdād Railway 27 Bb
Beroea 19 Cb
Berytus (Beirut) 15 Fd
Beshbalik 5 Db 7–9 11
Bessalu (Besalu) 37 Ha 38
Bessarabia 34 Ea
Betica 36 Hd
Beyazıt Mosque and Square 32 Ge
Beyoğlu 32 Gd
Beypazarı 31 Eb 33 Ba 34
Beyşehir 29 Ge 30 31 34
Bharōč, see Broach
Bharukachha 5 Dc
Bhatkal 46 Ec
Bhatnair 49 Bb
Bhera 50 Ba
Bhilsa 48 Bb
Bhomslas 53 Bb
Bhutan 13 Ec
Bibans 40 Da
Bīčagān L. 16 Bd
Bīdar 46 Ec 49–53
Bidjāya (Bougie) 40 Da Kd 42 43
Biga 29 Fd 30 31 34
Bigadiç 31 Ec 34
Bighū 37 Dd
Bihābād 16 Cc
Bihac 34 Aa
Bihār 24 Mh 47–53
Bihlişte 31 Cb
Bijapur (Bidjapur) 45 Ec 46 50–53
Bikaner 49 Bb 50 51
al-Bila 23 Ff
Bilağay (Blagaj) 31 Bb 34
Bila-Suwār 16 Aa
Bilbana opp. 14 Ec
Bilecik 26 Ba 31 34
Billiton (Biliṭūn, Belitung) 45 He 56 Cc
Bilma 8 Bd 9 -12 41
Bīmand 16 Cd
al-Bīnā 15 Cb
Binbirdirek Sarnice (Philoxenus) Cistern 32 Ge
Bindraban 51 Bb
Binkath 24 Cb, see Tashkent
Bint 17 Dd
Bir Aslu 9 Bc 10–12
Bir Dufan 43 Fb
Bir Ghanem 43 Fb
Bir Hakeim 43 Hb
Bir al-Gobi 43 Hb
Bir Um Grein 41 Ab
Birdjand 16 Dc 26 27
Birecik 26 Bb 31 32 34
Birgi 29 Ge
Birka 7 Bb
Bisha (Pisa) 1.2.v
Bisha 7 Cc 19 22 26
Bishāpūr (Shāpūr) 16 Bd
Bishlang 17 Ec
Biskra 7 Bc 40 42
Biskri 40 Db
Bist 20 Eb 25, see Bost, Bust

Bisṭām 16 Cb 24
Bisutūn 19 Db
Bitlis 26 Cb, see Badlis
Biyār 16 Cb
Bizerte (Banzart) 35 Jg 40 42 43
Bjelina (Peline) 34 Ba
Black Sea 19 Ca
Blagaj 34 Ba
C. Blanc 40 Da
C. Blanco 11 Ac
Blīda 42 Jd 43
Blitar 54 Og 55
Bliulaei 14 Ed Mh
Bobo Dioulasso 41 Bc
Bodrum 31 Dc 34
Boğaziçi (Bosphorus) 32 Hd If
Boğdan (Moldavia) 31 Da
Boghari (Achīr) 42 Ca Jd 43
Bogürdelen (Šabac) 31 Ba
C. Bojador 11 Ac
Bojonegoro (Jipang) 54 Nf 55
Bokhara, see Būkhārā
Bolu 26 Ba 29 31 34
Bolus 31 Gc 34
Bolvadin 31 Ec 34
Bombay (Thana) 12 Dd 13 46 51–53
C. Bon 40 Ea
Bonduku 41 Bd
Bone (in East Indies) 56 EFc
Bône (Būna) 35 Dc
Boni Cistern 32 Fd
Bonjol 56 Bb
Bono 41 Bd
Bor 26 Bb 31 34
Bordeaux (Bordāl) 1.1.v 35
Border seismic zone 18 Bb
Bordj Messouda 43 Eb
Borgu 41 Cc
Borneo (Barhinadvipa) 10 Ede 11–13 54–56
Bornu 5 Bd 6 9–12 41
Bosna (Bosnia) 13 Bb 30 31 34
Bosphorus (Boğaziçi) and Bridge 32 If
Bosra (Bostra) 15 Fd 19 Cb
Bost 19 Fb, see Bust
Bou Regreg (R.) 40 He
Bou Saada (Bū Saada) 40 Ca 42 43
Boudonitsa 30 Cc
Bougie, see Bidjāya
Bouira Sahari 40 Ca
Bourbon 13 Cf
Boyabat 31 Fb 34
Bozdoğan 31 Ec 34
Bozkır 31 Fa 34
Bozok 31 Fc 33 Cb
Bracara 36 Gc
Braga 38 Bb 39
Brahmanābād (Bamāramān, Mansūra) 19 Fc
Brahmaputra R. 47 Db 48–51 53
Brahui lang. 4 Dc
Brantas R. 54 Ib
Brashk (Cherchel) 40 Ca
Bratskii 12 Eb
Brazil slave trade 12 Be
Bregha 43 Gb
Bretons 5 Ab 6–8
Breznik 34 Cb, see Pireznīk
British interests 26 27 Ab Cb Dc 53
Broach (Barūdj, Barūza, Bharōč) 44 Eb 45–49
Brod (Despot Birōdi) 34 Ba
Broome 13 Fe
Bruges 11 Bb
Brunei 12 Ed 45 54–56
Brusa (Bursa) 22 Aa
Bu Ngem 43 Gb
Bū (Bou) Saada 40 Ca 42 43
Bual 56 Fb
Buāmia, Bilad 1.3.vi
Bubashtar 37 Dd
Bucharest 34 Da
Buda, Būdīn 31 Bd 33
Budaha 17 Fd
Budaun 47 Bb 48
Buddhists 5 Dd 6 7
Buhari (Būkhārā) 1.8.iv
Buitenzorg 56 Lf, see Pakuan Bogor, Pakuan Pajajaran
Bukellarion 28 Cab
Būkhārā (Bokhara, Nūmidjkath) 7 Dc 8 13 17 19 20 24 26 27
Bulala 41 Dc
Bulāy 37 Dd
Bulgaria 10 Bb 13
Bulgars 6 Cb 7–9 19 21
Bullīn 44 Ed
Būna (Bône) 7 Bc 40 Da 42
Bunābid (Djunābid) 16 Db
Buñar-ḥiṣar 31 Db 34
Bundjikath 24 Cc
Buraida (Burayda) 7 Cc 22 25–27
Burdj 16 Bc
Burdj-i Sangīn 24 Dc
Burdur 27 Bb 29–31 33 34
Bure 41 Bc
Bureba 37 Ea
Burgas 34 Db
Būrgōs (Thrace) 31 Db 34
Burgos (Spain) 36 Ea 37–39
Burgundy 8 Bb
Burhanpur 12 Dc 49–53
Burids 22 Bb
Burīyāna 37 Fc
Burma 13 Ec
Bursa (Brusa) 26 Aa 29–31 33 34
Burshāna 37 Ed
Burtuḳāl (Oporto) 37 Bb
Buru 55 Gc
Burudjird 16 Ac
Busa 41 Cc
Būshahr (Būshiḥr, Bushire) 12 Cc 13 26 27 45 46
Bushkānāt 16 Bd
Bushtaḳān 16 Db
Bust 17 Ec 20 24 47, see Bist, Bost
Buttamān mts. 17 Fa 24
Butung 56 Fd
Buwaiyhids (*Būyids*) 16 Bc 21 Ba–Ca 44
Buxar 53 Cb
Büyük Cami, Üsküdar 32 Id
Büyükdere 32 If
Buzen 34 Da
Būzgan 17 Db
Byzantines 5 Bb 6 Bc–Cb 7–10 15 21 22
Byzantium (Constantinople, İstanbul) 28 Ba 29

Cabeira 28 Da
Cabercium 28 Bb
Cabezarados 36 Dc
Cabinda 12 Be
Cabra 38 Dd
Cačak (Çaçka) 31 Cb 34
Cáceres 36 Cc 38 39
Cacheo 41 Ac
Cadara opp. 14 Ec
Cadi 28 Bb
Cádiz 36 Cd 38–40
Caesarea (Kayseri) 19 Cb 20 28
Caesarea (in Palestine) 14 15 Ed 19
Čaghāniyān 17 Fa 24
Çağlayık 31 Db 34
Cāhamānas 47 Bb
Čāhuk (Ṣāhuk) 16 Cd
Cail 10 Dd, see Kāyal
Cairo (Fustat) 22 Bb Ed 25 26 33 41 44
Čajniče, see Çayniçe
Calabar 12 Bd
Calahorra 38 Fa, see Kalahurra
Calapeni 14 Cc Lg
Calatañazor 36 Eb 39
Calatayud 36 Fb
Calcutta 12 Dc 13 52 53
Çaldıran 33 Hd
Calicut 6 Dd 7 8 10 11 13 48 53
la Calle (Marsa al Kharaz, Bastion de la France) 40 Da Kd 42 43
Callinicum (Callinicus) 5 Cc 19 Cb
Calon mons 14 Oh
Calonoros (Coracesium) 28 Cb He
Čalūs 16 Bb
Camacha 28 Db
Cambay (Kanbāya) 8 Dc 9 10 44 47–52
Cambil 39 Hc
Cambodia 12 Ed 45
Camdratiyas 47 Bb
Cameroons R. 41 Dd
Campanario 39 Dc
Čampaner, see Champaner
Çan 31 Dc 34
Çanakkale 29 Fd 31 34
canal (China) 8 Ec
Cananore, see Cannanore
Canara 53 Bc
Canary Isls. 13 Ac 41
Candar 29 Hd
Cane (QN', Ḥiṣn al-Ghurāb) 15 Db 19
Canik 30 Gb 31
Çankırı (Gangra) 29 Hd 30 31 33 34
Cannanore (Jurfattan) 11 Dd 48–53
Canton (Khānfū) 12 Ec 44 57
Cape Coast Castle 13 Ad
Capsina opp. 14 Fc
Caracal 53 Bc
Caralis L. 28 Bb
Carallia 28 Bb
Carcassonne 36 Ha 35 37
Cardamine ins. 14 Cd
Carman regia 14 Dc
Čarmangān 17 Fb
Carmania 14 Hc Ng
Carmona 38 Dd
Carnatic 53 Bc
Carpathians 19 Ba
Carrhae (Haran) 19 Cb 28
Carrión [de los Condés] 36 Da 38
Çarşamba R. 30 Fc
Cartàgena (Kartadjannat al-Halfā') 36 38 Fd 40 42 43
Carthage (Cartagena) 5 Bc 6 7 35 Ec
Casablanca (Dar Beida) 41 Ba 43
Caspian Sea 19 Ea 26
Cassanitae 14 Cd Li
Castamon (Castemonu, Kastamonu) 28 Ca 29
Castellón (de la Plana) 36 Fc 38
Castilblanco 39 Dd
Castile (Castilla) 9 Abc 10 11 32 38 39
Castillezos 42 Hd
Castle Ward (Madīna) 23 Ff
Castuera 36 Dc
Catalayud 38 Fb
Çatalca 31 Cc 34
Cataluña (Catalonia) 38 Gb 39
Catanitae 14 Dc Lg
Catara 14 Dc
Cattano 31 Bb 34
Caucasic languages 4
Caucasus mts. 19 Da
Cauvery R. 47–50 Bc 52 53
Cavana 14 Ec
Cawnpore 53 Cb
Çayniçe (Čajniče) 34 Bb
Cebreros 39 Db
Celaludin 33 Cb
Celebes (Sulawesi) 11 Ee 12 13
Çelebī bāzāri 31 Bb
Celenderis 28 Cb
cemeteries 23 Bc Db Gf 32 Ie
Central Africa, British 13 Ce
Çepni 33 Da
Cerablus 31 Gc 34
Cerasus 28 Id
Cerdaña 37 Ga 38
Cernovoda 34 Ea
Çernīçe (Sjenica) 31 Bb
Ceuta (Sebta, Sibta) 12 Ac 35 41–43
Ceuta, Strait of (Strt. of Gibraltar) 1.1.iv
Ceylon (Sinhala-dvipa, Serendib) 12 Dd 13 46 53
Chaban 9 Ed 10 11
Chabuata 14 Fc
Chad L. 8 Bd 10–12 41
Chad Arabs 41 Dc
Chagos archip. 13 De
Chahbar 27 Ec
Chalcedon 19 Ba 28 29
Chalcis (Āğrībōz) 34 Cc
Chaldia 28 Da
Chalkis (Syria) 19 Cb
Chalukyas (*Calukyas*) 5 Dd 8 44 47
Chalus 20 Db
Chalybon 28 Db, see Aleppo
Chaman 27 Eb
Chaman seismic zone 18 Eb
Champa 5 Ed 6–8 44 45
Champaner 46 Eb 50 51
Chandellas 47 Bb
Chanderi 48 Bb 50 51
Chandernagore 52 Cb 53
Chandpur 52 Bb
Chandragiri 51 Bc
Ch'ang-an 7 Ec 8
Changchun 57 Gb
Changsha 57 Fd
Chao-modo 12 Eb
Chaouya 43 Bb Ea
Charax (Characene) 14 Mf, near Apologus, al-Ubulla
Chargatha 14 Cd
Chariopolis 29 Fd
Charmen 34 Db
Charsianon 28 Cb
Chatramonitae (*Hadhramis*) 14 Ed Mi
Chattenia, see Atta
Chaul 10 Dd 46 47 49–52, see Saymūr, Shaiyūl
Chausa 51 Cb
Chelif, W. 40 Ca Jd 42
Chen-chiang 9 Ec
Chengchow 57 Fc
Chéng-tu 5 Ec 6 8 9 11
Chen-la 5 Ed 6 7
Cheras 47 Bc
Cherchel (Brashk) 40 Ca Jd 42 43
Cheribon 54–56 Mf
Chersonese prom. 14 Bb
Chersonesus 19 Ca
Chewa 12 Be
Ch'ia-sha 5 Dc 6 7, see Kashgar
Chiang-tu 5 Ec, see Yang-chou
Chiao-chih 5 Ec
Chidambaram 48 Bc
Chien-an 5 Ec
China Road 25 Ea
Chinese Empire 9 Ec–Fb 13 44 45
Chinese pilgrims 5 Dc, *traders* 12 Ed
Ching-chao 5 Ec 6 9
Ch'ing-hai 12 Ec
Chinguitti 41 Ab
Chinsurah 53 Cb
Chios 28 Ab
Chitor 10 Dc 47–53
Chittagong (Islamabad) 46 Gb 50–53
Chiu-chou 7 Ed 8
Chlemontzi (Hulumic) 34 Cc
Chliara 28 Fe
Choaspes R. 19 Db
Cholas (*Cola*) 5 Dd 8 9 44 47
Choma 28 Ge
Chonae 28 Ge
Chora Church (Kahriye Mosque) 32 Ed
Christianity 5 Bc
Ch'üan-chou (Zaiton) 8 Ec
Chu-yai 5 Ed
Cibotus 28 Gd
Cibyra 28 Bb
El Cid 38 Hc
Cide 34 Fb
Cilician Gates 20 Bb 31 34
Cinaedocolpitae 14 Bc Kh
Čipronica (Gibre) 34 Cb
Circars 53 Cc
Čirčik R. (Nahr Shāsh) 24 Db
Çirmen 31 Db
Çirpān (Čirpan) 31 Db 34
Cisr-i Ergene 31 Db 34
Cisr-i Muṣṭafāpāşa 31 Db
citadel (Madīna) 23 Ff
Citium 28 Cc
Čitōr 24 Ki
Čitrāl 17 Gb
Çitroz 30 Cb
Ciudad Real 36 Ec 38 39
Ciudad Rodrigo 39 Cb
Claudiopolis (N) 28 Ba Gd
Claudiopolis (S) 28 Cb
Climax mons 14 Dd Lj
Clissa (Kilīs) 34 Bb
Clysma (Suez) 19 Cb
Cnidus 28 Ab
Coca 39 Db
Cochin 11 Dd 13 46 48 53
Cocusus (Coxon, Göksun) 28 Db
Coimbra (Ḳulumriyya) 35 Ab 36–39
Colas, see Cholas
Collo (al-Ḳul) 40 Da Kd 42 43
Colomb Béchar 42 Ie 43
Colombo 11 Dd 13 46 53
Comana 28 Db
Comilla 52 Db
Comoro (Ḳumr) 10 Ce 12
Congo Kingdoms 11 Be 13
Conjeeveram 49 Bc 53, see Kansipura
Conrad III, route of 22 Ab
Constanta 34 Ea
Constantia (Salamis) 28 Cc
Constantine (al-Kusantina) 40 Da Kd 41–43
Constantinople (Istanbul) 5 Bb 6–9 11 19 22 27 29 30
Consuegra 36 Ec
Cooch Bihar 52 Cb
Coptos (Coptus) 14 Jg 19
Coracesium, see Calonoros
Coraco 14 Ca
Córdoba (Ḳurṭuba) 7 Ac 35–39
Coria (Ḳūriyya) 36 Cc 38
Corinth (Köridüs) 19 Bb 34
Çorli 31 Db 34, see Tzouroulos
Corodamum prom. 14 Gc
Coromanis opp. (Kuwait) 14 Db Mg
Coron 30 Cc
Çorum 30 Fb 31 33 34
Corycus 28 He
Cos 28 Ab
Cossacks 12 Cb
Cotiaeum (Kütahya) 28 Bb Ge
Cottabani 14 Gc Oh
courts (Old Turkish) 5 Db Eb 6
Coxon 22 Ba, see Cocusus
Craiova 34 Ca
Crateia 28 Ca Hd
Crete (Girid) 8 Bc 13 19 30
Crimea 11 Cb
Croatia 31 Aa
Cruz, R. da 41 Cd
Cryptus portus (Muskat) 14 Gc Oh
Ctesiphon 15 Gd 19
Ču R. 24 Db
Cuenca 38 Eb, see Kunka
Çukur bostan 32 Ee Fd
Curna 14 Cc
Cutch 48 Ab 50
Cuttack (Palmiras ?) 12 Dc 47–49 52 53
Cyprus (Kibris) 10 Cc 12 13 20–22 25–30 32
Cyrenaica 40 Ne 42 43
Cyrene (Skahat) 43 Hb
Cyzicus 28 Aa Fd 29

da Gama, Vasco 50 Bc 46
Dabīl 15 Gf
Dābūl 45 Ec 46 49–51
Dabūsiyya 24 Cc
Dacca 52 53 Db
Dachareni 14 Ec Mh
Daemonam 14 Bc
Dafina 15 Gf
Daghestan 26 Ca
Dagomba 10 Ad–Bd 41
Dahban 22 Gg
Dahistān 1.7.v
Dahlak (Is.) 19 Dd 46
al-Dahnā', Dahnā 15 Hef 19 Dc
Dahomey 13 Bd
Dahra 42 Ca Jd
Daima 5 Bd 6
Dalidjān 16 Bb
Dam 15 Gf
dam, Mārib 15 Bb
Damān 46 Eb 51–53
Damascus (Dimashk) 1.5.iii 5 Cc 6–9 12 14 15 19 20 22 25–27
Damāwand mt. 16 Bb 19
Dāmghān 16 Cb 19 20 25 26
Damiat (Damietta) 1.4.iii 19 Cb 22
Dandānkān 17 Db
Danes 5 Bb 6 7
Dāniya (Denia) 36 Gc 37 38
Danube R. (N. Danū) 1.3.vi 30 Db
Danzig 10 Bb 11
O. Daoud 43 Da
Dapha 14 Ca
Dār al-'Arā'is 15 Bc
Dār Beida (Anfa, Casablanca) 42 Ab He 43

Dār al-Salām 13 Ce
Dār al-Sulṭān 42 Ca
Dara 19 Db
Dārābdjird 16 Cd 19
Darawḳa 37 Fb
Darb al-Amir 22 Hg
Darb al-Arbain 41 Ebc
Darb al-Djināza 23 Gg
Darb Habābiyya 22 He
Darb al-Kebsy 22 Gg
Darb al-Salmān 22 Ge
Darb al-Sulṭān 22 Gf
Darb al-Tabūkiyya 22 Fe
Darb Wādī Sebeʿ 22 Gef
Darb al-Zubayda 22 Ge
Darband (Bāb al-Abwāb) 7 Cb 13 19 22 25–27 32
Dardjīn 16 Dd
Darende 30 Gc 31 34
Darende Pass 20 Bb
Darfārid 16 Cd
Darfur 5 Bd 6 7 12 41
Dargah 53 Bb
Darganata 26 Ea
Darghān 24 Bb
Darghash 17 Ec
Dār-i Āhanīn (Iron Gate) 17 Fb
Dār-i Alān 19 Da
Dār-i Tāziyan 17 Gb
Dār-i Tubbat 17 Gb
Darin 15 Ie, see al-Ḳaṭīf
Darʿiyya 19 Dc 27
Darkān 16 Cd
Darmashān 17 Ec
Darna (Derna) 40 Gb Ne 42 43
Daroca 36 Fb 38
Darrae 14 Bc Kg
Darzangī 17 Fb
Dasht-i Kavīr 16 Cb 24
Dasht-i Lut 19 Eb 24
Dastadjird (Irāḳ) 19 Db
Dastadjird (Ṣuḥār) 15 Jf
Dathina 19 Dd
Daulatabad, see Deogir (before 1338) 48 Bc 49–52
Abū Dāʾūdids 17 Fb
Daura 41 Cc
Davud Paşa Mosque 32 Ee
Dawʿān, W. 15 Db 19
Dawawida 40 Da
Dawraḳ 16 Ac
Dawraḳistān 16 Ac
Daww 15 He
Daybul 1.7.ii 5 Dc 6–10 19 20 24 25 44 46–48 52
Daylam 16 Ab
Dayradjān (Rīshahr) 16 Ac
Dazaifu 10 Fc
Dazimon 28 Da
Dazkırı 31 Ec 34
Dead Sea seismic zone 18 Bb
Debarwa 46 Ac
Debra 46 Ad
Debre 31 Cb 34
Decla (Mangalore) 52 Bc
Dedeağaç 34 Db
Dehibat 43 Fb
Dehra Dun 53 Ba
Deire opp. 14 Ce
Dela 14 Ee
Delhi, see Dihlī
Deli 56 Ab
d'Eli mt. 50 Bc
Dellys (Tadallis) 40 Ca 42 43
Delvīne 31 Cc 34
Demak 45 HIe 54
Demir Kapu 34 Db
Demirci 31 Ec 34
Dendi 41 Cc
Denghi Tepe 27 Db
Denia, see Dāniya
Denizli 29 Ge 31 33 34
Denmark 8 Bb 9–13
Denpasar 56 Pg
Deogir (Daulatabad) 9 Dd 10 48–52
Deorum Tutorum portus 14 Bd
Depok 56 Lf
Dera Ghazi Khan 50 Ba
Derbe 28 Cb
Derbend, Derbent, see Darband
Derna, see Darna
Desert Route 26 BCb
Despot Birōdi (Brod) 31 Ba
Deva 14 De
Develikarahisar 31 Fc 34
Dezful 26 Cb, see Dizful
Dhamār 15 Bb 22 46
Dharur 49 Bc
Dhat Irk 22 Gf 26
B. Dhiʾl Nun 37 Eb
Dhomokos (Domenek) 31 Cc 34
Dhū Ḳār 15 Hd 19
Dhufar 10 Cd 11 15, see Ẓafar
Dhuʾl Ḳadr, see *Dulkadir*
Dia 41 Bc
Diāba 1.2.vi
Dianae Oraculum (Salala) 14 Gd Ni
Dībadjāt (Maldive Isls.) 44 Ed
Miāh Didjla 1.6.iv
Didymateichon 29 Fd
Digema 14 Db
Dih-i Gūz (Hurmuz) 16 Cd
Dih-i Naw (Yengi-Kent) 24 Ba
Dihistān (W) 16 Ca 24
Dihistān (E) 17 Eb
Dihlī (Delhi) 8 Dc 9–12 21 24 46–53
Dijon 35 Ca
Dimashk, see Damascus
Dimetoka 30 Db 33
Dinavar 22 Db
Dioscoridis ins. (Socotra) 5 Cd 14 19
Dipa Negara 56 Cd
Dipalpur 49 Ba 50
Dirāca 31 Bb, see Durazzo
Dirāma 31 Db 34
Diu (Isl.) 12 Dc 45 46 50–53
Divane Ali 31 Db 34
Divrik (Divriği) 26 Bb 30 31 34
Diyāḳova 31 Cb 34
Diyarbakır (Amīd) 22 Cb 26 33
Diza 17 Eb
Dīzak 17 Ed
Dizbad (Ḳaṣr al-Rīḥ) 16 Db
Dizfūl 16 Ac 22, see Dezful
Dizfūl R. 16 Ac
Djāba Harandj 44 Hd
Djabal Abi Kubays 23 Cd
Dj. Ayr 23 Gh
Dj. al-Barānis 37 Dc
Dj. Djalūt 1.4.ii
Dj. Djauf 1.9.v
Dj. Djiyād 23 Bd
Dj. al-Fanna 23 Ac
Dj. al-Fiḍḍa 17 Db
Dj. Hindi 23 Bc
Dj. Ḳaiḳʿān 23 Bb
Dj. Kudā 23 Bd
Dj. Ḳufṣ 16 Dd
Dj. Laʿla 23 Cb
Dj. Sala 23 Gh
Dj. Ṭāriḳ (Gibraltar) 35 Ac 36 37 39
Dj. Uhud 23 Hg
Dj. ʿUmār 23 Ad
Djabala 19 Dc
al-Djābiya 19 Cb
Djabrīn (Labris) 14 Mh 15
Djaʿda 19 Dc
B. Djadām 15 Fe
Buḥ. Djādjān 1.9.iv
Djadjarm 16 Cb
Djado 41 Db
Djadu 43 Fb
Djaghatai 10 Db 11 21 25
Djahrum 16 Bd 26
Djakovo (Yāḳova) 34 Ba
Djalairids 25 Cb
Djalandi 5 Cc 15
Djalaula 15 Gd
Djalfūniyya (Kephalonia) 1.3.iv
Djālk 17 Ed 20
Djalo 42 Nf 43
Djam 17 Db
Djām (Fīrūzkūh) 17 Eb
Djamna (Jumna) R. 46 Eb
Djanāba (Ganawa) 16 Bd, 25
Djanbā 45 He
Djand 24 Cb Je
Djandzarūdh 16 Cc
Djanet 41 Cb
Djankent 24 Ie (Yengi Kent)
Djannabeh 20 Dc, Djannaba (Genava) 25 Dc
Buḥ. Djanūn 1.6.vii
al-Djār 19 Cc
Djarabub 42 Nf
Djarash, Djurash 14 Li 19 Dd
Djarba, see Djerba
Djarbāya 17 Fb
Buḥ. Djardjūn 1.8.v
W. Djarib 15 Ge
Djarkafort (Oxford?) 1.2.vii
Djarmaḳ 16 Cb
Djarmat 20 Db
Djarshīk 45 Ie
Djarwal 23 Bb
Djāsk 45 Cb 46
al-Djaudharīya 23 Dc
al-Djauf (Duma) 8 Cc 22
Djauf (E) 15 He
W. al-Djauf (Gawf) 15 Bb
Djāwa (Java) 45 He
Djawad, Ibn Abiʾl 37 Bd
Djayhūn R. (Djihūn, Oxus, Amu Darya) 11 Db 17 19 24 25 47–53
Djayyān 37 Ed, see Jaen
Djayzān, see Djīzān
al-Djazāʾir (Algiers) 7 Bc 40
Djazira 7 Cc
Djazira Danmarsha (Denmark) 1.3.vii
Djazira Dans 1.1.vii
Djazira Daran 1.1.iii
Djazira Tarīf (Tarifa) 37 Dd
Djazira Zarīn 45 Ce
Djazirat al- ʿArab 45 Bb
Djazirat al-Khadrā (Algeciras) 37 Dd
Djazirat al Sharḳiyya 37 Hc
Djazirat al-Tawīla (Ḳishm Isl.) 16 Cd
Djelfa 42 Je 43
Djenbara 1.2.v
Djenne 9 Ad 10–12
Djerba Isl. (Djarba) 32 Bb 35 40 42 43
Djerda, K. 43 Ea
Djerid 40 Ke 42 43
Djibāl 7 Cc 24
Djidda (Djudda) 7 Cc 10 11 19 22 23 44–46
Djidjal (Djidjelli) 40 Da Kd 42 43
Djihun R. (Anat.) 28 Ie
N. Djīhūn (Djayhūn) 1.8.iv 11 Db
Djindjāla 37 Fc
Djīra 16 Bd
Djirm 17 Gb
Djīruft (Djīraft) 16 Cd 20 24 26
al-Djiyād 23 Bd
Djiza 17 Ec
Djīzān (and Wādī) (Djayzān, Qizān) 19 Dd 22 45 46
el-Djof 43 Hd
Djofra 42 Mf
Djōl 1.1.vi
Djolef Cayor 41 Ac
Djuba R. 46 Bd
Djūdāwarī 44 Fc
Djudda, see Djidda
Djudham 19 Cc
al-Djufa 22 Ff
Djuhayna 19 Cc
Djulayla 15 Fe
Djulfar 45 Cb
Djunābīd (Bunābīd) 16 Db
Djundishāpūr 16 Ac
Djundūr 17 Gd
Djūr (Fīrūzābād) 16 Bd
Djurād 15 Ge–Hf
Djurbādhkan (Gulpāyagān) 16 Bc
Djurdjan (Gurgān) 19 Eb 20
Djusk 43 Fb
Djutham 15 Fd
Djuwah (Sindabūr) 45 Ec
Djuwayn (N) 16 Cb
Djuwayn (S) 17 Dc 20
Djuy-i Sulaymān 16 Dd
Djuyūm (-i Abū Aḥmad) 16 Bd
al-Djuzr 45 Bc
Djuzur al-Dīb (Dībadjāt), see Maldive Isls. 44 Ed 45
Djuzur al-Fāl, see Laccadive Isls.
Djuzur al-Ḳumr 45 Bf, see Comoro Isls.
Djūzurāt (Gujerat) 44 Eb 45
N. Dnābr (Dniepr R.) 1.5.vi
N. Dnast (Dniestr R.) 1.4.vi
Dobruja 30 Ea
Docimium 28 Bb
Doero R. see Duwayrah, W.
Doliche 28 Db
Dolmabahçe 32 Hd
Domana 14 Ec
Domenek (Dhomokos) 31 Cc 34
Don R. 32 Da
Donghai 8 Bd
Dongola (*Donkola*) 1.4.i 5 Cd 6–8 10–12 41
Donkey Drovers' Inn (Makka) 23 Bc
Dorylaeum 22 Ba 28 29
Dosareni (*Dawasir*) 14 Dd Mi
Draa, Moyen 42 Ac He 43
Dragoman Pass 31 Cb 34
Drava R. (N. Drawa) 1.3.vi 30 Ba
Dravida 6 Dd
Dravidian languages 4
Drin R. 31 Cb
Dueñas 37 Db
Dukagīn 31 Bb
Dukkala 40 Ab 43
Dulkadir (*Dhuʾl Ḳadr*) 30 Gc 33
Duma (Dūmat al-Djandal, Djauf, Dumaitha) 6 Cc 14 Cb Kf 15 19
Dupnica (Dūbnice) 31 Cb 34
Durağan 31 Fb 34
Durazzo 30 Bb, see Dirāca, Dyrrachium
Duruh 17 Dc
Dutch East Indies 13 Ee
Duwayrah, W. (Doero R.) 37 B–Eb
Düzce 31 Eb
Duzdap (Zahidan) 27 Ec
Dvarasamudra 48 Bc
Dvaravati 8 Ed 9 44
Dvipantara 7 Ed 9
Dwīn 19 Da
Dwird 43 Fb
Dyak 54 Dc 55 56
Dyrrachium 19 Aa, see Durazzo
Dzafar (Sapphar) 14 Lj
Dzungarian Gates 57 Cb

East Africa 13 Ce
Eastern Roman Empire 5 Ac–Cc
Eboda (ʿAbda) 14 Jf
Ebro R. 38 Fb, see Ibruh
Ecbatana 19 Db
Ecija 36 Dd, see Istidja
Edessa (Urfa) 19 Cb 22 28
Edfu 22 Ee
Edirne (Edrene, Adrianople) 26 Aa 27 29 30 31 33 34
Edirne Kapı (İstanbul) 32 Ed
Edjelé 43 Ec
Edremid (Edremit) 29 Fe 31 34
Eflāk (Wallachia) 31 Da
Eğin 31 Gc 34
Egra (Madaʾin Ṣaliḥ) 14 Cb Kg
Egri 31 Bd
Eğri Kapı (İstanbul) 32 Ed
Egri-bucak 31 Cb 34
Eğridir 30 Ec 31 34
Eğrigöz 30 Ec
Egri-ḳaṣri 31 Cb 34
Egypt 5 Bc 12 13 19 27
Egyptian Kitchen (Madīna) 23 Eg
Elana 14 Jg, see Aḳaba
Elassona (Alāṣōnya) 34 Cc
Elbistan 29 Ie 30 31 33 34
Elburz seismic zone 18 Cb
Elche 38 Fc
Eldigüzids 24 Ff
Elesari 14 Ce Lij
Eli, Mont d' 50 Bc, Kingdom 51 Bc
Ellichpur 48 Bb
Ellore 51 Cc
Elmalı 33 Bb 34
Elmina 41 Bd
Elvira 40 Ba
Emboliam vic. 14 Fe
Emerita (Merida) 36 Hd
Emesa (Homs) 19 Cb 28
Endires 31 Gb 34
Enfidaville 42 Ld 43
England 1.2.vii 9 Ab 10–12
Ennedi 41 Ec
Ephesus 19 Bb 28 29
Epiphania 19 Cb 28
Epirus 30 Cc
Erbil 26 Cb
Erciyas D. 29 He
Ereğli (Heracleia Pontica) 27 Ba 29–31 34
Ereğli (Cappadocia) 26 Bb 29 31 34
Eretna 30 Gc
Erevan 26 Ca 27
Erg occ. 43 Db
Erg or. 43 Eb
Erg d'Oubari 43 Fc
Eristhe opp. 14 Ee
Eritrea 13 Cd
Ermenek 30 Fc 31 34
Erupa 14 Ca
Erzerum 12 Cc 20 25 26
Erzincan 26 Bb 29 33
Esfahan (Isfahan) 25 Db 26
Eski Baba 33 Aa
Eski Zağra 30 Db
Eski- cumʿa 31 Db
Eskişehir (Dorylaeum) 26 Bb 29 31 34
Esla R. 38 Da
Eşme 31 Ec 34
Eşref 29 Ge
Estella 36 Ea
Eszek (Ösek) 34 Ba
Et Meydan (İstanbul) 32 Ee
Etawah 49 Bb
Ethiopia (Ḥabash) 7 Cd 8–12 44 45
Eudaimon Arabia (Arabia Emporium, ʿAdan) 15 Bc
Euphrates R. (Firāt) 15 Gd 19 25
Euspoena 28 Db
Evangelorum portus 14 Bd
Evora 35 Ac 36 38 39
Evreşe 31 Db 34
Extremadura 39 Cc
Eyüp 32 Ed
Ezbider 31 Gb 34

Fachi 41 Dc
Fadak 15 Ge
Fadjr 15 Fe
Fahradj (N) 16 Cc
Fahradj (C) 16 Dd
Fahradj (S) 17 Dd
Faḥṣ al-Ballūt 37 Dc
Faid, see Fayd
Faidjū 45 Gc
Failaka (Ichara) Isl. 14 Mg
Faines 1.1.vi
Fakiya (Umūr-fakīh) 34 Db
Fāknūr 44 Ec 45
Faladj 15 Hf
al-Falḳ 23 Cc
Famagusta (Māġūsa) 29 Hf 34
Fandarīna 44 Ec
Fang 7 Bd 8 9 11 12
Fanṣūr 44 Gd 45
Fārāb 24 Cb
Farabr 24 Bc
Farah 17 Ec 20 25 26
Farah-Rūd 17 Dc
Farasan Isls. 19 Dd
Shamāl Farghān 1.8.iv
Farghāna 24 Db, see Fergāna
Farhādgird 17 Db
Fariana 43 Eb
Faridpur 53 Db
Farighunids 17 Eb
Baḥr Faris (Baḥr al-Fārs) 7 Cc 24
Fārs 7 Cc 19 20 24
Faryāb 17 Eb
Faryumad 16 Cb
Fās, see Fez
Fasā 16 Bd
El Fasher (al-Fasher) 8 Bd 10 11 41
al-Fata Mosques 23 Gh
Fatih 32 Fe
Fātimids 8 Bc 9 21 44
Fatisa (Fatṣa) 29 Da 31 Gb 34
Ḳaryat al-Faw 14 Mi
Fayd 7 Cc 9 15 22 25
al-Fayyūm 19 Cc
Fazāra 19 Dc
Fazzaz 42 Ab He 43

Fener 31 Cc
Fenollet 38 Ha
Ferecük 31 Db 33 34
Fergāna (Farghāna) 19 Ga
Fethiye Mosque (İstanbul) 32 Fd
Fethü'l-Islām 31 Ca
Fevzi Paşa Caddesi (İstanbul) 32 Ed
Fez (Fās, Fès) 1.1.iii 7 Ac 8–11 40 42 43
Fezzan 5 Bc 6 7 12 13 41 43
Figuig 40 Bb Ie 42 43
Filali Sharifs 12 Ac
Filibe (Filibüs, Plovdiv) 1.4.vi 30 Db 31, see Philippopolis
Filōrinā 31 Cb 34
Finandj 45 Hd
Finike 29 Ge 31 33 34
Finns 5 Ba 6 7
N. al-Firāt (Frat) 1.5.iv 29 Ie, see Euphrates
Fīrūz (Pandjgūr) 17 Ed
Firrīm 16 Bb
Fīrūzābād (Djūr) 16 Bd 19
Fīrūzān (Khānlandjān) 16 Bc
Fīrūzkūh (W) 16 Bb
Fīrūzkūh (Djām) 17 Eb 24
Flores 54 Fd 55 56
Fōça (Anatolia) 31 Dc 34
Fōca (Balkans) 31 Bb 34
Focsani 34 Da
Fōnua 31 Cc
Foochow 57 Fd
Forcados 41 Cd
Forest, Rain 11 Bde
Formosa 12 Fc 13
Fort Nikolajevsk 13 Fb
Fort St. David 52 Bc
Fort St. George 52 Cc
Fort Sandeman 27 Eb
Foum Tatahouine 43 Fb
Fraga 36 Gb
Francovilla 30 Ca
Franks (Merovingian) 5 Bb 6–8 13 32 35 37
Frat, Nahr al-, see Firāt
French Railway 27 Ab
Frisians 5 Bb 6 7
Fu-chou 6 Ec 9 11 13, see Fugiu
Fugiu 10 Ec, see Fu-chou
Fulani (Peul) 41 Ac Bc
Fulo-Kondor 11 Ed
Fūmān 19 Db
Fūmin 16 Ab
Fu-nan 5 Ed 6
Fung 41 Fc
Furg 16 Cd
Fustat 7 Cc, see Cairo
Futa Jalon 41 Ac

Gabal Kadūr 15 Cb
Gabal Kanin 15 Bb
Gabal Tala' 15 Bc
Gabele (Gabela) 31 Bb 34
Gabès (Kābis) and Gulf 35 Ed 40 42 43
Gabrova 34 Db
Gades 7 Ac, see Cadiz
Gafsa (Ḳafṣa) 40 Db Ke 42
Gaia opp. 14 Cb
Galam 41 Ac
Galata 32 Ca
Galata Bridge and Tower 32 Gd
Galatz 34 Ea
Galicia 36 Hc 37–39
Galla 11 Cd 12
Galle (Horkand) 11 Dd 47
Gallipoli 29 Fd 30
Gamarkān (Kirkūk) 19 Db
Gambia 13 Ad
Ganāwa (Djanāba) 16 Bd
Ganda 7 Ce 9
Gandāwa (Ḳandābīl) 17 Fd
Gandhara 19 Fb, see Kandahar
Gandia 38 Fc
Gandj Rustāḳ 17 Eb
Ganga (Ganges) R. 46 Fb 47–53
Gangaikanda-Colapuram 47 Bc
Gangra (Çankırı) 28 Ca Hd 29
Ganjam 53 Cc
Ganzaca 19 Db
Gao 8 Ad 9–12 41 43
Garamantes 5 Bc
garden, walled (Makka) 23 Ba
Gardíz 17 Fc 19
Garha 51 Bb
Garhakatanga 51 Cb
Garian 40 Le 42 43
Garrovillas 39 Cc
Garumdé 41 Dc
Gates of China 44 Ib
Gaur (Lakhnauti) 10 Dc 48–51
Gavashir (Kirman) 25 Db
Gāvmāhā R. 16 Bb
Gawf, W. al- 15 Bab
Gawilgarh 50 Bb
Gaya 5 Dc 6 7 53
Gaza 5 Cc 14 19 22 25–27
Gebze 31 Eb 34
Gediz 31 Ec 34
Gediz R. 29 Fe
Gedrosia (Makrān) 19 Ec 14 Pg
Gegia 38 Da
Geikwars 53 Bb
Gelgel 54 Ed Pg
Gelībōlī 31 Db 34
Gemlik 31 Eb 34
Genava (Djannaba) 25 Dc 16
Genoese 10 Cb 12 30
Gerede 29 Hd 30 31 34
German Empire 8 Bb 9–12
Germaniceia (Marash) 28 Db
Germiyan 29 Ge 30
Geró 41 Bd
Gerona 35 Cb 36 37
Gerra opp. 5 Cc 14 Ec
Gerraei 14 Dc Mg
Geyve 26 Ba 29 31 34
Ghadamès 5 Bc 6 8 10–12 40–43
Ghaibūn 15 Db
Ghāna 1.1.ii 1.2.i 5 Ad 6–9
Gharb 40 He 42 43
Gharčistān 17 Eb
Ghardaiya 40 Cb Je 42 43
Dj. Gharghara 1.2.ii
Gharghūn 1.8.v
Gharnāṭa 40 Ba
Gharrar 11 Cd
Ghassānids 15 Fd 19
Ghat 9 Bc 10–12 41
Ghatafān 15 Ge 19 Dc
Ghaymān 15 Bb
Ghazipur 50 Cb
Ghāzna (Ghazni) 5 Dc 7 9 17 19–21 24–27 44 46 50
Ghaznawids 16 Db 17 Ed 21 44
Gheddaiya 43 Gb
Ghemines 43 Gb
Ghifar 15 Gf
Ghundidjān 16 Bd
Ghūr 17 Ec 24 47
Ghūri chiefs 17 Ec
Ghurmadj 37 Eb
Ghuzz 8 Cb 20 21
Gibraltar (Djabal Ṭarik) 13 Ac 35 39 42 43
Gibre (Čipronica) 31 Cb
Gijon 35 Ab
Gilān 16 Ab 21
Gilevci 33 Bb
Gilgit 51 Ba
Gingi 49 Bc 52
Giradçānīce 31 Ba
Giratha 14 Dc
Gīrebene 31 Cb 34
Giresun 29 Id 31 34
Giri 54 Ib Of
Girīd (Crete) 31 Dd 34
Girīne (Kyrenia) 31 Fd
Girnar 48 Bb 49
Giurgiu (Yer-gögi) 34 Db
Goa 11 Dd 12 48 50–53, see Sindapur (Panjim)
Gobir 41 Cc
Godāvarī (Godāwarī) R. 46 Ec 47–53
Goddua 43 Fc
Gog and Magog 1.10.v–vi
Gōgha 46 Eb
Gogra R. 48 Cb 49–53
Göksun (Cocusus, Coxon) 22 Ba 31 34
Gōlconda (Gōlkonda) 12 Dd 46 50–52
Gold Coast 11 Ad 13
Golden Horde (Kipchak Empire) 10 Cb–Db 11 30
Golden Horn (Haliç) 32 Fd
El-Goléa 41 Ca 42 43
Gölhisar (Anatolia) 29 Ge
Göl-ḥiṣār (Jezero) 31 Ba
Golubac 30 Ca
Gombroon (Bandar Abbas) 26 Dc
Gondar 46 Ac
Gondwāna 11 Dc 46 49–51
Gonja 41 Bd
Gorbeous 28 Cb, see Beinam
Gorda 14 Dc
Görice 31 Cb 34
Gorontalo 56 Fb
Goths 19 Ca
La Goulette 42 Ea Ld
Goulmina 42 Ab
Goundiourou 41 Ac
Gourlimine 42 Ac
Gowa 54 Ed 55 56
Göynük 31 Eb 34
Gračanica 34 Ba
Grada 14 Dd
Gradiska 34 Ba
Granada 10 Ac 35 36 38 39
Grand Bazaar (İstanbul) 32 Ge
Grand Trunk Road 53 Bb
graveyards (Makka, Madīna) 23 Bc Db Gf, see cemeteries
Greece 13 Bc
Greek Patriarchal Church (İstanbul) 32 Fd
Greenland 9 Aa
Gresik 54 Dd Ib 55 56
Guadalajara 35 Bb 36 38 39
Guadalete 36 Dd
Guadalquivir R. 38 Ed
Guadiana R. 38 Dc
Guadix 36 Ed 40
C. Guardafui 19 Ed
Guardo 39 Da
Guelma 42 Kd 43
Guemar 42 Ke
Guergour 42 Da Kd 43
Guernica 37 Ea
Gügercinlik 31 Ca
Guijelo 36 Db
Guinea, Portuguese 13 Ad
Guir, Haut 42 Bb Ie 43
Gujarat (Gudjarāt, Gujerat, Djūzurāt) 11 Dc 24 32 44 45 46 49–51
Gujeratis 9 Dd
Gül Mosque (İstanbul) 32 Fd
Gulbarga 48 Bc 49–51 53
Güle (Gyula) 31 Ca Cd 34
Gülek 31 Fc 34
Gülnar 31 Fc 34
Gulpāyagān (Djurbādhkān) 16 Bc
Gümülçine 30 Db
Gümüş 31 Ec 34
Gundeshapur 19 Db
Guntur 51 Cc 53
Gunung-Jati 54 Mf
Gunung Kidul 55 Ib
Gunung Sewu 55 Ib
Gurdjara 19 Fc
Güre 31 Ec 34
Gurgān (Djurdjan) 16 Cb 19
Gurgāndj 7 Cb 8 19 24–26
Gurun 10 Fe
Gurzivar 17 Eb
Güzelhisar 31 Dc 34
Guzgān 17 Eb
Gwādar 46 Db
Gwāliōr 24 Lh 52 53
Gwari 41 Cc
Gyim Pass 34 Da
Gyula (Güle) 34 Ca

al-Ḥabash (Ḥabasha, Ethiopia) 11 Cd 19 44
Ḥabbān 15 Cb
Hacci Bektaş 33 Cb
Hacıköy 31 Fb 34
Ḥācīoğli-bāzāri (Bazargik) 31 Db
Hadhramaut (Hadramawt) 6 Cd 7 11 14 15 19 45 (see Sūḳ Hadhramawt)
Hadhramis (Hadramites, Chatramonitae, Atramitae) 14 Ed Mi 15
Hadjar (al-Ḥadjr) 14 Mg Ng 15 He 19 Dc, see Hofuf
B. Ḥadjdjādj 37 Cd
al-Hadjla 23 ABd
Haduz 42 Ab
Hafar 15 He 22
B. Ḥafs 40 Da
ibn Ḥafsūn 37 Ed
Hagar bin Ḥumayd 15 Bb
Hagios Petros (Āyā-Petrī) 34 Ce
Ḥagr, W. 15 Db
Hāhla 40 Ab
Haidar (Haydar) Baba 33 Bb
Haifa 27 Bb
Haihayas 47 Cb
Hā'il (Arra) 14 Lg 15 19 22 27
Hai-nan 10 Ed 11
Ḥairīdj 45 Cc
al-Halaka 23 Db
Hālawand 17 Fb
Ḥaleb (Ḥalep, Aleppo) 29 Ie 31 34
Halha 12 Eb
Halī (Haly) 46 Bc
Haliç (Golden Horn) 32 Fd
Halicarnassus (Bodrum) 28 Ab
Halmahera 55 Gb 56
Halys fl. 19 Cb 28
Hama 20 Bb 22 25–27 29 31 34
Hamada de Tinhert 43 Ec
Hamada Tounassine 43 Bc
Hamadhān 6 Cc 8 16 20 22 24–27
Hamburg 10 Bb 11 13
Hamdān (Hamdānids) 15 Hh 19 Dd: 21 Ba
Hamdha 22 Gg
Hami 11 Eb 12 13 57
Hamit, Hamid 29 Ge 30 Ec 31 33
Hamitic languages 4
al-Ḥamma (Spain) 37 Ed
al-Hamma (Tunis) 40 Db
Hammamet and Gulf 40 Ea 42 43
B. Hammud 38 Dd
Hamsavati 6 Ed 8 9
Hamvārān 17 Fa
Hanakiyya 22 Gf
Hang-chou (Hangchow, Quinsay, Lith-an) 8 Fc 10 57
Ḥanifa 15 Hf 19
Hankow 13 Ec
Hanoi 12 Ec 13
Hānsī 24 Lh 48
Haouz 40 He 43
Happu 10 Fc
Hara Berezaiti 19 Eb
al-Ḥaram (Madīna) 23 Gf, (Makka) 23 BCcd
Harar 46 Bd
Harāt (W) 16 Cd
Harāt (Herāt) 17 Eb 24 46
Harāt al-Bāb 23 Bc
Harbin 57 Gb, see Kharbin
Hardwar 49 Bb 53
Ḥarīb, W. 15 Bb
Harī-Rūd 17 Db
Harith 15 Hg
Harmancık 31 Ec 34
Ḥarmanlı 31 Db 34
Harmozon prom. (Ormuz, Hurmuz) 14 Gc Og
Harran (Haran, Charrae) 22 Cb
Harşova, see Hırsova
Harūd R. 19 Fb
Harūn 20 Ab
Harūniye 31 Gc 34
Ḥarūrī 17 Ec
al-Hasa 12 Cc 21
Hasan Abdul 53 Ba
Hasan Baba 33 Ab
Hasanparlık 31 Gc 34
Ḥasanūyid Kurds 16 Ab
Haseki Cad. (İstanbul) 32 Ee
Hāshimgird 17 Fb
Ḥāsik 19 Ed 44
Haskova 34 Db
Hassan Arabs 41 Ab
Hassi Messaoud 43 Eb
Hassi R'mel 43 Db
Hastinks (Hastings) 1.2.vi
Hatra 19 Db
Hattīn 22 Bb
Ḥaṭvān 31 Bd
Hausa 9 Bd 10–12 41
Havāss-i Mahmūdpāşā 31 Db 34
Hawazin 15 Ge
Hawdha 5 Cc 15
Hawsam 16 Bb
Haydarābād (Nirūnkōt) 17 Fe
Haydar Paşa (Station, İstanbul) 32 If
Ḥayra-bōlī (Hayrabolu) 31 Db 33 34
Hazārasp 20 Ea 24 25
Hazārğirād (Razgrad) 31 Db
Hedjaz, see Hidjaz
Hei-an 9 Fc
Hekimhan 29 Db 31 34
Heliopolis (Egypt) 15 Ee 19
Heliopolis (Syria) 19 Cb
Hellin 38 Fc
Helmand R. 17 Ec 47–49 51–53
Hendek 29 Gd
Heracleia Cappadocica 22 Bb 28, see Ereğli
Heracleia Pontica 1.5.vi 28 Ba Gd 29 30, see Ereğli
Herāt 1.8.iii 6 Dc 8–11 19 20 25 27, Road 50 Aa, see Harāt
Hermanstadt 31 Da 34
Hermus fl. 28 Ab
Hersek 31 Bb
Hexamilion 29 Fd
Hidjāra, W. al- 37 Eb
Hidjaz 12 Cc 15 20, Railway 23 Egh
al-Hidjr (Egra, Madā'in Ṣāliḥ) 14 Cb Kg 15 Fe 19
Hidjra route 23 Hh
Hieron 28 Fe
Hierosolyma (Jerusalem, al-Kuds) 14 Kf 15
Himyar 15 Gh 19, see *Homeritae*
Hinaur 48 Bc 49–51, see Hunawār
Hind 1.9.ii 44 Eb 45 47
Hindi lang 4 Dc
Hindūshāhis 17 Gb
Hintāta 40 Ab
al-Ḥīra 15 Gd 19
Hırsova (Harşova) 31 Ea 34
Hisar 49 Bb
Ḥiṣn al-Ghurāb (Cane) 19 Dd
Ḥiṣn al-Hanash 37 Cc
Ḥiṣn Kayfa 22 Cb
Ḥiṣn al-Mahdi 16 Ac
Ḥiṣn-i Mansur 31 Gc 34
Ḥiṣn Tawas 33 Bb
Ḥiṣn ibn 'Umāra 16 Cd
Ḥiṣn al-Ward 37 Dd
Hispalis (Sevilla) 5 Ac 36
Hīt 19 Db 22
Dj. Hodna 40 Ca Kd 42 43
Hofei 57 Fc
Hofuf 27 Cc, see Hadjar
Hoggar 5 Bc 6 7 9–12 41
Holkar 53 Bb
Holland 13 Bb
Hollandia 56 Jc
Holwan 20 Cb 22
Holy Roman Empire 10 Bb 11
Homeritae (Himyarites) 14 De Lj
Homs (Libya) 40 Le 42 43
Homs (Syria–Emesa) 20 Bb 22 26 27 29 31 34
Hōnan 5 Ec 6 9
Honaz 31 Ec 34
Hondo 12 Fc
Hong-kong 13 Ec
Hor 7 Db
Horcajo 39 Dc
Horkand (Galle) 47 Cd
Hormuzd 19 Db, see Ahwāz
Hosadurg 48 Bc 49
hospital (Makka) 23 Ba
Hova 5 Ce 7
Hoyran 31 Ec 34
Hoysalas 9 Dd 47 48
Baḥr al-Hozar 1.7.v
HRBT 15 Bb
Hsi-an (Hsi-an-fu) 11 Ec 12, see Sian
Huang-ho 5 Db
B. Hud 38 Fb
Hudavendigār 31 Ec 34
al-Hudayda 45 Bc 46
Hudhayl 15 Hf 19
Hue 13 Ed

Huelva 36 Cd 38 40
Huesca 38 Fa, see Osca, Washka
Huete 36 Eb 38, see Wabdha
Hugli 51 Cb 52
Huhehot 57 Fb
Hulbuk 17 Fb 24
Ḥulumic (Chlemontzi) 31 Cc
Hulwān 19 Db
Humayun 51 Ba
Hun 43 Gc
Hunawār 46 Ec, see Hinaur
Ḥunayn (Honayn, Beni Saf) 40 Ba Id 42 43
Hungary 9 Bb 10–12 30
Huns 6 Db
Huraydah (MḌB) 15 Db
Ḥūrbişte 31 Cb
Hurmuz (Hormuz, coastal) 5 Cc 6 8–11 21 24–26 32 46
Hurmuz (Hormuz, Dih-i Gūz) 16 Cd
Hurmuzshahr 16 Ac, see Ahwāz
Husain (*Hüseyn*) *Gazi* 33 Cab
Ḥuṣn al-'Urr 15 Da
Hussaynids 42 Da
Ḥuwayza 16 Ac
Huzū 16 Cd
Hyaila 14 De
Hyderabad (Deccan) 51 Bc 53
Hyderabad (Sind) 17 Fe 27, see Haydarābād (Nirūnkōt)

Iabri 14 Cb
Iala 14 Fd
Iambia vic (Yanbu) 14 Bc
Iathrippa (Madīna) 14 Cc
Iazd 1.7.iii, see Yazd
Ibād 15 Gd
Iberia (Caucasus) 5 Cb 6 19
Iberia (Spain) 36 Hc
Ibi 22 Gg
Ibil 7 Cb 8
Ibiza 39 Gc
Ibn Saud 27 Cc
Ibrā'īl 31 Da 34
W. Ibruh 37 Fb, see Ebro
Ibṣāla 31 Db, see Ipsala
Icaria 28 Ab
Içel 31 Fc
Iceland 9 Aa
Ichara (Failaka Isl.) 14 Eb Mg
Icheriden 42 Jd
Ichthyophagi 14 Fc Nh
Ichtimān (Iḥtimān) 31 Cb 34
Iconium (Konya) 19 Cb 28
Idar 50 Bb
Idhadj (Mālamīr) 16 Ac
Idicara 14 Db
'Idim, W. 15 Db
Idjil 41 Ab
Mt. Idris 42 Ab
Idrisids 8 Ac
İdrum 16 Cd
Ife 5 6 10 Bd 11 12 41
Ifni 42 Ac Hf
Ifrīkiya 7 Bc
al-Īgharayn 16 Ac
Igir ad-Yattuf 35 Ad
Iharana 9 Ce 10
Iḥtimān (Ichtimān) 31 Cb 34
Iklīd 16 Bc
Īlāk (Angren) R. 24 CDb
Il-basan 31 Bb
Ilbīra 37 Ed
Ilek Khans 21 BCa
Ilgin 31 Ec 34
Ili (R.) 12 Db 24
Ilkhans 10 Cc–Dc 21 29
Illyricum 19 ABa
Ilok 31 Ba
Ilorin 41 Cd
Ilyāsids 16 Cd
In Azawa 41 Cb
In Gall 41 Cc
In Salah 41 Cb
In Zize 41 Cb
Inapha 14 Dc
Indarpat (Delhi) 49 Bb
Indian Empire 13 Dc
Indian traders 12 Cd
Indo-European languages 4
Indonesians 5 Ce
Indore 53 Bb
Indrafūrā 45 He
Indrapūrā 5 Ed 6–9
Indus R. (N. Mihran) 17 Fd 19 24 25 47–53
İne 31 Dc 34
İnebaḥti (Naupaktos) 31 Cc
Inebolu 27 Ba 31 34, see Ionopolis
Inecük 31 Db 34
Inönü 31 Ec 34
İnöz 31 Db 34, see Ainos
Iobaritae 14 Fd Ni
Iodisitae 14 Db Mg
Iokun (*Kwararfa*) 41 Cd
Ionopolis 28 Ca
Ipek 31 Cb 34
Ipsala 30 Db, see Ibṣāla
Irada ('Irdh) 14 Ec Mh
Irāhistān 16 Bd
'Irāḳ 7 Cc 8 20 32
Irbil 19 Db 22
'Irdh, see Irada
Ireland (Djaz. Irlanda) 1.1.vii
Irīg 31 Ba
Irish 5 Ab 6 8 9 11 12
Iritae 14 Dd Mh
Irkutsk 12 Eb 13
'Irmā', W. 15 Cb
Irminiya (Armenia) 7 Cb
Irmiye (Armyro) 31 Cc
Iron Gate (on Danube) 34 Ca
Iron Gate (Dar-i Ahanīn) 17 Fb 24 Cc
Irşova (Orsova) 31 Ca
Irtish (Irtysh) R. 13 Db
Isākce 31 Ea
Isaurians 19 Cb
Işbāt 31 Cb
Iṣfahān 7 Cc 8 10 12 16 19 20 24–27 44
Isfara'in (Isfarayin) 16 Cb 20
Isfīdjāb, N. (Aris R.) 24 Cb
Isfirlīg (Svrljig) 31 Cb
Isfizār (Sabzawar) 17 Ec
B. Ishak 37 Fd
İshaklı 31 Ec 34
Ishbīliya (Sevilla) 37 Cd 40
Ishkāmish 17 Gb
Ishkāshim 24 Dc
Ishkīmish 17 Fb
Ishtikhān 24 Cb
Isias mons 14 Bc
Isık Göl 24 Le
Işıklı 31 Ec 34
Işīm 31 Bb
Iskaf 17 Dd
Iskenderiye (Egypt–Alexandria) 1.4.iii 7 Bc 8
Iskenderiye (Balkans–Dukagin, Scutari) 31 Bb 34
Iskenderūn (Alexandretta) 1.5.iv 29 31 34
Iskilip 31 Fb 34
Islamabad (Chittagong) 52 Db
Işlimye (Slivno) 31 Db
Ismail 31 Ea 34
Isma'ilis 24 Gf
Ismil 31 Fc 34
Isparta 31 Ec 34
Iṣṭabba 37 Dd
Iṣṭahbānāt 16 Cd
Iṣtakhr 6 Cc 16 19 20, see Persepolis
İstanbul 1.4.vi 26 27 31 33 34
Istānköy (Kos) 31 Dc 34
Istanoz 31 Ec 34
Istārova, Istarovo 31 Cb 34
Istib 31 Cb 34
Istidja 37 Dd, see Ecija
Istifan 31 Fb 34
Istife (Thebes) 31 Cc
Istiklāl Cad. 32 Gd
Istōkī 31 Ca
Italy 8 Bb 13
Itamus portus 14 Db
Ithar opp. 14 Db
Itrablus 7 Bc, see Tripoli
Iuliopolis 28 Ba
Ivlāhōr 31 Cc
Ivory Coast 11 Ad 13
Ivraca (Vraca) 31 Cb
Ivranya (Ivranj) 31 Cb 34
Ivrindi 31 Dc 34
Izdin (Lamia, Zeytuni) 31 Cc
Izlādī 31 Cb, see Zlatica
İzmir 31 Dc 33 34, see Smyrna
İzmit (Izmid, Nicomedia) 26 Aa 29 31–34
İznik (İsnik, Nicaea) 29 Ba 31 33 34
İzvornik (Zvornik) 31 Ba

Jabalpur 53 Bb
Jaca 36 Fa 37 38
Jacobabad 26 Ec 27
Jaen 36 Ed 38 40, see Djayyān
Jaffa 26 Bb 27
Jaffna 52 Cd
Jagodina (Yāğōdīna) 34 Cb
Jaipur 51 Bb 53
Jaisalmer 49 Bb 50–53
Jajce (Yaca) 34 Ba
Jajnagar (Orissa) 48 Cb 49
Jakarta (Sunda Kalapa, Batavia) 55 Cd Lf
Jalón R. 38 Fb
Jalor 50 Bb
Jambi 12 Ee 54–56
Janju 7 Ec
Japan 10 Fc 12
Japara 54 Dd Nf 55 56
Jativa 36 Fc 38
Jatnapatam 10 Dd
Jats 52 Bb 53
Jaunpur 49 Cb 50–52
Java 11 Ee 12 13 54–56
Javanese lang. 4 Ee
Java Major (Sri-Vijaya) 10 Ed
Jaxartes R 19 Fa
Jefren 40 Le 42
Jenne (Djenne) 41 Bc
Jerez 38 Cd
Jerez de los Cabelleros 36 Cc
Jerusalem (Hierosolyma, al-Kuds) 7 Cc 9 14 15 22 25–27
Jesselton 56 Ea
Jezero (Göl-ḥiṣār) 34 Ba
Jhelum R. 47 Ba 48–50
Jidda 26 Bc, see Djidda
Jih-pen (Wo) 9 Fc, see Japan
Jipang (Bojonegoro) 54 Nf 55
Jirdān, W. 15 Cb
Jodhpur 47 Bb 51 52
Jogyakarta 55 Ih 56 Nf
Johore 54 Bb 56
Jolo 54 Fa 56
Jubo 11 Ce
Jucar R. 38 Ec
Juchen 8 Fb
Juda 41 Cd
Jullundur 48 Ba
Junagadh 49 Bb 50
Junnar 50 Bc
Jurfattan (Cannanore) 48 Bc
Jutes 5 Bb

Kābis (Gabès) 40 Eb Le
Kābūl 6 Dc 7 8 10 12 17 19 20 24–26 44 46–52
Kābūl R. 17 Fb
Kābūlshāhs 17 Fb
Kabylie 40 Ca Jd 42
Kāçānik 31 Cb 34
Kadah 10 Ed
Kadambas 47 Bc
Kadarang 10 Ed
Kadiri 54 Of 55 56
Kadrandj 44 Hc
al-Ḳaf 14 Kf
Kaffa 30 Fa 31 32 34
Kafiristān (Kafarestan) 17 Gb 26
Kāfirnihan R. 24 Cc
Ḳafṣa (Gafsa) 40 Db Ke
Kafsids 10 Bc
Kahfa 15 Ge
Kahriye Mosque (İstanbul) 32 Ed
Kāhta 30 Gc
Ḳā'in 16 Dc 24
Kairouan (Kayrawan, Kairwan) 8 Bc 35 40–43
Kajoran 55 Ib
Kakatiyas 47 Bc 48
Kakhetti 26 Ca
Ḳāḳulla 44 Gd
Kākūyids 16 Bc
Ḳal'a B. Hammād (B. Abbès) 40 Da 42
Ḳal'a-yi Dīkdān (Ḥiṣn ibn 'Umāra) 16 Cd
Ḳal'a Djabal Hindi 23 Bc
Ḳal'a Djiyād 23 Bd
Ḳal'a Filfil 23 Cc
Ḳal'at-i Nādirī 17 Db
Ḳal'a Rabāḥ 37 Ec
Ḳal'a-yi Safīd 16 Bc
Kalāh 7 Ed 10 44
Kalahari 11 Bf
Kalahurra 37 Fa, see Calahorra
Kalanau 48 Ba
Kalansar 50 Ba
Kalār 16 Bb
Ḳalāṣ Steppe 24 Cb
Ḳal'at Ayyūb 37 Fb
Ḳal'at Huwwāra 40 Ca
Kalāvrita 31 Cc 34
B. Kalb 15 Fd 19
Kalecik 31 Fb 33 34
Ḳalghradun 1.3.vi
Ḳalhāt 45 Cb 46
Kālif 17 Fb 24
Kālikat (Kālikūt, Calicut) 45 Ec 46
Kalimantan (Borneo) 11 Ed–e
Kalinga 5 Dd 6 9 47
Kalinjar 24 Mh 47 48 51
Ḳalkan-delen 31 Cb
Kalpi 49 Bb
Kalyana 5 Dd
Ḳalyūsha 37 Fc
Kamakura 10 Fc
Kamarān Isls. 46 Bc
Kamaru (Kamarupa) 7 DEc 48 52
Kamenkirād 31 Ba
Kamerun 13 Bd
Kamīn 16 Bc
Kamnūrīyya 1.1.ii
Kampar R. 54 Bb
Djab. al-Ḳamr 1.4.i
Djaz. al-Ḳamr (Malai) 1.9.i
Ḳāmrūb (Lakshmibūr, Kāmta-Kāmrūp) 44 Gb 50 Cb
Kanauj (Kanaudj, Kanawj) 24 Lh 44 47–51
Kanbāia (Kanbāya, Cambay) 1.7.ii 44 Eb 45
Ḳanbalī (? Balīn) 17 Fe 44
Ḳanbalu, Madagascar 8 Cef
Ḳanbalū, Pemba 10 Ce
Kanbūsa 45 Hd
Kanchi (Kanci, Kandjā) 44 Ec 47 50, see Kansipura
Kan-chou 7 Ec 9–12
Kandābīl (Gandāwa) 17 Fd 25
Ḳandahār (? Tigīnābād) 1.8.ii 7 Dc 8 9 12 17 20 25–27 44 46–52, see Gandhara
Kandak 17 Fa 24
Kandıra, Kandırı 29 Gd 31 Eb 34
Kandy 46 Fd 53
Kane emporium (Bir 'Ali) 14 Ee Mj
Kanem 5 Bd 6 8–11 41
Kangaba 41 Bc
Kangala 41 Bd
Kangan 46 Cb
Kangawār (Kangiwār, Ḳaṣr al-Lusūs) 16 Ab
Kangra (Nayarkot) 47 Ba
Kanīje 31 Bd
Ḳanīṭ 37 Dd
Kannanūr (Kananūr) 45 Ec 46, see Cannanore
Kano 9 Bd 10–12 41
Kansipura (Conjeeveram) 5 Dd 6–9, see Kanchi
Ḳānṣū 12 Eb 44 Ia
Ḳantara al-Hidjara (Stone Bridge) 17 Fa
Kanwa (battle) 50 Bb
Kanyakubja 7 Dc
Kao-li 9 Fc
Kapı Dağı 31 Db 34
Kapisi 5 Dc
Kappadokia 28 Cb
Kara 48 Bb
al-Ḳara 15 Ge
Kara Dağları 29 Hd
Kara Gümrük (İstanbul) 32 Fd
Kara Khitai 9 Db 10
Ḳara Ḳum Desert 16 Da 24
Ḳara-ağaç 31 Db 34
Karachi (Karashi) 13 Dc 27 45
Karadj-i Abu Dulaf 16 Ac 22 Db
Karadj-i Rūdhrāwar 16 Ab
Ḳara-ferye 31 Cb 34
Karahisar 34 Ec
Karahisar-i şarki 33 Da
Ḳarākhānids 9 Db 17 21 24
Ḳarākhitay 9 Db 21 Bb 24
Karakoron 10 Eb
Karakuay 37 Ec
Karaman 25 Bb 29 30 33, see Larande
Karamanlis 42 Fb
Karapınar 26 Bb 31 34
Karashi, see Karachi
Karasi 29 Fe 30 31 34
Karasu Yeñicesi 31 Db 34
Karātigīn (Rāsht) 17 Ga 24
Karbala 22 Cb Gd 27
Ḳardhīra 37 Ed
Karīmātā 45 Ie
Karīnābād (Karnabat) 31 Db 34
Ḳarīnayn (Barakdiz) 17 Eb
Ḳaritene (Karytaena) 31 Cc 34
Ḳarḳana (Kerken, Kerkena) Isl. 40 Eb 42
Karkisiya (Karkissiya) 7 Cc 22
Dj. Karkuniyya 1.7.v
Karkūya (nr. Zarandj) 17 Dc 25
Karli Ili 31 Cc
Karlsburg (Karlsberg) 31 Ca 34
Karlstadt 34 Aa
Ḳarluks (*Turkish slaves*) 9 Db 17 Ga 24
Ḳarmatians 8 Cc 9 20–22 44
Karmīna 24 Bb
Ḳarmūna 37 Dd
Karnabat, see Karīnābād
Karnal 53 Bb
Karnasuvarna 47 Cb
Ḳarnīn 17 Ec
Karpuzlu 31 Dc 34
Karrān 17 Ga 24
Kars (Cilicia) 31 Fc 34
Kars (Georgia) 26 Ca 27
Karta 55 Ib
Karta Sura 55 Ia Nf
Ḳartādjannat al-Ḥalfā' (Cartagena), Ḳartadjena 1.1.iv 37 Fd
Karu (*Quoja*) 41 Ad
Karūkh 17 Eb
Karūki 1.3.vii
Ḳarūḳīyya 1.7.vi
Karūn R. 19 Eb
al-Ḳarura 23 Cc
Karwar 52 Bc
Ḳaryāt al-Bīdh 16 Bc
Ḳaryāt 'Abd al-Raḥmān (Abāda) 16 Bd
Ḳaryāt al-Faw 14 Mi
Ḳaryatayn 22 Ge
al-Ḳasaba 1.3.ii
Kāsān 19 Ga 24 Db
Kasarkand 20 Ec
Kasba 17 Ea
Ḳāshān 16 Bb 24 –26
al-Kashāshīya 23 Cd
Kāshgar (Kāshghar) 5 Dc 6–12 24 51, see Ch'ia-Sha
Ḳashka Darya 24 Cc
Kashmīr [al-Khāridja] (Kasmira) 1.8.ii 13 Dc 24 44 47–53
Ḳashṭamūni 1.5.v, see Kastamonu 28 Ca 30 31 33 34
Kashtāra 1.3.iv
Ḳashṭilyūn 37 Fc
Kāsī 47 Cb
B. Kāsī 37 Fb
al-Ḳasīm 15 Ge 19
B. Kasim 38 Fc
Kasma 45 Gc
Kasmira (Kashmir) 11 Dc
Ḳaṣr Abi Dānis 37 Bc
Ḳaṣr Aḥnaf 17 Eb
Ḳaṣr-i Kand 17 Dd, see Kasarkand
el-Ḳaṣr el-kebir (Ḳaṣr Kutāma) 42 Ab
Ḳaṣr al-Lusūs 16 Ab
Ḳaṣr al-Rīh (Dizbad) 16 Db

Ḳaṣr Ṣaliḥ 40 Eb
Ḳaṣr-i Shīrīn 19 Db
Kastamonu (Kastamoni, Ḳashṭamūni) 28 Ca 30 31 33 34
Ḳasṭulūna 37 Ec
al-Ḳaṭar 19 Ec 27 45
Kāth 17 19 Ea 20 24 26
Katha (Yazd) 16 Cc
al-Ḳaṭīf 19 Dc 26 27 46, see Darin
Ḳaṭīgūrā 1.9.ii
Katimantan 12 Ed–e, see Borneo
Katra 48 Cb
Katsina 9 Bd 11 12 41
Ḳaṭwan Steppe 24 Cb
Kaūda 22 Hg
Kaulam (Kawlam, Quilon) 46 Ed 48, see Kūlam
Kausambi 6 Dc
Kavala (Kavalla) 30 Db 31 32 34
Dasht-i Kavir 24 GHg
Kawar 41 Dc
Ḳawra 37 Cd
al-Ḳaws ('Marble Arch') 43 Gb
Kawshī 45 Hb
Kaya 7 Fc
Kāyal 46 Ed, see Cail
Ḳays Isl. (Kish) 16 Bd
Kayseri 22 Ba 25 26 29–31 33 34
Kazak (*Kazakh*) 12 Db 57
Kazan 13 Cb
Kazan khanate 11 Cb
Kazan Pass 31 Db
Kazanluk (Aḳça-Kizanluk) 34 Db
Kāzarūn (Kazerūn) 16 Bd 25–27
Keban 26 Bb 31 34
Kebbi 10 Bd 11 41
Kebili 42 Ke 43
Kebsud 33 Bb
Keçiborlu 31 Ec 34
Kedah 54 Ba 55 56
Le Kef 40 Kd 42 43
Kefe, see Kaffa
Kei 56 Hd
Kelantan 9 Ed 54 56
Kelaris 51 Bc
Kelat 25 Ec 47 51
Kelibia 40 Ld 42 43
Kelkit R. 29 Id
Kemer 31 Dc 34
Kemerlü 33 Db
Kenadza 43 Cb
Keraits 8 Eb 9 10
Kerak 22 Bb
Kerch (Kertch, Kers) 30 Ga 31 34
Kermanshah 16 Ab 26 27
Keşan 29 Fd 33
Kesik Köprü 34 Fc
Kesriye 30 Cb 31 34
Keumala 56 Aa
Khabarovsk 13 Fb
Khabb, W. 15 Ba
Khabīs (Bardasīr) 16 Cc
Khābr 16 Bd
Khabūshān, see Khūčān
Khāḳān Ādkash 1.9.vi
Khaladj 17 Fc
Khaldjand 25 Ea, see Khodjand
Khaldjis (*Khaljis*) 21 Cb 48
Khalfāt 45 Cc
Khalidj al-Anklishin 1.1.v
Khalkhāl 16 Ab
Khamit 15 Aa
Khamlydj 7 Cb 8
Khanbalik (Ta-tu) 10 Ec, see Peking
Khanbāyat 46 Eb, see Cambay
Khāndēsh 46 Eb 49–52
Khanfar 46 Bc
Khānfū (Khānfūā, Kuang-chou), see Canton, Sincalan
Khānlandjān (Fīrūzān) 16 Bc
Khar 26 Db
Khārak Isl. 16 Bd 46 see Khardj
Kharba 1.9.v
Kharbin 13 Fb, see Harbin
Khardj 45 Cb, see Khārak Isl.
Kharga 7 Cc 41
Kharīdj 44 Cc
Kharḳān 16 Bc
Kharkov 13 Cb
Kharraḳān 16 Ab
Khartoum 13 Cd
Khash 20 Ec, see Khwāsh 17 Dd
Khath'am 19 Dd
Khawr 17 Ed
Khaybār (Khaibār) 1.5.iii 15 Fe 19 22 23
Khaylam, N. (Narin R.) 24 Db
Khazar, Buḥ. al-(Caspian Sea) 1.7.v 24 Ge
Khazars 5 Cb 6–8 19 21
Kherson 5 Cb 7 30
Khīr 16 Cd
Khirkhir 1.10.iii
Khirki (Aurangabad) 51 Bc
Khiva (Khiwa) 12 Db 13 24–27
Khmer (Ḳmār) 8 Ed 9–11 44
Khocho, Turfan 5 Db 7–9
Khodjand (Khaldjand) 6 Db 24 26 27
Khoisan 5 Be 9 11
Khokand 12 Db
Khokars 49 Ba
Khorāsān (Khurāsān) 7 Cc–Dc 19 20 24 46
Khorāsān Road 22 Cb 50 Aa
Khotan 5 Dc 6 8–12 24, see Yu-t'ien
Khoy 25 Cb
Khūbdhān 16 Bc
Khūčān (Khabūshān) 16 Db
Khudjanda 24 Cb, see Khodjand
al-Khuḍrā 45 Ae
al-Khuḍrā, W. 15 Da
Khulm 17 Fb 24
Khūr 16 Cc
Khurāsān, see Khorāsān
Khūriyān-Mūriyān (Kuria Muria Isls.) 19 Ed 46
Khurkhur, W. 15 Da
Khurmudj 16 Bd
Khurr, W. 15 Gd
Khurramābād 16 Ac 22
Khūsb 16 Dc
Khushnamī 44 Gc
Khusrūgird 16 Bc
Khuttal 17 Fb 24
Khuwār 16 Bb
Khuwi 22 Ca
Khuzā'a 19 Cc
Khuzdār (Ḳuṣdār) 17 Fd 19 20 25
Khūzestān (Ahwāz) 16 Ac 19 26
Khwādja Čisht 17 Eb
Khwāf 17 Db 25
Khwārazm (Khwārizm) 7 Db 8 19 20 24–26
Khwārazm, Buḥ. al-(Aral Sea) 1.8.v 24
Khwarazm Shahs 24 He
Khwāsh (N) 17 Ec
Khwāsh (S) 17 Dd 20
Khyber Pass 19 Gb
Kiafi (*Kâfi*) *Baba* 33 Bb
Kiao-chow 13 Fc
Kibris (Djaz. Ḳibros, Cyprus) 1.5.iv. 31 Fd 33 34
Kibyrraioton 28 Bb
Kich 25 Ec, see Kiz
Kiev (Kiāū) 1.5.vi 7 Cb 9–13
Ḳīkān, see Kizkānān
Kilāb 19 Dc
Kilādine (Kladanj) 31 Ba
Kilakarai 46 Ed
Kilī 31 Ea 34
Kılıç Ali Paşa Mosque (İstanbul) 32 Gd
Kılıc Arslan II 28 Ge
Kilifi 10 Ce
Kilikia 28 Cb
Kilimani 9 Ce
Kilīs (Clissa) 31 Bb 34
Kilwa (Wamīzā) 8 Ce 9–12 45
Kimak 7 Db 8 9
Ardh al-Kīmākīyya min al-Ātrāk 1.10.iv
Kināna 15 Gf 19
Kinda, Kindites (*Minaei*) 5 Cc 14 CDc Li 15 19
Kipchaks (*Golden Horde*) 10 Cb–Db 24
Kirağuyūfce (Kragujevac) 31 Ca 34
Kīrang 17 Eb
Kiratova 31 Cb 34
Kircali 33 Aa
Kirensk 12 Eb
Kirğa 31 Aa
Kirghiz 4 CDb 7–9 11 12 57
Kirin Prot. 12 Fb
Kirk-chik 5 Eb
Kırk-kenise, Kırk Kilise 30 Db 33 31 Db 34
Kirkuk (Gamarkān) 19 Db 26
Kirmān (Gavashir) 7 Cc 10 16 19 20 24–27 46
Kirmanshah 22 Db, see Kermanshah
Kirmasti 31 Eb 34
Kırşehir 29 He 30 31 33 34
Kirthar mts. 19 Fc
Kish (N) 17 Fa 24
Kish (S, Rudbar) 17 Ec
Kish (Ḳays) Isl. 17 Bd
Kishm Isl. (Djaz. al-Tawila) 16 Cd 45 Cb 46
Kishmar 16 Db
Ḳishn (Tritus portus) 14 Ni 46
Kiss 41 Bd
Kistna R., see Krishna
Kitan 6 Eb 8
Kitara 7 Cd 9 11 12
Kitāwa 45 Be
Kitchen, Egyptian (Madīna) 23 Eg
Ibn al-Ḳiṭṭ 37 Dc
Kiz 17 Ed 20, see Kich
Kızıl-ḥisar 31 Dc
Kızıl Ḳum 19 Fa 24
Kızılbaş 33
Kizkānān (Ḳīkān) 17 Fd 20
Kızkulesi (Laeander Tower) 32 Hd
Kladanj (Kilādine) 34 Ba
Klungkung 55 Pg 56
Ḳmār, see Khmer
Knights of Rhodes 29 Fe
Koa 14 Ee
Koca Mustafa Paşa Cad. and Mosque 32 Ee
Koca-eli 31 Eb 34
Koçhisar 31 Fb 34
Kodur, see Kūrā
Kohat 27 Fb
Ko-ku-pye 5 Fb
Kolar 52 Bc
Kolhapur 53 Bc
Ḳolōneia 28 Db
Ḳolōnya 31 Cb 34
al-Ḳolzum (Suez) 1.5.iii
Komombo 22 Ef
Ḳomr, see Ḳumr
Konarak (Puri) 53 Cc
Ḳōnīce 31 Cb 34
Königsberg 13 Bb
Kongo (Congo) 12 Be
Konya (Iconium) 13 Cc 22 25–27 29 31 33 34 1.5.v
Kopal 52 Bc
Kōpān 31 Ba
Köprili 31 Cb 34
Kora 53 Cb
Kordofan 7 Bd 41
Korea (Korye) 10 Fc 12
Köridüs (Corinth) 31 Cc
Ḳorōn (Koroni) 31 Cc 34
Korykos 30 Fc
Kosarai 34 Ba
Kosi R. 47 Cb 50 53
Kōşk 31 Dc 34
Kosovo 30 Cb
Kostānīce (Kostajnica) 31 Ba 34
al-Kostanṭīna (Constantinople) 1.4.vi
Köstendil 30 Cb 31 34
Djaz. al-Ḳoṭroba al-Gharb 1.7.i
Koufra (Kufra) 43 Hd
Koumbi Saleh (Kumbi Saleh) 9 Ad
Kouribga 43 Bb
Koyulhisar 31 Gb 34 33 Da
Koyun Baba 33 Ca
Ḳōznīk 31 Cb
Krādis 1.2.v
Krak of Montreal 22 Bb
Krakatau 55 Kf 56
Kraljevo (Alaca-ḥiṣār) 34 Cb
Krānganūr 46 Ec
Krasnovarsk 12 Eb
Krasnovodsk 13 Cc 27
Kratons 55 Nf
Krawang 55 Lf
le Kreider 43 Db
Krīm (Crimea) 31 Fa 32
Krishna (Kistna) R. 46 Ec 47–53
Kronstadt 31 Da 34
Kroya 30 Bb
Krupa 34 Ba
al-Ksar 40 Aa, see el-Ḳaṣr el-kebir
Ksar al-Souk 42 Bb
Dj. Ksour 40 Bb 42 43
Kua-chou 5 Eb 6
Kuang chou-fu (Khanfu, Canton) 1.9.i 6 Ec 7–12 44
Kubā 24 Db
Ḳūba road 23 Fh
Ḳubādhiyān 17 Fb 24 Ce
Küçük Aya Sofya (İstanbul) 32 Ge
al-Kuds, see Jerusalem
Kudus 54 Nf 55
Kue-chi 5 Fc
Kufa (Nadjaf) 6 Cc 7 8 20 22 26
Ḳūfičīs 16 Cd
Kufra 7 Bc 8 13 41, see Koufra
Kūhbanān 16 Cc
Kuhestan 26 Db
Ḳuhistān-i Abū Ghānim 16 Cd
Kuhistān seismic zone 18 Eb
Kuka 9 Bd 10–13
Dj. Ḳūḳāya 1.6–8.vii
Kūkū 1.3.i
al-Ḳul (Collo) 40 Da Kd
Kula 31 Ec 34
Kūlam [Malay] 45 Ed 44, see Kaulam, Quilon
Djaz. Kūlam Mali 1.8.i
Kuldja 57 Cb
Kulumbū (Colombo) 45 Ed
Ḳulumriyya (Coimbra) 37 Bb
Ḳulzum, Baḥr al- 7 Cc–d 44 Ab
Ḳum 1.7.iv 12 Cc 16 20 25 26
Ḳum R. 16 Bb
Ardh al-Ḳumānīyya 1.5.vii
Kumanova 30 Cb
Kumari (Comorin) 5 Dd 6–8
Kumbi Saleh 41 Bc, see Koumbi Saleh
Kumidjis 17 Fa 24
Ḳūmis 16 Bc
Ḳūmisha 16 Bc
al-Ḳumr (Mozambique) 11 Cef 44 45
Ḳumr Isls. 8 Ce 45
Kumul 8 Eb 9
Künbet D. 29 Id
Kun-chou 5 Ec
Ḳunfida 22 Gg
Ḳūnīyya (Konya) 1.5.v
Ḳūnka 37 Eb, see Cuenca
Kunkan 45 Ec
K'un-lun 9 Ed
Kunming 57 Ed
Kupang 55 Fe 56
Kur R. 16 Bc
Kūrā (Kodur) 47 Bc
Kurān 16 Bd
Ḳurayya 14 Kg
Kurbus 40 Ea
Kurdestan 26 Cb
Kurds 16 Ab Cd
al-Ḳurḥ, Sūḳ and Wadi 15 Fe
Kurham 51 Bb
Kurī 16 Cc
Kuria Muria Isls 27 Ed, see Khūriyān-Mūriyān
Kurikan 5 Eb 7 8
Ḳūriyya 37 Cc, see Coria
Kurk 16 Dd
Ḳurḳūb 16 Ac
al-Kurma 27 Cc
Kurn al-Manāzil 22 Gf
Kurnool 48 Bc 50 51
Kurram R. 17 Gc
Ḳurşunli (Kuršamlija) 31 Cb 34
Kurts 21 Cb 25
Ḳurṭuba (Cordoba) 37 Dd 40
Kus 22 Ee
Kuş Kavak 33 Aa
al-Kusantina (Constantine) 40 Da Kd
Ḳuṣayr 46 Ab
Ḳuṣdār, Kusdur 47 Ab, see Khuzdār
Kushāniyya 24 Cb
Kūhbanān 16 Cc
Kūsī-ḳaṣri 31 Db
al-Ḳusuriyya 22 Hf 26
Kūsūy 17 Db
Kuta Gedé 55 Ib
Kütahya 30 Ec 31 33 34
Kutaraja 54 Aa 55 56
Ḳutb Shāhis 50 Bc 51
Kuṭruh 16 Cd
Kūtum 16 Ab
al-Kuwait (Coromanis opp.) 14 Mg 19 27
Kuznetsk 12 Db
Kwararfa (*Iokun*) 41 Cd
Kweiyang 57 Ed
Kyoto 10 Fc 11 12
Kyrenia (Girine) 34 Fd
Kyushu 9 Fc 12

Laba 14 Bb
Labada 1.5.vi
Labda 40 Eb, see Lepda
Labla 37 Cd, see Niebla
Lablūna (Avlōnya) 1.3.iv
Labuan 13 Ed 56
Labris (Djabrin) 14 Mh
Laccadive Isls. 8 Dd 13
Lachchera 14 De
Ladik 29 Ge
Laeander Tower (Kızkulesi) 32 Hd
Laeanitae, Laeeni 14 Db Mg
Lāft 16 Cd
Lāghir 16 Bd
Laghouat (al-Aghwat) 40 Je 42 43
Lagos 13 Bd 41
Lāhidjān 16 Bb
Laḥig 15 Bc
Lahore (Lahōr, Lāhūr) 10 Dc 12 13 24 44 47–53
Laja 40 Ba
Lajazzo 29 He, see Ayas
Laka 1.4.iii
Laḳant (Alicante) 37 Fc Hd
Lake Kingdoms 9 Ce
Lakhmids 15 Gd 19
Lakhnauti (Gaur) 46 Fb 48–50
Lakshmibūr (Ḳāmrūb) 44 Gb
Dj. Lālān 1.9.iv–v
Laleli Mosque (İstanbul) 32 Fe
Lalibela 46 Ac
Lalla Maghnia 42 Bb Ie
Laltha 14 Ec
Lambri 11 Ed, see Lāmurī
Lamdiya (Médéa) 40 Ca Jd
Lamego 37 Cb
Lāmghān 17 Gb 47
Lamia (İzdin, Zeytuni) 34 Cc
Lampsacus 28 Fd
Lampung 55 BCc
Lamu (Lamūh) 45 Be 46
Lāmurī (Rāmnī, Lambri) 44 Gd 45
Lamus 28 He
Lanchow 57 Ec
Landjabālūs 44 Gd
Landjashukā 45 Hd
Langa Cad. (İstanbul) 32 Fe
Langarud 26 Db
Lang-chou 8 Fc
Langres 35 Da
Laodiceia Catacecaumene 28 Cb
Laodiceia ad Lycum (of Phrygia–Ladik, Lādiḳiyya) 1.5.v 19 Bb 28 Bb Ge 29
Laodiceia (of Syria–Latakia) 19 Cb 28
Laos, Laotien 11 Ed 45
Lapethus 28 Cc
Lāpsek (Lāpseki) 31 Db 34
Lār 16 Cd 19 21
Lār Rulers 25 Dc
Lar fl. 14 Fc Lh
Lara 38 Ea
Lara Kidul cave 55 Ib
Lara Sea 47 ABc
Larache (al-Ara'ish) 40 Aa Hd 41–43
Laranda (Lārende, Karāmān) 28 Cb He 29 30
Larandān, see Lurdagān
Larbaa, O. 43 Db
Laredo 38 Ea
Lārida 37 Gb, see Lérida
Larisa (Larissa, Yenişehir-i Fener) 30 Cc 34
Larmān (Rahma) 44 Gc
Lasem 55 Nf

Ardh Laslanda 1.4.vii
Lasura 48 Bb
Latakia 22 Bb 31 34, see Laodiceia of Syria
Laththa 14 Dd
Latvia 9 Bb
Lāwān Isl. 16 Bd
Lawiks 17 Fc
Lawraka 37 Fd
Lazica 19 Da 5 6
Ledesma 39 Cb
Lefke 31 Eb 34
Lefkoşa (Nicosia) 31 Fd
León 7 Ab 9 37–39 Da
Leondari 30 Cc 34, see Livāndār
Lepanto 32 Cb
Lepda (Labda, Leptis Magna) 1.2.iii 40 Eb 43
Leran 54 Ib
Lérida (Lārida) 35 Cb 36 38
Leş 31 Bb 34
Lesbos 28 Ab 29, see Midillü
Leskofca (Leskovac) 31 Cb 34
Leucosia 28 Cc
Lhasa 7 Ec 8 11 12 57
Li 9 Ed
Libanos 46 Ad
Libanotofera regio 14 Fd
Liberia 13 Ad
Libya 19 Bc 41–43
Lidoriki 34 Cc, see Ōlendorik
Lifao 55 Fd
Lillo 39 Ec
Limassol 29 Hf
Limnae L. 28 Bb
Limni (Lemnos) 31 Dc 34
Lindjeh 27 Dc
Lisbon (Lisboa, Lissabon) 13 Ac 35 38 39, see Olisipo
Lishtar 16 Ac
Lith-an (Quinsay) 9 Fc
Lithuania 9 Bb 10
Liu-ch'iu 5 Fc 7–10
Liun (Lyon) 1.2.v
Livādya (Livadia) 31 Cc 34
Livāndār (Leondari) 31 Cc 34
Livkand 17 Fb
Livno 34 Bb
Ljubinje 34 Bb, see Lübin
Llerena 36 Cc 39
Loango 9 Be 12
Lodis 47 Ba
Lōfca (Loveč) 31 Db 34
Logar R. 17 Fb
Logroño 36 Ea
Loja 39 Hc
Lombards 5 Bb 6 7 35
Lombok 54 Ed 55 56
London (Londras) 1.2.vi 13 Bb, Highway (İstanbul) 32 Ed
Lopadium 28 Ba Gd
Lophburi 8 Ed
Lop-nor 5 Db 10
Lorca 36 Fd 38 39
Louis VII's route 22 Bb
Loulon 28 Cb
Lo-yang 8 Ec
Lübin (Ljubinje) 31 Bb 34
Lucanites sinus 14 Db
Lucknow 53 Cb
Ludhiana 53 Ba
Lugana 14 Db
Lugo 36 Ca 38
Lūğoş (Şepeş) 31 Ca 34
Lukāgha, Djaz. 1.3.vii
Lūkīn 44 Hb
Lūlūa 1.8.ii
Dj. Lunia 1.2.ii
Lurdagān (Larandān) 16 Bc
Lurestān 16 Ac 26
Lurs 16 Ac
Lusignans 22 Bb
Lusitania 36 Hc
Dasht-i Lut 24 Hg
Lykandos 28 Cb
Lyon 35 Ca, see Liun
Lystra 28 Cb

Ma'an 15 Fd 19 22 27
Ma'bar (India) 44 Ec 48
Ma'bar (Yaman) 22 Gg
Mabruk 41 Bc
Macae 14 Fc Nh
Macao 12 Ec
Macassar 11 Ee 13 54–56
Maccala 14 Ee
la Macea 42 Jd
Macedonia 30 Cb 34
Machara 14 Bc
Māçin 31 Ea
Macoraba, see Makka
Macre 28 Ge
Madagascar 11 Cef 13
Mada'īn Ṣaliḥ (Egra, al-Ḥidjr) 14 Kg 22 26 27
Ma'dan, Ma'din b. Sulaim 15 Gf 22 Gf
Madeira Isl. 13 Ac 41
Ma'den-i İpek 31 Ca
Madhhidj 15 Ig 19 Dd (*Madhidj* 15 Hg)
Madhmīniyya 24 Ab
Madiama 14 Bb
al-Ma'din 37 Bc
Madīna (al-Madīnat al-Nābī, Iathrippa, Yathrib) 7 Cc 9–14 15 22 23 25–27 44 46
Madīnat ibn al-Salīm 37 Dd
Madiun 55 Nf 56
Madjakisa (Ceuta) 35 Gg
Madjerda R. 40 Da 42
Ardh Mādjūdj (Magog) 1.9–10.vi
Madras (Fort St. George) 12 Dd 13 52 53
Madrid 36 Eb 39
Madūra Isl. 45 Ie 54–56
Madūra (S. India) 48 Bd 49 52
Madyanā 45 Gd
Maeander fl. (Menderes R.) 28 Bb
Mafia 46 Be
Magadha 9 Dc
Magalğara, see Miğalğara
Magelang 55 Ha Nf
al-Maghrib 7 Ac 40
al-Maghrib al-Aksa 40 Ab
al-Maghrib al-Awsat 40 Cab
Maghūn 16 Cd
Maglai 34 Ba
Magnesia (Manisa) 28 Ab 29
Magog (Mādjūdj), see Gog
Magulaya 14 Dd
Māğūsa (Famagusta) 31 Fd
Magyars 7 Cb 8 Bb
Mah al-Baṣra (Nihāwand) 16 Ab
Mah al-Ṣīn 45 Hd–Ic
Mahaban 53 Bb
Mahail 22 Gg
Mahā'im 45 Ec
Maḥal 45 Ed
Māhān 16 Cc
Mahanadi 47 Cb 48 53
Maharādja Isls. 44 He
Mahareg 43 Fb
Mahdia, al-Mahdiya 8 Bc 40 42 43
Mahé 52 Bc 53
Maḥmūd, Ṣultan 47 Bb
Mahra 11 Cd 15 19
Mahrattas 12 Dd, see *Marathas*
Mahrūhān 16 Ac
Ma'id (Philippine Isls.) 9 Fd
Ma'in 15 Ba 19
Mainpuri 49 Bb
Ma'it 44 Hd 45
Majapahit (Java) 10 Ee
Majdanpak 34 Ca
Majunga 12 Ce 13
Maḳ(a)dishū, see Mogadishu
Ardh Maḳadūniyya 1.4.v, see Macedonia
Makhyah, W. 15 Da
al-Ma'kil 40 Ea
Makka (Mecca, Macoraba) 1.5.ii 5 Cc 6–15 22 23 25 26 44 46
Maḳra 40 Da
Makran 7 Dc 19 20 24 26 44 45
Maksumlar 33 Db
Maktar 43 Ea
Mākū 19 Db
Makuria 5 Cd 6 9
al-Ma'laa cemetery (Makka) 23 Db
Malabar 44 Ec 45 48 53, see Male, Mulaībār
Malacca (Mal'aka) 11 Ed 12 45 46 54–56
Málaga (Mālaḳa) 7 Ac 35–37 40 42 43
Malagina 28 Ba Gd
Malagon 39 Ec
Malai (Djaz. al-Ḳamr) 1.9.i
Mālamir (Idhadj) 16 Ac
Malang 54 Of 55 56
Malatya (Malatiya, Melitene) 19 Cb 20 25 28–30 33
Malaya 13 Ed, see Malai
Malayan languages 4
Malayu 5 Ee 6 7
Malazgird 20 Cb 25 26, see Manzikert
Maldive Isls. 8 Dd 10 13 46 51
Male 5 Dd 6, see Malabar
Malḥān 44 Gd
Mali 41 Bc
Malichae 14 Cc Lh
Malichu 14 Ce
Malik Ibrahim's grave 54 Ib
Malīla (Melilla) 40 Ba Id 42 43
Mālin 17 Eb
Malindī 9 Ce 10–12 44–46
Malkapur 50 Bb
Mallada opp. 14 Eb
Mallorca (Majorca, Māyurka) 37 Hc 39
Malta 13 Bc 32 41
Mālwā 5 Dc 6 7 9 12 24 44 46–52
Mamala vic 14 Cd
Mamarusi 41 Bc
Mamistra 28 He, see Mopsuestia, Misis
Mamluks 10 Bc 11 21 25
Māmṭīr 16 Bb
Mamūn 20 Cb
Manadhira 15 Gd
Manaḳabaw 45 Gd, see Minankabau
al-Manākha 23 Fg
Manārat al-Ḳurūn 22 Gd
Manāstīr (Monastir) 30 Cb 31 34
Manavgat 29 Ge
Manchuria 12 Ec 13
Manchus 12 Db
Djaz. al-Mand 1.7.i
Mandaeth vic. 14 Ce
Mandali 26 Cb
Mande 8 Ad
Mandistān 16 Bd
Mandjarūr 44 Ec 45, see Mangalore
Mandu 50 Bb 51
Manfia 45 Ae
Mangalore (Manjarur, Decla) 48 Bc 50 52 53
Mangaruth 5 Dd, see Mangalore
Mangishlaḳ 24 Ge
Manila 12 Fd 13
Manipura 5 Dd, see Purī
Manisa (Magnesia) 29 Fe 31 33 34
Manitae 14 Dc Lh
Manjarur, see Mangalore
Mānkīr 44 Ec
Manḳūna 1.5.i
Mānshān 17 Eb
Manṣūra (Bamāramān, Brahmanābād) 7 Dc 8 17 24 25 44
Manubli 1.3.v
Manūdjān 16 Cd
Mānyakheta 47 Bc
Manzikert 9 Cc, see Malazgird
Mara metrop. 14 Dd
Marada 43 Gc
Maragha 20 Cb 22 25
Maran 56 Dc
Maraş (Germaniceia) 22 Bb 28 29 31 33 34
Marasda 14 Cd
Marathas 53 Bb, see *Mahrattas*
Marathonisi 34 Cc
Marbella 36 Dd 39
'Marble Arch' (al-Ḳaws) 43 Gb
Mardache opp. 14 De
Mardin 25 Cb 26
Mare Rubrum 14 DEe M–Oj
Mareth 43 Fb
Marghinān 24 Db
Mārib (Mariama) 5 Cd 14 15 Bb
Mārida, see Mérida
Marimatha (Tarim) 14 Fd Mi
Marinids 10 Ac 40 Bb
Maritsa R. 30 Db
Maritsa seismic zone 18 Ec
Marmara (Lydia) 29 Fe
Marmara Sea 29 Gd
Marmaris 29 Ge 34
Marrakesh (Marrakuch) 9 Ac 10–13 40–43
Marsā Farūkh 35 Hg
Marsa al-Kharaz (Bastion de la France) 40 Da Kd
Marseilles (Masīlia, Mashiliya) 5 Bb 13 Bb
Marṭabān 45 Gc 46
Martapura 54 Dc 55
Martyropolis 19 Db
Marw-i Rūdh 17 Eb 20
Marw-i Shāhidjān (Merv) 17 Db 24
al-Marwa 23 Cc
B. Marwan 37 Cc
al-Mas'a 23 Cc
al-Masamma Ghassara 40 Ba
Mascara 40 Jd 42 43
Masdjīd Bilal 23 Cd
Mashiliya 1.2.v, see Marseilles
Mashīz 16 Cd
al-Mashkar 15 If
Mashkel 17 Ed
al-Masīla (Msila) 40 Ca 43
Masira (Sarapidis Ins.) 14 Gd Oh, see Moseira
Masḳaṭ (Muscat) 15 Jf 19 44 46
Masonitae 14 De Mj
Masrukān C. 16 Ac
Maṣṣawa 46 Ac
Massilia 5 Bb, see Marseilles
Mastang 17 Fd
Mastiḥ 1.3.iii
Masulipatam 51 Cc 53
Māt 31 Cb
Mata opp. 14 Db
Matacum vic. 14 Fd
Mataram 12 Ee 45 55
Matghara 40 Cb
Mathura, see Muttra
Dj. Matmata 40 Db 42 43
Maucosmas metrop. 14 Ec
Mauretania 5 Ac 43 Bb
Mauritius 13 Ce
Mawara [al-Nahr] 7 Db 20
Mawr, W. 15 Ab
Mawshiq (Muza) 15 Ac
Mawsil, see Mosul
Mayafarikin 22 Ca
Maybudh 16 Cc
Mayfa'ah 15 Cb
Mayhana 17 Db
Māyin 16 Bc
Maylapūr 46 Fc
Maymana (Yahūdān) 17 Eb
Maymurgh 24 Cc
Mayṭ 46 Bc
Mayūrḳa, see Mallorca
Mazagān (Tit) 41 Ba 42 43
Māzandarān 24 Gf
Mazarak 31 Cc 34
Djab. Mazdjār 1.8.v
Djazā'ir b. Mazdjāni 1.1.iii
Mazdurān 17 Db
Mazzouna 40 Jd 42
Mbunda 11 Be 12
MDB (Huraydah) 15 Db
Meclisi Mebusan Cad. (İstanbul) 32 GHd
Medain 6 Cc
Medan 56 Ab
Médéa (Lamdiya) 40 Ca Jd 42
Medellín 38 Dc
Médenine 43 Fb
Media 19 Db
Medina, see Madina
Medina del Campo 36 Db
Medina Sidonia 36 Dd 38 39
Medinacelli (Medinaceli) 36 Eb 38
Mediterranean Sea 19 Bb
Medōke 31 Cb
Meerut 47 Bb 49
Meğāra 31 Cc 34
al-Meghili 43 Hb
Megrī 31 Db
Mehedia (Port Lyautey) 42 Ab 43
Mehmet ii Fatih Mosque (İstanbul) 32 Fd
Meknes, see Miknāsa
Mekri 31 Ec 34
Melanudium 28 Fe
Melilla (Malīla) 12 Ac 41
Melitene, see Malatya
Membidj 20 Bb
Memencha 43 Ea
Menado 56 Fb
Menambis regia 14 Dd
Mende 41 Ad
Menderes (Maeander) R. 29 Fe
Menemen 33 Ab 31 34
Menlik 31 Cb 34
Menorca, see Minurka
Mentawei 56 Ac
Menteşe 29 Ge 30 31 34
Menuthias 5 Ce
Mequinenza 36 Gb
Merapi 55 Ia
mercenaries 33 Hc
Mercia 6 Ab
El-Merdj 43 Hb, see Barḳa
Mérida (Marida, Emerita) 35 Ac 36–39
Merina 9 Ce
al-Meriyya 1.1.iv
Merkits 9 Eb
Meroë 5 Cd 8 9
Merovingian Franks 35 Cab
Mers el-Kebir 40 Id 42
Mersin 27 Bb
Mértola 38 Cd
Merv (Marw) 5 Dc 6 8 9 11 13 19 20 24–27
Merzifon 29 Hd 30 31 33 34
Mesene, see Characene
Meshed 26 Db
Mesopotamia 28 DEb
Messina 1.2.iv
Metlaoul 43 Eb
Metropolis 28 Bb
Mevlana Kapı (İstanbul) 32 Ee
Mewar 50 Bb 51
Beni Mguild 43 Cb
Miahs 53 Ab
Mianeh 26 Cb
Midillü (Lesbos) 31 Dc 34
Midnapur 53 Cb
Mien-tien 12 Ec
Miğalğara (Magalğara) 31 Db 34
Miḥrān (Indus) R. 17 Fd 44 46
Mihrimah Mosque (İstanbul) 32 Ed
Miknāsa (Meknes) 40 Ab 42 43
Mila 40 Da
Milās 29 Fe 30 31 34, see Mylasa
Miletus 28 Ab Fe 29
Miliana 40 Ca 42
Millet Cad. (İstanbul) 32 Ee
Mīna (nr. Makka) 23 Dac
El-Mina 11 Ad
Minab 20 Dc
Minaei (*Kindites*) 14 CDc Li 15
Minankabau Empire 55 Ab–Bc, see Manaḳabaw
Minazdjird 22 Ca
Mindanao 54 FGa 55 56
Ming Empire 11 Ec 45
R. Miño 37 Ba 38
Minurka (Menorca) 37 Ib 39
Mir 'Āli 32 Dc
Mir Jumla 52 Db
Mirand 22 Ca
Mirzapur 53 Cb
al-Misfala (Makka) 23 Ad
Mishḳāṣ 45 Cc
Mishṭah (MSṬT) 15 Da
Misis 31 Fc 34, see Mopsuestia, Mamistra
Misivrī 31 Db 30
Miṣr (Egypt) 7 Bc 32
missionaries 33 He
Mistra 30 Cc
Misurata (Misrāta) 40 Fb 41–43
al-Misyal 23 Bd
Mitidja 40 Jd 42
Mitrovica (Mitrofiçe, Mitrofcacuḳ) 30 Ba 31 34
Miyāna 16 Ab
Mizda 43 Fb

Mizistre 31 Cc
Mnasaemanes 14 Cb Lg
Mocha portus (Mokha, Mukha) 6 Cd 7 14 15
Moclin 39 Hc
Mocritae 14 Dd
Modiana 14 Bb
Modon (Motōn) 30 Cc 31 34
Mōdonice 31 Cc
Mogadishu (Maḳadishū) 8 Cd 9–13 45 46
Mogador 42 Ab 43
Moghan 26 Cb
Mohāc (Mohacs) 31 Ba 32 34
Mo-ho 5 Fb 6
Dj. Moḳaṭṭam 1. 5. ii
Mokha, see Mocha
Mokissos 28 Cb
Moldavia (Boğdan) 10 Bb 31 34
mole (İstanbul) 32 Ge
Molina 36 Fb 38
Moluccas 11 Fd
Mombasa 9 Ce 10–13 44–46
Monastir (Balkans) 30 Cb, see Manastir
Monastir (Tunisia), see al-Munastir
Monemvasia (Benefşe) 30 Cc 34
Mongol Imperial Highway 29 HIe
Mongolia 12 Eb 13
Mongolian lang. 4 Db
Mongols 9 Eb 47 48
Monomotapa Kingdom 9 Ce–f 10 11
Mont Maior 1.1.v
Montalban 38 Fb
Montefrio 39 Hc
Montiel 38 Ec
Mopsuestia 19 Cb 28, see Mamistra, Misis
Mora 31 Cc
Morava 31 Cb 34
Morella 38 Fb
Morocco 12 Ac 13 41–43
Moron 38 Dd
Moros 56 Fa
Morotai 55 Gb 56
Moscow 9 Cb 10 11 13
Moseira 13 Cc, see Masira
Mossamedes 13 Be
Mossi 9 Ad–Bd 11 41
Mostaganem, see Mustaghanim
Mōstār 31 Bb 34
Mōsul (Mawṣil) 1.6.iv 8 Cc 19 20 22 24–27 33
Motōn, see Modon
Moulouya, W. (W. Muluya) 40 Bb 42 43
Mozambique 9 Ce 10–13
MSṬT, see Mishṭah
Msun 40 Bb
al-Mu'askar 17 Ec
Müdanya 31 Eb 34
Mudgal 49 Bc 50
Mūdja 44 Hb
Mudurnu 34 Eb
Mughul Empire 52
Mughuls 12 Dc
Muğla 29 Ge 30
B. Muhallab 37 Ed
Muḥammadiyya (Ray) 16 Bb
Muḥammad ibn Kasim 47 Ab
Muharraḳ (Aradus) 14 Gc Ng
Muḥit, Baḥr al- 7 Cd
Muḥtādjids 24 Cc
Mukalla 7 Cd 15
Mūḳān 16 Aa
Mukden 12 Fb 13
al-Mukhā (Mocha) 15 Ac 19 45 46
Mukri 7 Fb
Mūl Djāwa 44 HIe, see Java
Mula 36 Fc
Mulaībār, see Malabar
Multān (Mulasthanapura) 1.7.ii 5 Dc 6–9 13 17 19 24 27 47–53
W. Muluya, see W. Moulouya
al-Munakkab 37 Ed, see Almunécar
al-Munastir (Monastir) 40 Ea 42 43
Munbasa, see Mombasa
Mundir 47 Bb
Mundhir [*b. Ibrahim*] 37 Dd 47
Mundjan 17 Gb
Munk 17 Fa 24
Muntshūn 37 Gb
Murād 19 Dd
Murcheh Khurt 26 Db
Murcia 36 Fd 38 39
Murghāb R. 17 Eb 24
Murow 9 Cb
Murshidabad 52 Cb
Mürted 31 Dc
Murzuk 7 Bc 8–13 41 43
Mūsa ibn Nusayr 35 Cc
Musāfirids 16 Ab
Mushaynika 15 Ba 22
Muskat (Cryptus portus) 8 Cc 9–12 14
Muskat and Oman 27 Dc
Muslim colonists 7–9 Dc 47 Bc Cb
Mustaghanim (Mostaganem) 40 Ca 42 43
Musus 43 Hb
Mut 31 Fc 34
Muttra (Mathura) 5 Dc 44 47 48 52 53
Muza emporium (Mawshiq) 14 Ce 15
Muzaffarids 25 Cb–Dc
B. Muzain 38 Bd
Muzdaḳān 16 Ab
Mylasa 28 Ab, see Milās
Myosormos 14 Ab Jg
Myra 28 Bb
Myrcia 35 Bc, see Murcia
Myriocephalum 28 He
Mysore 12 Dd 51–53
Mzabites 43 Db

Nabal (Naples) 1.2.v
Nāband 16 Cc
Nābil (Nabeul) 40 Ea 43
Nablus 26 Bb
Nacla 14 Ba
Nadir Shah's Empire 26 Db
Nadiya 47 Cb 48
Nādjabārī 45 Gd
Nadjaf (Kufa) 22 Gd 25
Nadjd 7 Cc 19 27
Nadjrān (Nagāra, Ukhdud) 7 Cd 8 15 19
Nafta (Nefta) 40 Db 42 43
Dj. Nafūsa (Nefousa) 40 Eb Le
Nagara metrop. (Nadjrān) 14 Ed Li
Nagarahāra 17 Gb
Nagasaki 12 Fc
Nagd Marqad 15 Bb
Nagilla navali 14 Fd
Nagoya 7 Fc 8 9
Nagpur 13 Dc 53
Nagran, see Nadjran
Nahavand 26 Cb
Naīl, O. 42 Cb 43
Dj. O. Naïl 43 Db
Nain (Nā'in) 16 Bc 26
Naipāl, see Nepal
Nakhichevan 26 Cb 27
Nakhla 19 Dc
al-Nakhoala 23 Gg
Nakhshab, see Nasaf
Nakşa, see Naxos
Nalu Baga 41 Ac
Nalut 43 Fb
Nanchang 57 Fd
Nan-chao (Nan-chaw) 6 Ec 7 8 44
Nander 50 Bc
Nan-hai 5 Ec
Nanking 57 Fc
Nanning 57 Ed
Napataei (*Nabataeans*) 14 Cb Lg
Napegus vic. 14 Cd
Djaz. al-Nar 1.2.iv
Nara 7 Fc
Narbo, Narbonne 7 Bb 35–38 36 Ic
Nārda 31 Cc, see Arta
Nareitae 14 Ec Nh
Narin R., see N. Khaylam
Narmahda R. 47–52 Bb
Narmashīr 16 Dd
Naryān 17 Eb
Nasā 16 Db 19, see Nisa
Nasaf (Nakhshab) 17 Ea 24
Nashrān 1.10.iii
Nasik(a) 7 Dc 50
Naṣpides 40 Ba
Nasratabad (Sanidj) 20 Dc, see Sibih
Barr al-Nāt 45 Fc
Naṭanz 16 Bc
Nātil 16 Bb
Naupaktos (İnebaḫti) 34 Cc
Nauplia (Anābolī) 34 Cc
Navarra (Navarre) 9 Ab 10 11 35 37–39
Nawbandadjān 16 Bc
Nawdjay 16 Cb
Nawīda 17 Fb
Naxos (Duchy–Nakşha) 30 Dc 31 34
Nayarkot (Kangra) 47 Ba
Nazwā 46 Cb, see Rustaḳ
Ndongo 11 Be
Nea Paphos 28 Cc
Nebranta 1.2.ii
Necuveran Isls. 10 Ed
Nedjd, see Nadjd
Nefud 20 Cc
Negapatam 10 Dd 50–53
Negombo 46 Ed 52–53
C. Negro 11 Be
Negroponte 30 Cc
Nellore 48 Bc 50–53
Nemesus 28 Cc
Nemours (Tawat) 43 Ca
Neocaesareia 28 Id
Nepal (Naipāl) 7 Dc 13 44
Nesca 15 Ba
Nestorians 5 Cd 6 Dd Ed 8 Eb
Sa. Nevada 40 Ba
Nevesin, Nevesinje 31 Bb 34
Nevreḳōb 31 Cb 34
Nevşehir 31 Fc 33 34
New Guinea 56 HI c
Nfis 42 Ab
Ngonde 11 Ce
Nguni 5 Ce
Niani 10 Ad 11 12 41
Nias 55 Ab 56
Nicaea (İznik) 19 Ba 22 28 29 31
Nicomedia (İzmit) 19 Ba 22 28 29
Nicopolis (Pontus) 28 Da
Nicopolis (Nikopol, Nigbōlī) 30 Db 34
Nicosia (Lefkoşa) 29 Hf 34
Niebla 36 Cd 38 39, see Labla
Nif 29 Fe
Nigbōlī, see Nicopolis
Niğde 28 He 29–31 33 34
Niger Kingdoms 12 Ad, R. 41 Bc
Nigeria 13 Bd
Nih 17 Dc
Nihā 45 Gd
Nihāwand (Māh al-Baṣra) 16 Ab 19 22
Nikki 41 Cd
Nikopol, see Nicopolis
Niksar 22 Ba 29 31 33 34
Nīl (Nile) R. 1.1.i 1.4.i 19 Cc 41 44
Nilotics 8 Cd
Ninève (Nineveh) 19 Db
Nioro 41 Bc
Nīrīz 16 Cd
Nirun 47 Ab
Nīrūnkōt (Haydarābād) 17 Fe
Niş 11 Bb 30 31 34
Nisa 7 Cc 20, see Nasā
Nişāb 15 Cb
Nishāpūr (and Shādyākh) 5 Cc 7 16 19 20 24–26
Nisibin (Nisibis) 5 Cc 20 25–28
Baḥr Niṭas (Euxine) 1.5.vi
Niyān 44 Gd
Nizam Shahis 50 Bc
Nkole 9 Be
Nobatia 5 Cc
Nogay 31 Ga
Nok (culture) 5 Bd
Norsemen 5 Ba 6 9 10 12 13
Northumbria 6 Ab
Nosy Mamuk 9 Ce
Nosy Manfa 9 Ce
Nova (Novi) 31 Bb 34
Nova Zagora (Zağra-i cedid) 34 Db
Novgorod 9 Cb
Novgorod Lands 9 Ca 10 11
Novibazar (Yeñi-bāzār) 34 Cb
Novōberde 31 Cb 34
Ntusi 9 Ce
Nūbia 1.4.i 5 Bd 44
Nufīlīa 43 Gb
Nukād-i Ḳuraysh 17 Fa
Nuḳra 22 Ge 26
Numidia 5 Bc
Nūmidjkath (Būkhārā) 17 Ea
B. dhu'l Nun 38 Fc
Nupe 11 Bd 41
Nūr 24 Cb
Nusarkembangan 55 Mf
Nushki 27 Ec
Nusr el-Din 33 Cb
'NWḌ ('Uqlah) 15 Cb

Oaditae 14 Bb Kg
Ob R. 13 Db
Obraca 14 Cb
Oca 38 Ea
Ocelis emporium 14 Ce Lj 15
Ocsonoba 36 Cd, see Ukshūnuba
Odessa 13 Cb 34
Od. Nun 41 Ba
Oghuz (*Oguz*) 5 Eb 16 24
Oghuz Yabghu 24 Bb
Oğlan Sheyh 33 Ba
Ohrī 30 Cb 31 34
Oinaeum 28 Id, see Ünye
Oirats 9 Eb 11
Ok Meydan (İstanbul) 32 Gd
Olaphia 14 Dc
Olba 28 Cb
Olekminsk 12 Fa
Ōlendorīk (Lidoriki) 31 Cc
Oleshe 9 Cb
Ölgün-Bār 31 Bb 34
Oliola 37 Ga
Olisipo 7 Ac, see Lisbon
Olivenza 38 Cc
Olova (Olovu) 31 Ba 34
'Ōman ('Uman) 6 Cc 7 11–13 15 20 27 47
'Ōman, Sea of 26 DEc
Omani Fontes 14 Fc
Omani traders 12 Cd
Omanitae 14 Ni
Omanum emporium 14 Fd
Omarkot 26 Ec
Ommana (Sadidj) 14 Pg
Omsk 12 Db 13
Oña 38 Ea
Ongole 53 Cc
Oporto (Burtuḳal) 37 Bb
Opsikion 28 ABb
Optimaton 28 Bab
Oran (Wahran) 32 Ab 40–43, see Oron
Ordu 29 Id 30 31 34
Orenburg 13 Cb
Organa 14 Gd
Orihuela 38 39 Fc
Orissa (Warīsa) 5 Dc 44 45 48–53, see Jajnagar
Orkney Scots 8 Ab
Orléansville 42 Jd 43
Ormuz (Hurmuz) 14 Og
Oron 9 Ac 12 see, Oran
Orsova (Irşōva) 30 Ca 34
Orta Yol (Kol) 31 Db: Fc
Ortakçi 31 Ec 34
Ortokids 22 Ca
Osca 36 Fa, see Huesca, Washka
Ösek (Eszek) 31 Ba
Osman Pazar (Ala-kenīse) 34 Db 31
Osmancık 29 Hd 31 33 34
Ostama 14 Bb
Ōstorova 31 Cb 34
Otranto 32 Ba
Ottoman Empire 11 BCb 26
Ouargla (Wargilān, Wargla) 40 Ke 42 43
Ouarsénis 40 Jd 42 43
Ouarzazate 43 Bb
Oubari 43 Fc
Oudh 48 Cb 52 53
el Oued 42 Db Ke 43
Oued Zem 43 Bb
Ouezzan 42 Ab He 43
Oujda 42 Bb Ie 43
Ouled Naīl 42 Cb
Dj. Ouled Naīl 43 Db
Ouled Sidi Shayku 42 Cb
Ouzouzouite 43 Bb
Oviedo 35 37 Da 38
Oxus R. (Amu Darya, Djayhūn) 19 Fa 24 47–53
Oyo 41 Cd
Özbeks 11 Cb 12 26 27, see *Uzbeg*
Ozī 31 Ea 24
Özkend 24 Ke, see Uzkand

Padang 54 Bc 55 56
Padri 56 Ac
Pagan 5 Ec 6–10 44
Pagerrujung 54 Bc
Pahandj 45 Hd
(Pahang 54 Bb 56)
Paipert (Baiburt) 28 Jd 29
Pajang 54 Dd Nf 55
Pakpattan (Ajudhan) 48 Ba 53
Pakuan Bogor (Pakuan Pajajaran, Buitenzorg) 54 Cd Lf 55
Pala Kingdom 7 Dc
Palamut 31 Dc 34
Pal'as 44 FGb
Palembang 12 Ee 54–56
Palencia 36 Da 38 39
Palia Zompi 28 Bb
Palībandj 45 He
Pallars 37 Ga 38
Pallavas 7 Dd
Palma 39 Hc
Palmas, C. 41 Bd
Palmiras (Cuttack) 47 Cb
Palmyra 19 Cb
Pamekasan 54 Of 56
Pāmirs 24 Dc 27
Pamplona 36 Fa 37–39
P'an-p'an 7 Ed
Panarukan 54 Of 55
Pancorva 37 Ea
Pānçova (Pancsova) 31 Ca 34
Pandjāb, see Panjab
Pandjdih 17 Eb
Pandjgur Fīrbūz 17 Ed 25 Ec 27
Pandjhīr 17 Fb
Pandjikath 17 Fa 24
Pandjwāy 17 Ec
Pandurangga 10 Ed
Pandyas 9 Dd 47
Panhandj 44 Hd
Panidos 29 Fd
Panipat 50 Bb 51 53
Panjab 12 Dc 13 24 47
Panjim, see Sindapur
Pao-an 57 Ec
Paoting 57 Fc
Papal States 10 Bb 12
Paphlagonia 28 Ca
Paphos, Nea 28 Cc
Papuans 54 Ic 55
Paramānas 47 Bb
Parapamisus mts. 19 Fb
Pārghar 17 Fb
Pariaman 55 Bc
Paris 13 Bb
Parlais 28 Bb
Parnassus 28 Cb
Paros (Bare) 34 Dc
Parsis 48 Bc
Parwān 17 Fb 24
Pase, Pasei 46 Gd 55 Aa, see Samudra Pasei
Pastrana 39 Eb
Pasuruhan 54 Ib Of 55 56
Patali, Pataliputra 5 Dc 6 Dc
Paṭan (Anhilwada) 47 Bb 49 51
Patara 28 Bb
Pate 46 Be
Pati 54 Nf 55
Patna 10 Dc 11 12 48–53
Paurae 28 Hd, see Bafra
Payas 31 Gc 34, see Baiae
Pazarcik 31 Gc 34
Pazarjik (Tatar Pazari) 31 Db 34
Pazarköy 31 Eb 34
Pečeneg Lands 24 Ab
Peçuy (Pećs) 31 Ba 34
Pedīr 46 Gd
Pedroche 36 Dc
Pegu 10 Ed 11 12 45 46
Peking 11 Ec 12 13 57, see Khanbalik, Ta-tu
Peline (Bjelina) 31 Ba
Pelusium 14 Jf
Pemba (Kanbalu) 10 Ce 46
Penaconda 51 Bc

Penang 13 Ed
Penanggungan 54 Ib
Pengging 54 Nf 55
Penner R. 47 Bc 48 53
Peñon de Velez (Bādis) 42 Ba
Pepper Coast 11 Ad
Pera Mosque 32 Gd
Perak 55 Bb 56
Perākīn (Paracin) 31 Cb 34
Pergamum (Bergama) 19 Bb 28 29
Perge 28 Bb
Perīm 46 Bc
Perlak 10 Ed 54
Persepolis 19 Eb, see Istakhr
Persians 49 Bd
Persis 14 Ga
Pervane 29 Hd
Peshāwar 17 Gc 25–27 48–52
Peshwa 53 Bc
Peterwardein 30 Ba
Petit Jean 43 Bb
Petra 14 Ba Kf 15
Petric 31 Cb 34
Peul (*Fulani*) 5 Ad
Pharan, Prom. prope 14 Ab
Pherrai 29 Fd
Phigea 14 Db
Philadelphia (Asia Minor) 28 Ge 29 30
Philadelphia (Palestine) 19 Cb
Philby's route 22 Gf
Philippeville (Skikda) 40 Da 43
Philippines 12 Fd 13
Philippopolis (Filibe) 34 Db
Philita 28 Ge
Philomelium 28 Bb
Philotera portus 14 Ab
Philoxenus Cistern (Binbirdirek Sarnice) 32 Ge
Phnom-Kuleh 8 Ed
Phnom Penh 10 Ed 12
Phocaea 29 Ab 30
Picts 5 Ab 6
Pien 8 Ec
Pierèd 55 Ib
Pilaşce (Belušic) 31 Cb 34
Pilāv 31 Bb 34
Pilevne (Pleven) 31 Db 34
Pilgrim Roads, Sudan 11 Bd, Arabia 22; to Santiago 36 BFa
pilgrims 5 Dc 6 DEd 33 He
Pir Baba 33 Ca
Piremedi 31 Cb 34
Pirepōy (Pryeopolje) 31 Bb 34
Pirespe 31 Cb 34
Pireveze (Preveza) 31 Cc 34
Pireznīk 31 Cb, see Breznik
Piri Dede 33 Ca
Piriştine 31 Cb 34, see Priština
Pirīzrin (Pizīrin) 31 Cb 34
Pirlepe 30 Cb 31 34
Pirot (Şehir-Köyi) 34 Cb
Pisa 9 Bb 10, see Bisha
Pitesti 34 Da
Pitheca 28 Gd
Pizīrin 34 Cb, see Pirīzrin
Plassey 53 Cb
Pleven (Pilevne) 34 Db 31
Ploznik 30 Cb
Plymouth 13 Ab
P'o-hai 6 Fb 7 8
Podandos (Pozanti) 28 Cb
Poemanenum 28 Aa
Poitiers 7 Bb 35
Poland 9 Bb 10–12
Polovtsians 9 Cb
Polvoraria 37 Db
Polybii Ins. 14 Bc
Polybotus 28 Bb
Polygars 12 Dd 52
Pompeiopolis (Cilicia–Soli) 28 Cb
Pompeiopolis (Paphlagonia) 28 Ca
Pondicherry 12 Dd 52 53
Ponferrada 36 Ca
Pontevedra 36 Ba
Pontianak 56 Cc
Pontus Euxinus (Black Sea) 19 Ca
Poona 49 Bc 52 53
Porson 28 Ca
Port Arthur 13 Fc
Port Darwin 13 Fe
Port Lyautey (Mehedia) 43 Bb
Port Said 13 Cc
Port Sūdān 22 Fg 27
Porto (Oporto) 37 Bb 38 39
Porto Novo 52 Bc
Portugal 9 Ab 10 12 13 32 39 41–43
Pozanti, see Podandos
Pōzarefce (Pozarevac) 31 Ca 34
Požega (Pōzeğa) 30 Ba 31 32 34
Pracana 28 He
Pratiharas 21 Aa 44 47
Pravac, Pravadi 30 Db 34 Db
Prayag, Prayāk 44 Fb 49 Cb
Préveza 32 Cb, see Pirevse
Priego 39 Eb
Prio fl. 14 Mi
Priština 30 Cb, see Piriştine
Prizren 30 Cb, see Pirīzrin
Prome 12 Ed
Prophet's Birthplace (Makka) 23 Cc
Prophthasia 19 Fb
Prostanna 28 Bb
Provence 8 Bb
Prusa (Bursa) 28 Ba
Prusias 28 Gd
Prussia 12 Bb
Pryeopolje 34 Bb, see Pirepōy
Prymnessus 28 Bb
Pseudocetus 14 Ce
Pteleon 30 Cc
Pteria 28 Ca
Ptolemais 19 Cb
Ptolemais Epitheros 14 Bd Ki
Pudnu opp. 14 Cd
Puente del Arzobispo 36 Dc 39
Pulicat 46 Ec 50 52
Pulwar R. 16 Bc
Puri (Konarak) 49 Cc 53, see Manipura
Pūshang 17 Db
Pushkar 53 Bb
Pushtu lang. 4 Dc
Pylae 28 Gd
Pyong-yang 5 Fc
Pyramus fl. (Djihun) 28 Db
Pyrenees 37 Ga
Pyu 7 Ec 8

Qatabanians 15 Dc
Qizān, W. 15 Aa, see Djīzān
QN' (Cane) 15 Db
Quelimane 11 Ce
Quengianfu 10 Ec
Quetta 27 Eb
Quilon (Kaulam) 10 Dd 11 48–52
Quinsay (Hang-chou) 10 Fc 9
Quoja (*Karu*) 41 Ad

Rabat 42 Ab He 43
Rabigh 22 Ff
Rača 31 Ba 34
Rada'a 22 Hh
Rādkān 16 Db
Rādōmir 31 Cb 34
Radōs, see Rhodes
Radōscuk 31 Db 34
Rādoviște 31 Cb 34
Raghdan 22 Gf
Ragusa (Raghusa) 1.3.v 30 Bb 31 34
Rahma (Larmān) 44 Gc
Rahova 31 Db
Rahūn 44 Fd
Raichur 48 Bc 51
Raichur Doab 50 Bc
Railway, Berlin-Baghdad 27 Bb, Hidjaz 23 Egh, Trans-Siberian 13 Db
Raisūt 7 Cd 44
Rajamahandri (Rajamundri) 47 Cc 49–51
Rajputana 12 Dc 13 47–50
Rajputs 8 Dc 44 Eb
Rakandj 45 Gb
Rakhyah, W. 15 Cb
Rakka 20 Bb 22 25
Rām Shahristān 17 Dc
Ramhormuz 20 Cb
Ramazan 29 He
Rameshwara 48 Bd
Djaz. al-Rāmī 1.8.i 47 Ca
Ramitan 24 Bc
Raml 'Alidj 15 Ge
Ramlat Sab'atain 15 Cb
Rāmnī (Lāmurī) 44 Gd
Rampur 53 Bb
Rangoon 13 Ed
Rano 41 Cc
Ranthambhor 47 Bb 48 49
Ranya 15 Gf
Ra's 'Asir 46 Cc
Ra's Fartak (Syagros prom.) 14 Ge Ni
Ra's Ḥafun 46 Cc
Ra's al-Ḥadd 46 Cb
Ra's al-Kalb 16 Bb
Ra's al-Khaymah 27 Dc 46
Ra's al-Makhbaz 40 Eb
Rāsht (nr. Caspian) 16 Ab 26
Rāsht (Ḳarātigīn) 17 Ga
Rashtruktas 47 Bc, see Rastrakuta
Rāsk 17 Dd
Djaz. Raslanda 1.2.vii
Rasova 31 Cb 34
Rasova (on Danube) 34 Da
Rastrakuta 7 Dc, see Rashtruktas
Rasulids 10 Cd 25
Ratheni 14 Dd
Ravenna 5 Bb
Rāwar 16 Cc
Rawwafa 14 Kg
Ray (Rey, Rayy, Ragha, Muḥammadiyya) 5 Cc 6–10 16 19 20 25 26
al-Raydā' 15 Bc
Raydah 15 Bb
Rāyīn 16 Cd
Rayyū 37 Dd
Beni Razin 38 Fb
Razgrad (Ḥazārğirād) 34 Db
Rāzluḳ 31 Cb 34
Red Sea 19 Cc
Refresco 41 Ac
Regama opp. 14 Fc
Rembang 56 Nf
Resafa 22 Cb
Rēwand, see Rīwand
Rewari 49 Bb
Rhapta 5 Ce
Rhizas 28 Jd
Rhodes (Rhodus, Rudus) 1.5.iv 19 Bb 25 28–31 34
Rhodesia 13 Bef
Riaño 39 Da
Ribacorza 37 Ge
Ribāṭ-i Ab-i Ushturān 16 Cc
Ribāṭ-i Dihistan 16 Ca
Ribāṭ-i Farāwa 16 Ca
Ribāṭ al- Fath 40 Ab
Ribāṭ-i Ḥafṣ 16 Cb
Ribāṭ-i Ḳanṭara-yi Kirmān 17 Dc
Ribāṭ-i Kārwān 17 Fb
Ribāṭ-i Kish 17 Ec
Ribāṭ Shakir 35 Ad
Dj, Rif 40 HId 42 43
Riga 10 Bb 11 12
Rigar 17 Fa
Rijeka 34 Aa
al-Rīm 45 Ae
W. Rima 15 Ab
Rimnik 34 Da
Rio de Oro (Spanish Sahara) 13 Ac 43
Rio Muni 13 Bd
Rio Salada 42 Ba
Rīshahr (Dayradjān) 16 Ac
Rivshārān 17 Eb
Rīwand (Rēwand) 16 Db
Riyadh 22 Hf 27
Riyāh 40 Ab
Rodosto 29 Fd
Rohri (Rūr) 27 Ec
Rome 7 Bb 35
Roncesvalles 35 36 Fa 37
Ronda 40 Aa, see Runda
Rosellón 38 Ha
Rothenthurm Pass 34 Da
Roza 53 Bb
Rub' al-Khālī 19 Ec
Rudbar 20 Eb, see Kish (S)
Rudhān 16 Cc
Rūdnīk 31 Ca 34
Ruha (Urfa) 33 Db
al-Rukhadj 17 Fc 47
Rumania 13 Bb
Rumeli Hisar 32 If
Rumelia 32 Ba
Rumkale 31 Gc 34
Rūmlū 33 Cb
W. Rumma 15 Ge
Runda 37 Dd 38 39, see Ronda
Rūr 17 Fd, see Rohri
Russia 1.4.vi 1.6.vi 9 BCb 10 12
Rūssuḳ (Ruschuk) 31 Db 34
Rustaḳ (nr. Nazwā) 15 Jf
Rustamdār 16 Bb
Rustamids 35 Jh
Ruwayk 15 Cb
Rūy 17 Fb
Rūyān 16 Bb
Rwanda 9 Ce

Sa (Taourirt) 40 Bb
Sa'ala 1.10.i
Šabac (Bogürdelen) 34 Ba
Sabaeans (*Sabaei*) 14 Dd Li 15 Dc
Sab'atain, Ramlat (Şayhad) 15 Cb
Sabbatha metrop. 14 Ed
Sabība (Sbeitla) 40 Da 43
Sabirs 5 Db
Sabratho 43 Fb
Saburkhwast 20 Cb 22, see Shāpur Khwāst
Sabzawār (Bayhaḳ) 16 Cb 19 26
Sabzawār (Isfizār) 17 Ec
Sacacia vic. 14 Ce
Sachalitae 14 Ni
Sachalites Sinus 14 Fd Ni
Sachle 14 Ee
Ṣa'da 15 Aa 19 22
Ṣād-djām 45 Fb
Sa'di dynasty 41 Bb
Sadidj (Ommana) 14 Pg
Sadjids 8 Cc
Ṣadrapatam 45 Ec
Saduan 22 Gg
Sadūsān, see Sharūsān
al-Safa 22 He
al-Safa (Makka) 23 Cd
Safakus (Sfax) 40 Eb Le 42 43
Safāwīds 11 Cc–Dc 52
Saffārīds 17 Dc 21
Safi (Asfi) 40 Ab He 41–43
Safīd-Rūd 16 Ab
Safranbolu 30 Fb
Safru 40 Bb
Sağ Yol (Kol) 31 Dc: Ea
Sagar 48 Bc
Sagdana 14 Gb
Sāghand 16 Cc
al-Saha 23 Ff
Sahara 40 Cc 42 43
Saharanpur 49 Bb 53
Sahel 40 Ea Ld
Sahip Ata 29 Ge
La Sahla 38 Fb
Sahmar 16 Bb
Ṣaḥra Lūr 16 Ac
Ṣāhuk (Čāhuk) 16 Cd
Şahzade (Şehzade) M. 32 Fe
Saida 43 Db
Saigon 12 Ed 13
St. Andrew (K.M.P. Mosque) 32 Ee
St. George 32 Ee
St. Helena 13 Ae
St. Irene 32 Ge
St. John (Knights) 25 Ab 34
St. Mary Pamm. (Fethiye Mosque) 32 Fd
St. Mocius Cistern 32 Ee
SS. Sergius and Bacchus (K.A.S. Mosque) 32 Ge
St. Theodosia (Gül Mosque) 32 Fd
Sakalkand 17 Fb
Sakastān, see Sīstan
Sakenitae 14 Bb Kf
Sakhalin 12 Fb
Saḳiḳ 15 Ge
Sakız (Chios) 31 Dc 34
Salā (Salé) 40 Ab He 42 43
Saladian Sherifs 40 HIe
Salaga 9 Bd 10–12 41
Salala (Dianae Oraculum) 14 Ni 15 route 22 Hh
Salamanca 36 Db 38 39
Salamis (Constantia) 28 Cc
Salar 57 Ec
Salas de los Infantes 36 Ea
Saldaña 38 Da
Saldjuks 9 Cc–Dc 10 20 21
Salghurids 24 Gh
Salihids 35 Hg
B. Salim 40 Fb
Salma 14 Db
Salma 14 Cb
Salma 14 Cc
Salmān 22 Gd
Salobrena 39 Hd
Salona (Salone) 30 Cc 31
Ṣalūnik (Salonica) 1.4.v 30 Cb
Ṣam, see Syria
Sam (*Sham*) *Bayadi* 33 Db
Sama 31 Dc 34
Samahidj (Delma?) Isl. 15 If
Samākov 30 Cb 31 34, see Samokov
Samana 48 Bb 49
Samanatha, Sōmnāth, Sūmanāt 48 Bb
Samangān 17 Fb
Sāmānids 8 Dc 17 20 21 24
Samara (Samarra) 20 Cb 22
Samarinda 55 Ec 56
Samarkand 5 Db 6–8 11 13 17 19 20 24–27
Samatya Cad. (İstanbul) 32 Ef
Samavamsis 47 Cb
Samāwa 22 Hd
Sambava 9 Ce
Sammān 15 He
Samnan (Semnan, Simnān) 20 Db 26
Samokov 32 Ca, see Samakov
Samos 28 Ab 29
Samosata, see Samsat
Samothrace 30 Db, see Semādirek
Samoyeds 8 Db
Sampang 54 Jb Of 55–56
Samsat (Samosata) 19 Cb 20 28
Samsun (Amisus) 25 Ba 29–31 33 34
Samudra Pasei 54 Aa, see Pase
Sān 17 Fb
San Esteban de Gormaz 36 Eb
San Millan 37 Hc 38 Ea
Sana', W. 15 Db
Sana'ā' 7 Cd 15 19 22
Sanābād 16 Db
Sānbūr 31 Bd
Sandakan 56 Ea
(Djaz.) Sandān 1.7.i 44 Eb
Sandıklı 29 Ge 31 34
Ṣanf 44 Hc
Sanfīn 44 Gc
Sangarios fl. (Sakaria) 19 Cb 28
Sanglič 17 Gb
Sanhadja Berbers 9 Ac 41 Ac–Bb
Sanidj (Nasratabad) 20 Dc, see Sibih
Sanina opp. 14 De
Sant Yaḳub 1.1.v, see Santiago
Santa Cristina 36 Fa
Santa Maria de Algarve 38 Cd
Santa Maura (Aya-mavra) 34 Cc
Santander 38 Ea
Santarém 36 Bc 38
Santiago 36 Ba 37–39, see Sant Yaḳub
Sapha 14 Ec
Saphtha 14 Db
Sapphar (Dzafar) 14 De Lj
Sappharitae 14 De
Saraca 14 De
Saraceni 14 Bb Jf Kg
Saragossa (Zaragoza) 35 Bb
Sarai 10 Cb
Sarajevo 34 Bb, see Saray
Sarakhs 1.7.iii 17 Db 19 20 24 27
Saraḳusṭa 37 Fb, see Zaragoza
Sarandīb (Ceylon), see Serendib
Sarapidis 14 Gd Oh, see Masira Isl.
Sarāw 16 Ab
Sarawak 13 Ed
Saray 31 Bb, see Sarajevo
Saray Kapısı (Sublime Porte) 32 Ge
Sarbadars 25 Db
Sarcoe (Sarkoè) 14 Ec Nh
Sardinia (Sardāniyya) 1.2.iv 12 Bc
Sardis (Sardes, Sart) 19 Bb 28 29 31 34
Sargadwari 49 Bb
Sargal Isl. 11 Ed
Sārī 16 Bb

Saris 31 Gc 34
Sarjan 26 Dc, see Sirdjan
Şarkışla 31 Gc 34
Sarkoè Polis 14 Nh
Sarsūtī 24 Kg 48
Sart 29 Fe, see Sardis
Saruhan 29 Fe 30 31 34
Sārūk 16 Ab
Sarus fl. (Sihun) 28 Cb
Sarvon 14 Ed
Sarwān 17 Ec
Sarwistān 16 Bc
Sarwistān 16 Bd
Sassanids 5 Cc–Dc 15
Satāla 28 Da
Satara 52 Bc 53
Sātgāon (on Hugli) 10 Ec 48
Sātgāon (Chittagong) 49 Cb 50
Satif (Setif) 40 Da Kd 42 43
Satladj R. (Sutlej)
Sava R. 32 Ba
Save 14 De
Savoy 12 Bb
Sāwa 16 Bb 19
al-Sawadiyya 22 Hh
Sawahīl 11 Ce
Sawākin, see Suakin
Sawrān 24 Cb
Sawrashtra 19 Gc
Saxons 5 Bb 6 7
Şayḥad (Ramlat Sab'atain) 15 Cb
Şayḥūn R. (Syr Daryā) 24 Ba
Saymūr (Chaul) 46 Ec
Sayyid dyn. 49
Sayyīd al-Shuhadā'a 23 Fe Hg
Scotland (Djaz. Skūsīyya) 1.2.vii
Scots 5 Ab 6 9–12
Scutari (Dukagīn) 30 Bb
Scutari (Üsküdar) 26 Aa 29
Sea of Darkness 1 (ii)
Sea of Gog and Magog 1 (ii)
Sea of Khazar (Caspian) 1 (ii)
Sea of Pitch 1 (ii)
Sea of Syria (Mediterranean) 1 (ii)
Sebasteia (Sivas) 7 Cc 22 28
Sebha 41 Db 43
Sebinkarahisar 31 Gb 34
Sebkha d'Idjil 10 Ac 11 12
Sebou R. 40 He
Sed Samallagi 14 Lh
Segedīn, Szeged 31 Ca
Segovia 36 Db 38 39, see Shaghubiyya
Şehir-köyi 31 Cb, see Pirot
Sehwan 48 Ab 53
Seilan (Ceylon) 9 Dd 10, see Serendib
Seksār (Szegszard) 31 Ba 34
Selangor 54 Bb
Selānik (Salonica) 31 Cb 34
Selçuk roads 29
Selefke (Seleuceia of Cilicia) 28 Cb 29 31 34
Selefke (Silifke, Seleuceia Pieria) 28 Cb
Selendi 31 Ec 34
Seleuceia (Mesop.) 5 Cc 14 Lf
Selima 41 Eb
Selymbria 29 Ba
Semādirek 31 Db 34, see Samothrace
Semarang 54 Nf 55 56
Semendire (Smederova) 31 Ca 34
Semipalatinsk 12 Db 13
Semirečye (Yeti-Su) 24 Db Lb
Semitic langs. 4
Semnan, see Samnan
Sena 11 Ce
Senegal R. 13 Ad 41
Sengguruh 54 Og
Sennar 5 Cd 6–12 41
Senoussis 42 Nf
Sens 35 Ca
Senufo 41 Bd
Şepeş (Lūğōş) 31 Ca 34
Sera metrop. 5 Ec
Serampur 52 Cb
Serawak 56 Db
Serbia 9 Bb 13 30
Serbrenice 31 Ba
Serbs 7 Bb
Serendib (Sikaldīb, Seilan, Ceylon) 1.8.i 5 Dd 8 46–48
Serfiçe 31 Cb 34
Sergiopolis 19 Cb
Seringapatam 52 Bc 53
Serpa 38 Cd
Settat 42 Ab
Setúbal 38 Bc
Sevastopol 13 Cb 34
Sevilla (Hispalis) 36 Cd 35 38 39
Seybousse R. 42 Da
Seychelles 13 Ce, see Zarīn
Seydi Gazi 33 Bb
Seydişehir 31 Ec 34
Seyitgazi 31 Ec 34
Sfax 40 Le, see Safakus
Sha 9 Ec
Shabānkāra Kurds 16 Cd
Shabwa 15 Cb 19
Shādyākh (and Nishāpūr) 24 Hf
Shaghubiyya 1.1.v, see Segovia
Shāhadrūdj 1.8.vi
Shahis 47 Ba
Shahr-i Bākak 16 Cc
Shahr-i Naw 45 Hc
Shahr-i Zur 20 Cb
al-Shahrīya 23 Fg
Shahriyār R. 16 Bd
Shāh-Rūd 16 Ab
Shahrukhis 11 Db 49 Aa
Shahruwā 16 Cd
Shaiyūl 45 Ec, see Chaul
Ibn Shakir 37 Ed
W. Shakūra 37 Ec
Shalamba 16 Bb
Ibn-al-Shāliya 37 Ec
al-Shām 7 Cc
Shama 41 Bd
Shamakha 22 Da
Shamīrān 16 Ab
Shammar, Dj. 19 Dc
Shanbā 45 Hc
Shanghai 13 Fc 57
Shang-tu 10 Eb
Shant Madjial 1.1.vi
Shant Mahlo 1.1.vi
Shantabariyya 37 Eb
Shantamariyyat al-Gharb 37 Cd, see Santa Maria de Algarve
Shantarīn 37 Bc, see Santarém
Shāpūr (Bishāpūr) 16 Bd 20 Dc
Shāpur Khwāst (Sabur Khwast) 16 Ac
al-Sharaf 37 Cd
Sharāt, Dj. al- 37 Db
Shārat Kashtīla 37 Fa
Sharayya 23 Da
Shari R. 41 Dc
Sharifis 42 Aa–Bb
Sharif's Palace (Makka) 23 Dc
Sharīsh 37 Cd
Sharjis 49 Cb
Sharūsān (Sadūsān) 17 Fd
N. al Shās 1.8.iv
Shāsh (Tashkent) 19 Fa 24
N. Shāsh (Čirčik R.) 24 Db
B. Shassen 42 Bb
Shāṭ 37 Ed
Shāṭidjām 45 Gb, see Satgaon (Chittagong)
Sha-t'o 8 Ec
Shāwghar 24 Cb
Shaykh Mahmud (Makka) 23 Ba
Ouled Sidi Shayku 42 Cb
Shenyang 57 Gb
Sherda 41 Db
Shi'b 'Ali 23 Cd
Shibām (Aqyān) 15 Ab
Shibām (Hadramawt) 15 Db 19
al-Shiḥr 11 Cd 12 15 22 45 46
Shikkabanāriya 40 Da
Shikoku 12 Fc
Shilb 37 Bd, see Silves
Shilluk 11 Cd
Shing-i 'Abbādī 17 Db
Shipka Pass 31 Db 34
Shīrāz 7 Cc 8–10 16 19 20 24–27 44 46
Shīrāzis 10 Cd
Shīrīn R. 16 Bc
Shīrs 17 Fb
Shīrvan 26 Ca
Shott el-Chergui (Shergui) 40 Je 43
Shott el-Djerid 40 Db Ke 42 43
Shott el-Hodna 40 Jd 43
Shua-piu-fu 7 Fb 8
al-Shu'ayba 19 Cc
al-Shubayka (Makka) 23 Bc
Shūdhar 37 Ed
Shughnān 17 Gb 24 Dc
al-Shuhadā'a 23 FGe
W. Shukr 37 Fc
Shūlīyān 45 Ec
Shūmān 17 Fa
Shūr R. 16 Cd
Shūrīya 37 Eb, see Soria
Shurma 22 Gf
Shurmīn 17 Eb
Shushtar (Tustar) 15 Hd 16 19 26
Shūshū 45 Gd
Shwaref 43 Fc
Siak 54 Bb 56
Siālkot 24 Kg 47–50 Ba
Siām 11 Ed 12 45
Sian 57 Ec, see Hsi-an
Siberut 56 Ac
Sibī 7 Dc 17 Fd 20 25–27
Sibih (Sibidj) 17 Dd, see Sanidj
Sibir 8 Db 10 11
Sibolga 56 Ab
Sibor 6 Dc, see Supāra
Sibta (Sebta, Ceuta) 40 Aa
Sicily (Sikiliyya) 10 Bc 12
Sidayu 54 Ia
Side 28 Bb
Sidi Cheikh, O. 43 Db
Sidi Ferruch 42 Jd
Sidi Shayku, O. 42 Cb
Sidi-bel Abbès 43 Ca
Sidim Sultan 33 Ca
Sidjilmasa, see Sijilmasa
Sidjistān 20 Eb 44, see Sīstān
Sidra 43 Gb
Sierra Leone 11 Ad 12 13
Sif-i Muzaffer 16 Bd
Sif-i 'Umāra 16 Cd
Sif-i Zuhayr 16 Bd
Sigetvār (Szigetvar) 31 Ba 34
Sighnāḳ 24 Cb Je
Siguenzá 38 Eb
Sih Dih (Djarmak) 16 Cb
Sihām, W. 15 Ab
Sīhbān 17 Fd
Sihun R. (Aral) 11 Db
Sihun R. (Anat.) 28 He
Sijilmasa (Sidjilmasa) 8 Ac 9–12 40 41
Sijistān, see Sistan
Sikaldīb (Ceylon) 47 Cd, see Serendib
Sikandra 51 Bb
Sikasso 41 Bc
Sikhs 52 Ba 53
Djaz. Sikiliyya 1.2.iv, see Sicily
Şiklōs (Siklos) 31 Ba 34
Sīksawa 40 Ab
Djaz. al-Sila 1.10.i
Silaharas 47 Bc
Sīlān (Ceylon) 44 Fd 45, see Serendib
Şile 31 Eb 34 30
Silifke 33 Cb
Silistra (Silistre, Silistria) 30 Da 31 Da 34
Silivri Kapı 32 Ee
Silla 5 Fc 6 7, see Korea
Silos 38 Eb
Silves 38 Bd, see Shilb
Simancas 37 Db
Simirun 16 Bc
Simla 53 Ba
Simnān 16 Bb, see Samnan
Simṭorna 31 Bd
Şīn (China) 1.10.ii 44 HIb 45 47
Sinai 19 Cc
Sinawen 43 Fb
Sincalan (Khanfu) 10 Ec, see Canton
Sind 7 Dc 13 19 24 44 45 50
Sinda 53 Ba
Sindapur (Sindebur, Djuwah, Goa, Panjim) 10 Dd 44 45 48 49
Sindhia 53 Bb
Sine Salum 43 Ac
Singapore, Sindjāfūrā 45 Hd 13 Ed 56
Singaraja 56 Ed
Singidunum 19 Ba
Singkil 54 Ab
Sinhala-Dvipa 5 Dd 7
Sining 57 Ec
Şīnīs 1.10.ii
Sinitic langs. 4
Sīnīz 16 Bc
Sinkiang 57 Cb
Sinop (Sinope) 7 Cb 19 22 25 28 29 31 32 34
Sintzi Pass 31 Cb 34
N. Şīnu (Seine) 1.2.vi
Sinūboli 1.5.vii
Sinus Arabicus 14 Bb–e
Sinus Persicus 14 E–Gb
Sinus Sachalites 14 Fd
Sira 52 Bc
Sirāf 5 Cc 7–11 16 19 20 44
Sirdjan (Sirdjend) 16 Cd 20, see Sarjan
Sirem 31 Ba
Sirendīb (Ceylon), see Serendīb
Sirhan, W. 15 Fd
Sirhind 48 Ba 49–53
Sirişnik (Slavinja) 31 Cb 34
Sirkeci (İstanbul station) 32 Ge
Sironj 52 Bb
Sīrōz 30 Cb 31 34
Sirte 7 Bc 40 42 43
Şirwāḥ 15 Bb
Sis 29 He 31 34
Sisar 22 Db
Sīsīān 1.10.iv
Sīstān (Sijistan, Sakastān) 5 Cc 8 19 21 24 25
Sivas (Sebasteia) 19 Cb 25 26 29 30
Sivastan 48 Ab
Siverek 33 Db
Sivrihisar 34 Ec
Sīwa 7 Bc 8 9 12 40 41
Sjenica (Çeniçe) 34 Bb
Skahat (Cyrene) 43 Hb
la Skhira 43 Fb
Skikda (Philippeville) 40 Da 43
Djaz. Skūsīyya, see Scotland
Slatina 31 Da 34
Slave Coast 11 Bd
Slavinja 34 Cb, see Sirişnik
Slavonic langs. 4 Bb
Slavs 5 Bb 6 7 19
Sliven (Slivno, Islimiye) 30 Db 34
Slonta 43 Hb
Slunj 34 Aa
Smolensk 9 Cb 11
Smyrna (İzmir) 13 Bc 22 25–30
Smyrnoferae regiones 14 Dc Ee
B. Snous 43 Cb
Soa 28 Bb
Soaca 14 Bb
Soandos 28 Cb
Soba 5 Cd 6 7 10
Sobrarbe 37 Fa
Socotra Isl. (Soḳoṭra, Suḳūṭrā, Dioscoridis ins.) 1.6.i 5 Cd 7 8 10 11 13 19 44–46
Socratis 14 Cd
Socuellamo 39 Ec
Sofāla [al-Nabr] 1.8.i 8 Ce 9–12 47
Sofya (Sofia) 30 Cb 31 34
Soğdak 31 Fa
Sogdia 19 Fb
Söğüt 31 Eb 34
Şoḥār 1.6.ii, see Şuḥār
Sokhna 9 Bc 10–12, see Sukna
Sokoto 13 Bd
Djaz. Soḳotra, see Socotra
Sol Yol (Kol) 31 Db: Eb
Soli 28 Cc
Solis oraculum 14 Fc
Sōlnoḳ 31 Bd
Solons 11 Fb
Solor 55 Fd
Soluk 43 Hb
B. Somadih 38 Ed
Somaliland and *Somalis* 9 Cd 13
Sōmnāth 8 Dc 47–49 51, Sūmanāt
Sonārgāon 11 Ec 48
Sonda 49 Ab
Songhai 10 Bd 11 41
Sophta 14 Fb
Sora 14 Da
Soria 36 Eb 38 39, see Shūrīya
Sosippi portus 14 Ce
Sotha 5 Bf
Souk Ahras 42 Kd 43
Soummam R. 40 Jd 42
Sous R. 40 He
South-West Africa 13 Bef
Sozopol 30 Db 32
Sozopolis 28 Ge
Spain 12 Ac 13 36–42
Spalato (Split) 31 Bb 34
Srebrnica 34 Ba
Sribuza 44 He
Sriksetra 7 Ed 8 9
Srīnagar 24 49 Ba 51 53
Srivijaya (Sumatra) 5 Ee 6 7 9 10
Stara Zagora 34 Db, see Zağra-i 'atik
Stavropolis 28 Ge
Steppes, Basses 40 Da
Sthaneswara 5 Dc 6 7, see Thaneswar
Stone Bridge (Ḳantara al-Hidjara) 17 Fa
Suakin (Sawākin) 9 Cd 10–12 22, 27 45
Sūbakh 17 Fa
Sublaeum 28 Ge
Sublime Porte, see Saray Kapısı
Şubr 15 Bc
Su-chou 6 Ec 7 9 10 11 12
Sūdān 1 (ii) 13
Sudanese 6 Bd
Suez (Suways, Clysma, Arsinöe) 22 Ed 32 46
Sufāla, see Sofala
Sufayna 22 Gf
N. Sughd (Zarafshān) 17 Fa 24
Suğla 31 Dc
Şuḥār 15 Jf 19 44 45, see Dastadjird
Suhraward 16 Ab
Sui Kingdom 5 Ec
Es Suk 41 Cc
Sūḳ al-Ahwāz 16 Ac
Sūḳ al-Arba'a 16 Ac
Sūḳ Dubā 15 Je
Sūḳ Ḥabāsha 15 Gg
Sūḳ al-Habb 23 Dbc
Sūḳ Hadhramawt 15 Hg
Sūḳ Ḥamza 40 Ca
Sūḳ Keram 40 Ca
Sūḳ al-Ḳurḥ 15 Fe
Sūḳ al-Layl 23 Ccd
Sūḳ al-Rustāḳ 16 Cd
al-Sūḳ al-saghīr 23 Bd
Sukadana 54 Cc 55
Sukāwand 17 Fc
Sukayr 22 Cb
Suket 49 Ba
al-Suḳia 22 Fe
Sukkur 27 Ec 49 52 53
Sukna 43 Gc, see Sokhna
Suḳūṭra, see Socotra
Sulawesi (Celebes) 12 EFe
B. Sulaym 15 Gf 40 Da
Sulaymān mts 19 Fc
Süleymaniye Mosque 32 Ge
Sullūm 40 Gb
Sultan D. 29 Ge
Sultan Ahmet Mosque 32 Ge
Sultan Selim Mosque 32 Fd
Sulṭāna 23 Ee Gh
Sultāniya 22 Db
Sultan-önü 31 Ec 34
Sulu Isls. 11 Ed 56
Sulu Kule 32 Ed
Sūmāl, Barr al- 44 Bd 45, see Somaliland
Sūmanāt 44 Eb, see Sōmnāth
Sumatra 11 Ede 12 13 45 46 54–56
Sumba 54 EFd 55 56
Sumbawa 54 Ed 55 56
Sumedang 55 Lf
Šumen 30 Db, see Şumni
Sumenep 54 Of 55 56
Summa 12 Ad
Şumni (Šumen) 31 Db 34
Sunda Kalapa (Jakarta, Batavia) 54 Cd Lf
Sundanese 54 Lf
Sung 9 Ec 44
Dj. Sūnīyya 1.8–9.vi
Supāra 44 Ec (Sibor, Surparak)
Şūr 1.6.ii 46 Cb
Surabāya 45 Ie 54–56
Surakarta 55 Ib 56 Nf
Sūrat 12 Dc 45 46 49–53
Surdūd, W. 15 Ab
Surkhān R. 17 Fa 24 Cc

Surmak 16 Bc
Surt (Sirte, Sort) 1.3.iii 40 Fb 42 43
Suru 7 Cc 25, see Shahruwā
Sūs (Susa) 16 Ac 19
Sūsa (Sousse) 40 Ea Ld 42 43
Susa (Appolonia) 43 Hb
Sūṣām (Samos) 31 Dc 34
Sūsan 16 Ac
Susiana 14 Ea Mf
Susu 41 Ac
Sutlej R. 19 Gc 46–53
Suwayd 40 Ca
Suways, see Suez
Sūyāb 24 Db
Svishtov (Ziştovī) 34 Db
Svrljig (Isfirlig) 34 Cb
SW (Saua, Ta'izz?) 15 Bc
Swamps, Great ('Irāḳ) 24 Fg
Swedes 5 Bb 6–10
Switzerland 13 Bb
Syagros prom. (Ra's Fartak) 14 Ge Ni
Sycae 28 He
Sydeni 14 Bb Kg
Syene 14 Jh
Sylaion 14 Dd
Synnada 28 Bb 29
Syr Darya (Ṣayḥūn R.) 24 Cb Ke
Syracuse 7 Bc
Syria 34 Gd: Syrian Sea (Mediterranean) 1 (ii)
Szeged (Segedīn) 31 Ca 34
Szegszard (Seksār) 31 Ba 34
Szigetvār 31 Ba 34

Tāb R. 16 Bc
Tabāla 1.6.ii 15 Gf 19 22
Ṭabaristān 7 Cc 16 19 20
Tabarka (Tabarca) 40 Da Kd 42
Ṭabas-i Gīlakī (Kileki, Ṭabas al-Ṭamr) 16 Cc 20
Ṭabas Masīnān, Ṭabas al-'Unnāb 17 Dc
Tabassa (Tebessa) 35 Dc 40 42 43
Tabrīz 1.6.iv 7 Cc 8–10 12 13 16 20 24–26
Tabūk 7 Cc 9 14 15 19 22 25–27
Ṭabūnī 1.6.vii
Ṭaburmīn (Taormina) 35 Lg
Tadallis (Dellys) 40 Ca
Tademaït 43 Dc
Tadjiks 57 Cb
W. Tādjuh 37 Cc
Tadla 42 Ab He
Tadmekka 9 Bd
Tafalla 38 Fa
Tafilalet 41 Ba
Tafilelt 40 Ie 42 43
Tagala lang. 4 Fd
Tağ-ardi 31 Db 34
Taghaza 9 Ac 10–12
al-Taghlabiyya 1.6.iii, see al-Ta'labiyya
Taghlib 15 Gd
Taguine 42 Je
Tāhart (Tahert, Tiaret) 35 Ig 40 Ca 42 43
Tahirids 11 Cd
Ṭāhiriyya 24 Bb
Ta-hsing 9 Ec, see Ta-tu
Taḥt al-Rīḥ 45 Fc–Hf
Tā'if (al-Tayf) 15 Gf 19 22
Taīmā' (Taymā', Thaema) 14 Kg 15 19 22 27
T'ai-wan 11 Fc
T'ai-yüan 5 Ec 6 9–12 57
Ta'izz (SW?) 15 Bc 22
Tajo R. 38 Cc, see W. Tādjuk
Ibn Takit 37 Dc
Takrit 22 Cb
Ṭaksim 32 Ed Hd
Tākurunnā 37 Dd
Ṭalabīra 37 Dc, see Talavera
al-Ta'labiyya 22 Ge, see Taghlabiyya
Ṭālaḳān 17 Fb 24
Ṭalamanka 37 Eb
Talamba 49 Ba
Talande (Atlante) 31 Cc
Talas (Ṭarāz) 7 Db 24
Talas R. 24 Db
Talavera 36 Dc 38, see Ṭalabīra
Tālish 16 Aa
Talkad 47 Bc
Ta-lo 9 Ec 8
Talpurs 53 Ab
Tamān 31 Ga 34
Tamatave 13 Ce
Tamīm 19 Dc
Tamir 15 He
Tamra 15 Hf
Tamralipti 5 Dc 6–9
Tamrān 17 EFb
Tāna (India) 7 Dd 8 44
Tana (Azov) 10 Cb 11
Tanas (Ténès) 40 Ca Jd 42 43
Tanaṣārī 45 Gc
Taudeni 10 Ac 11 12 41
Ṭandja 7 Ac, see Tangier
Tanezrouft 41 Bb
T'ang Empire 6 Ec 7 8
Tangier (Tandja, Tanger) 7 Ac 10 11 35 40 42 43
Tangut 5 Ec 6 9
Tanimber 56 Hd
Tanjore 48 Bc 50 52 53
Dj. Ṭanṭana 1.2.ii
Tanūkh 15 Gd
Taourirt 42 Ie 43, see Sa, Taurirt
Tapi (Tapti) R. 46–53
Tarablus, see Tripoli
Tarain 47 Bb
Tarakan 56 Eb
Ṭarasūna 36 Fb
Ṭarāz, see Talas
Tarbela 50 Ba
Ibn Ṭarbisha 37 Dc
Tarentum 7 Bb
Tarhala 31 Dc 34
Tarhuna 40 Le 42
Tarifa 36 Dd 40 42 43, see Djaz. Tarif
Dj. Ṭāriḳ (Gibraltar) 40 Aa
Tarīm (Marimatha) 7 Cd 14 15 19 22 46
Tarragona (Tarraco, Tarrego, Tarrakūna) 1.1.iv 37 Gb 38
Tarsus 19 20 Bb 22 25 26 28 29 33
Tartars (*Tatars*) 5 Eb 10 Eb 57
Tarūdant (Taroudant) 10 Ac 11 12 40 42 43
Tārum 16 Cd
Tārūtī 45 Bb
Tashkent (Shāsh, Binkath) 11 Db 13 19 25 26
Taşköprü 31 Fb 34
Tatar Pazari (Pazarjik) 31 Db
Tatta 47 Ab 49 51–53
Tatta L. (Tuz Göl) 28 Cb
Ta-tu (Khanbalik) 10 Ec, see Peking
Taudeni 10 Ac 11 12 41
Taungū 46 Gc
Taurirt 7 Bc 9–12, see Taourirt
Taurus (Toros) mts. 19 Cb 28 29
Tavas 29 Ge 31 34
Tavira 39 Cd
Tavium 28 Cb
Tavşanlı 30 Ec 31 34
Ṭawāhī 45 Gc
Tawat (Nemours) 40 Ba 43
Ṭawāwīs 24 Bc
al-Ṭawīl 37 Fc
Tāwurghā 35 Lh
Taxila 6 Dc
al-Tayf 19 Dc, see Tā'if
al-Tayyar 23 Efg
Ṭayyi' 15 Ge 19
Taza 40 Bb 42 43
Tazerbo 41 Eb
Tebessa, see Tabassa
Tebet, see Tibet
Teda 41 Dc
Tefeni 33 Bb
Tegal (Tegalwangi) 54 Mf 55
Tegheza 41 Bb
Tehāma, Buḥaīre 1.9.v
Tehran 13 Cc 27
Tehuda 35 Dc
Teke Ili 29 Ge 31 33
Tekedda 9 Bd
Tekke Turkmans 27 Db
Tekkelü 33 Cb
Tekrūr 1.1.i 10 Ad 11 41
Tekye 31 Fb 34
Tel Başir 31 Gc 34
Tel Hamdun 31 Gc 34
Telangut 5 Eb
Telegraph, Coastal 27 DEc
Telingana 48 Bc 49
Tell, Haut 40 Da
Telmessus 28 Bb
Telokbetung 56 Cd
Teluch 28 Db
Telugu lang. 4 Dd
Tembayat 54 Nf 55
Temesvar 34 Ca, see Timişvar
Temne 41 Ad
Tenere 41 Cb–Dc
Ténès, see Tanas
Teniet el-Had 43 Da
Tensift Hawz R. 40 Ab He
Tepe-delen 31 Bb 34
Tephtice 28 Db
Terme 29 Id 30
Termez 26 Eb, see Tirmidh
Ternate 10 Fd 54 Gb 55 56
Teruel 36 Fb 38, see Tīrūl
Terung 54 Ib
Teşani (Tešenj) 31 Ba 34
Tete 9 Ce 10 11
Tetouan (Tiṭṭāwan) 40 Aa Hd 42 43
Teutons 9 Bb 10 11
Thabba 14 Dd
Thadj 14 Mg
Thaema 14 Kg, see Taīmā'
Thaemae 14 Db Mg
al-Thaghr al-Adnā 37 Bc
al-Thaghr al-A'lā 37 Fb
al-Thaghr al-Awsaṭ 37 Db
Thaḳif 15 Hf 19 Dc
Thakka 44 EFa
Thamūd 15 Da
Thamydeni/*Themuditae* 14 Bb-Cb Kg
Thānā (Bombay) 9 Dd 49, see Tāna
Thanuitae 14 Dc Mg
Thanes(w)ar 44 Eb 47 53, see Sthaneswara
Thapaya 14 Cb
Thāra (Tīz) 44 Db
Tharo 14 Fc
Thasos 30 Db
Thauana 14 Fd
Thauba 14 Ca
Thebes (Greece—İstife) 34 Cc
Thebes (Egypt—Thebae opp.) 5 Cc 14
Themuditae, see *Thamydeni*
Theodosiopolis 19 Db 28, see Erzerum
Thessalonica 19 Ba, see Ṣalūnik
Thessaly 34 Cc
Thialemath 14 Fe
Thrace 19 Ba 34
Thrakesion 28 Bb
Thumala 14 Cc
Thumna 14 Dd
Thuris 14 De
Thyateira (Akhisar) 28 Ab 29
Tiagar 14 Ec
Tiaret, see Tāhart
Tiberias 19 Cb
Tibesti 5 Bc 6 7 9–12 41 43
Tibet (Tebet, Tüpüt) 1.9.iii 5 Dc 7–12 45
Tichit 41 Bc
Tidore 54 Gb 55 56
Tien-Shan-Nan-Lu 12 Dc
Tientsin 57 Fc
Tiflīs (Tiphlis) 7 Cb 8 25 26
Tigīnābād (Ḳandahār?) 17 Ec
Tigris R. (Dicle) 14 Da 19 25
Tihama (*Tehama*) 15 Ff 19
Tiku 54 Ab
Tiḳves 31 Cb 34
Tilimsān, see Tlemcen
Till 17 Ec
Timbuktu 8 Ad 9–13 41
al-Timimi 43 Hb
Timimoun 42 Jf 43
Timişvar (Temesvar) 31 Ca 34
Timmissao 41 Cb
Tīmōk 31 Cb
Timor 13 Fe 54–56
Timur 11 Cc 25
Timür-ḥiṣār 31 Cb 34
Timurids 11 Cc–Dc
Tindouf 41 Bb
Tingis 35 Ac, see Tangier
Tineo 38 Ca
Tinnevelly 50 Bd
Tiphlis, see Tiflīs
Tirābōlice 31 Cc, see Tripolitz
Tire 31 Dc 34
Tireboli 31 Gb 34, see Tripolis
Tirḥāla (Trikkala) 30 Cc 31 34
Tirhut 48 Cb
Tirmidh, Tirmiz 17 Fb 20 Eb 24, see Termez
Tirnova (Ṭirnovi, Turnova) 30 Db 31 34
Tīrūl 37 Fb, see Teruel
Tit (Mazagan) 40 Ab 42
Titalya 53 Cb
Titel 31 Ca 34
Tiṭṭawan, see Tetouan
Titteri 40 Ca Jd 42 43
Titulcia 36 Eb
Tiyūma 44 Hd
Tīz 9 Dc 17 20 25, see Thāra
Tizi Ouzou 42 Jd
Tj. Priok 56 Lf
Tlemcen (Tilimsān) 8 Ac 10–12 40–43
Tmessa 43 Gc
Tmutorokan 9 Cb
Tobolsk 13 Db
Tobruk (Tuburk) 7 Bc 40 42 43
Tocharistān 19 Fb
Tochi R. 17 Gc
Togo 13 Bd
Tokat 26 Ba 28–31 33 34
Tokuz 33 Cb
Toledo (Toletum) 7 Ac 35 36 38 39, see Tulayṭula
Tomar 38 Bc
Tomaras 47 Bb
Tomos Pass 34 Da
Tōmōvica 31 Cb 34
Tomsk 12 Db 13
Tongkin (Tongking) 12 Ec 13
Top Kapı 32 Ed
Tophane 32 Gd
al-Tor 22 Ee, see al-Ṭūr
Toraja 54 Fc 55 56
Tordesillas 38 Db
Torgur 12 Cb
Toro 36 Db 37 38
Toros Dağ 29 He, see Taurus mts.
Torsburg Pass 34 Da
Tortosa (Ṭurṭūsha) 36 Gb 37–39
Tosya 29 Hd 31 34
Toulouse 35 Cb 36 Ga
Touggourt, see Tuḳḳurt
Tours 35 Ca
Toyran 31 Cb 34
Tozeur 42 Ke 43
Trabzon (Trapezus, Trapezunt, Trebizond) 5 Cb 8–11 19 21 25 26 28 29 33 34
Traghan 43 Fc
Trajan's Gate 34 Cb
Tralla portus 14 Ee
Tralles 28 Ab
Tranquebar 52 Bc
Trapezunt, see Trabzon
Trans-Alai mts. 24 Dc
Transoxiana 24 Jf 26
Transylvania 31 CDa
Travancore 53 Bd
Travnik 34 Ba
Trebizond, see Trabzon
Trengganu 54 Ba 55 56
Trichinopoly 53 Bc
Trikkala, see Tirḥāla
Trincomalee 52 Cd 53
Tripoli (Atrāblūs, Tarablūs) (Libya) 5 Bc 6 7 9–13 32 35 40–42
Tripoli (Syria) 19 Cb 20
Tripolis (Chaldia), see Tireboli 28 Da
Tripolitania 40 Le 42
Tripolitz (Tirābōlice) 34 Cc
Tritus portus (Ḳishn) 14 Fe Ni
Trstenik 34 Cb
Ṭrūiyya 1.6.vii
Trujillo 36 Dc
Tsangpo R. 48 Cb 49 50
Tsinan 57 Fc
Tsonga 5 Cf
Tuareg 5 Ac 6 41
Tuat 13 Ac 41
Tūban 45 Ie 54–56
Tubbat 44 FGa
Ṭubna (Batna) 40 Da 43
Tuburk, see Tobruk
Tudela 36 Fa 38, see Tuṭīla
Tudela [de Duero] 39 Db
B. Tudjib 37 Fb
Tudmir 37 Fc
Tu-fan (Tüpüt) 8 Cc, see Tibet
Tughluks 48 49
Tuḳḳurt (Touggourt) 40 Db Ke 42 43
Ṭukhāristān 24 Cc 47 Ba
Ṭulayṭula 37 Dc 35, see Toledo
Tulca 31 Ea 34
Tulun Bunar 33 Ab
Tulunids 21 Aa
Tulwān 45 Ec
Tumasik 54 Bb
Tumkath road 24 Db
Tumma 41 Db
Tumna' 15 Bb
Tūn 16 Dc
Tundzha R. 30 Db
Tungh hsiang 57 Ec
Tungus 10 Eb 12
Tunis 9 Bc 10–13
Tunisia 12 Bc 13 42 43
Tunisian Gulf 40 Ea
Tūnkath 24 Cb
Tunūs, see Tunis
Tüpüt, see Tibet
al-Ṭūr (Sinai) 19 Cc 46, see al-Tor
Turaba 15 Gf 19 22 27
Turaythīth, see Turshīz
Turcomans, see *Turkomans*
Turfan (Khocho) 5 Db 9 11 12 57
Turgurt 7 Bc, see Tuḳḳurt
Turhal 31 Gb 34
Turkestan 13 CDb
Turkish lang. 4 Cc
Turkomans 11 Cc 12 Cb 27 Db 33 Db
Turks 5 DEb 6 7 17 EFc
Turk-Sib Railway 13 Db
Turnova 34 Db, see Tirnova
Turnu(-Severin) 34 Ca
Turshīz (Turaythīth) 16 Cb 20
Ṭurṭūsha, see Tortosa
Ṭūs 1.7.iv 16 Db 19 24
Tuscany 12 Bb
Tustar (Shushtar) 16 Ac
Tuticorin 50 Bd 52
Ṭuṭidjām 45 Ed
Tuṭīla 37 Fa, see Tudela
Tuy 36 Ba 37 38
Tuzar 40 Db
Tuzla 29 Fe
Tyana 22 Bb 28
Tylus 14 Gc Ng, see Baḥrain Isl.
Tyre (Tyrus) 5 Cc 19
Tyriaeum 28 Bb
Tzouroulos 29 Fd, see Çorli
Tzympe 29 Fd

Ubangi, U. 13 Bd
Ubbadha, Ubeda 36 Ec 38 37 Ec
al-Ubulla 15 Hd 19 44, see Apologus, near Charax
Uch 24 Kh 47 48
Udaipur 51 Bb 53
Udeni 14 Cc Lg
'Udhra 19 Cc
Udjān 16 Bc
Uganda 13 Ce
Ugro-Finns 6 BCa
Uighurs 5 Cb 7 Eb 9 Dc 57
Ujjain (Udjdjain), Ujjayana 5 Dc 8 Dc 24 44 47–53
Ukair 15 Ie
'Ukayl 19 Dc
'Ukāz 15 Gf 19
'Ukda 16 Bc
Uklīsh 37 Ec
Ukshūnuba 37 Bd, see Ocsonoba
Ukur 55 Lf
al-'Ula 15 Fe 26
Ulubad 31 Eb 34
Uluborlu 31 Ec 34
Uludağ 29 Ge
Ulukışla 26 Bb
Ulunids 8 Cc

al-'Umān ('Omān) 19 Ec 20 44 45
Umūr-fakīh (Fakiya) 31 Db
Unaiza 15 Ge
Unās 16 Cc
United Kingdom 13 Ab
United Provinces [of Agra and Oudh] 13 Dc
University (İstanbul) 32 Ge
Unḳūdja 44 Ae
Ünye 31 Gb 34, see Oinaeum
'Uqlah ('NWḌ) 15 Cb
Ural-Altaic (Turkic) languages 4
Urdunn 20 Bb
Urfa (Ruha) 25 Bb 26 33
Urgandj (Urgenč) 24 Bb 27 Ea
Urgel 37 Ga
Uri 41 Ec
Urmia 22 Cb
Ursh al-Yaman 37 Ed
Urshudhūna 37 Dd
Urumchi 12 Db
Uşak 27 Ab 31 34
'Usfan 22 Ff
Ush 24 Db
al-Ushbūna 37 Bb 35, see Lisbon
Ushbūrḳān 17 Eb
Ushnuh 22 Cb
Ushrūsana 24 Cb
Ushūna 37 Dd
Üsküb 30 Cb 31 34
Üsküdar (Scutari) 26 Aa 31–34
Ust Strelka 13 Fb
Ustaclu 33 Da
Usturūmca 31 Cb 34
Utkala 47 Cb
Uṭrār 24 Cb Je 25
Uwal 15 Ie
Uyvār 31 Bd
Uzbeg lang. 4 CDb 57, see *Özbeks*
Ūzice (Užice) 31 Bb 34
Uzkand (Uzkent) 7 Db 20 24, see Özkend

Valabhi Valabhipur 5 Dc 7 47 Bb
Valencia (Balansia) 36 Fc 38 39
Valladolid 36 Db 38 39
Valspir 38 Ha
Valtoz (Valtos) 31 Cc 34
Vālyeva 31 Ba 34, see Valyevo
Van 25 Cb 26
Varanāsi (Banaras) 5 Dc 47
Varāt 31 Cd
Varay 31 Fb
Vārdār 30 Cb 31 34
Varna 30 Db 31 34
Vartān 16 Aa
Vasco da Gama 11 CDd 46
Vasconia 39 Ea
Vatapi 5 Dd 6
Velesīn 31 Cc
Velez Rubio 39 Hc
Velika 31 Ba
Vellore 51 Bc 52
Venice 8 Bb 9–12 25 35 41
Vera 36 Fd 39
Verawal 49 Bb
C. Verde 11 Ad
Verkhature 12 Db
Vidīn 30 Cb 31 32 34
Vienna 9 Bb 13
Vijayanagar 11 Dd 45 46 49–51
Vikramapura 47 Db
Villa Alhacemas 42 Ba
Villacastin 39 Db
Vince 31 Cb 34
"Vinland" 9 Aa
Visby 7 Bb
Vişeğirād (Višegrad) 31 Bb 34
Visigoths 5 Ab 6 36
Vize 34 Db
Vizegapatam 13 Dd 52
Vlachs 10 Bb
Vladivostok 13 Fb
Vodena (Vōdīna) 30 Cb 31 34
Volga R. 32 Da
Volga Bulgars 9 Cb
Volo 34 Cc
Volona 14 Dd
Volta R. 41 Cd
Vona 31 Gb 34
Vōnice (Vonitsa) 31 Cc 34
Vorochta 14 Gb
Vōstīce (Aegion) 31 Cc 34
Vraca (Ivraca) 34 Cb
Vrlika 34 Bb
Vulçitrin 31 Cb 34
Vulḳovār (Vukovar) 31 Ba 34
Vurla 31 Dc 34
Vyadhapura 5 Ed 6 7

Wabdha 37 Eb, see Huete
Wadai 11 Bd 12 41
Wadan 41 Ab
Waddan 42 Mf 43 Gc
Wadhāk Canal 24 Ab
Wadhār 24 Cc
Wādī Baṭhān (al-Seil) (Madīna) 23 Fg
Wādī Halfa 27 Bc
Wādī Fatima 23 BCa
al-Wādī al-kabīr 37 Dd
Wadjda 40 Bb
al-Wadjh 22 Fe
al-Wadjha 23 Ef
Wagadugu 41 Bc
Wahhābis 26 Cc
Wahran (Oran) 40 Ba Id
Waihind 47 Ba
Wajo 55 Fc
Wakasha 22 Gg
Wakhān 1.8.iii 17 Gb 24
Wakhsh R. 17 Ga 24
Waḳisā 22 Gd
al-Wāḳ-Wāḳ 1.9.i 47 Ca
Walata 41 Bc
Walili 35 Ad
Wall (Great) 5 Eb
Wall (Gurgān) 16 Cb
Wall (Transoxiana) 24 Cb
Wallachia (Eflāk) 30 Da 31 34
Wallen 41 Cb
Walmū 37 Fb
Walwālīdj 24 Cc
Wamīzā (Kilwa) 45 Ae
Wara 41 Ec
Waraghsar 24 Cc
Warāmīn 16 Bb
Warangal (Sultanpur) 48 Bc 49 50
Wargilān (Ouargla, Wargla) 40 Db Ke 41 Ca
Warīsa (Orissa) 45 Fb
Warsaw 13 Bb
Wāshgird 17 Fa 24
Washka 37 Fa, see Huesca, Osca
B. Wasin 40 Cb
Wasit 15 Hd 26
B. Waṭṭas 40 Eb
Wattasids 11 Ac
Wazīr Ḥān 31 Eb 34
Wazirabad 51 Ba
Wazzan 43 Fb
Webi Shabella 46 Bd
Wei-hai-wei 13 Fc
Wessex 8 Ab
Wo (Jih-pen) 7 Fc 9, see Japan
Wolof States 12 Ad
Wu-ch'ang 12 Ec
Wuhān 57 Fc

Yabghūkath 24 Cb
Yābisa (Ibiza) 37 Gc
Yabrīn 19 Dc
Yaca (Jajce) 31 Ba
Yadavas 47 Bb 48
Ardh Yādjūdj (Gog) 1.10.v
Yaghma 24 Db
Yāğōdīna (Jagodina) 31 Cb 34
Yahudān (Maymana) 17 Eb
Beni Yahwar 38 Dd
Yākova (Djakovo) 31 Ba 34
Djaz. al-Yākūt 1.10.iii
Yakutsk 13 Fa
Yalamlam 22 Ff
Yalova 29 Gd 31 34
Yalvaç 29 Ge
Yamāma 6 Cc 7–9 15 19 20 22
al-Yaman 1.6.i 7 Cd 12 15 44 45
Yamato 5 Fc
Yaminis 47 Ba
Yamūna (Jumna) R. 47–53 Bb
Yanaon 52 Cc 53
Yānbōli (Yambol) 31 Db 34
Yanbu' (Yanbo, Iambia) 14 Kh 15 19 22 27 46
Yang-chou 6 Ec 7 8 11
Yanina, Yanya 30 Cc 31 Cc 34
Yanova 31 Cb
Yarim 22 Gh 46
Yarkand 12 Dc
Yatağan 33 Bb
Yatenga 10 Ad 11
Yatenga 41 Bc
Yathrib (Madīna) 1.5.ii 5 Cc 15 19
Yazd (Katha) 7 Cc 16 20 25–27, see Iazd
Yazd-i Khwast 16 Bc 20 26
Yedi Kule (İstanbul) 32 Ef
Yedi Kule Kapı 32 Ef
Yendi Diari 41 Bd
Yengi-kent, Djankent (Dih-i Naw) 24 Ba
Yeni Han 29 Db
Yeni Il 33 Cb
Yeni Valide Mosque (İstanbul) 32 Ge
Yeñi-bāzār (Novibazar) 31 Cb
Yenişehir (Asia Minor) 31 Ec 34
Yenişehir-i Fener (Larisa) 30 Cc 31
Yeniseisk 12 Eb 13
Yerebatan Saray (Basilica) Cistern (İstanbul) 32 Ge
Yer-gögi (Giurgiu) 31 Db
Yeşil İrmak 29 HId
Yeşilköy 32 If
Yezo 12 Fb
YLṬ 15 Bb
Yokohama 13 Fc
Yoruba 12 Bd 41
Yozgat 33 Cb
YṬL 15 Bb
Yu-chou 7 Ec 8
Yumen 10 Eb
Yün-nan 9 Ec 12
Yu-t'ien 5 Dc 6, see Khotan

Zaaram regia 14 Bc
al-Zāb 40 Da
Zab R. 20 Cb
Zābadj 44 Hde
Zabag 7 Ee
Zabīd (W.) 8 Cd 15 Ab 19 22
Zābul 27 Eb, see Zarandj
Zābulistān 17 Fc 19
Zadjd 45 Db
Zadrīma 31 Bb 34
Ẓafār (Yaman) 15 Bb 19 44 45
Ẓafar ('Oman) 44 Cc 45, see Dhufar
Zafi Raminia settlements 9 Cf
Zafra 39 Cc
Zaghouan 43 Fa
Dj. Zaghouan 40 Ea
Zağra, Eski (Stara Zagora, Z.-i 'atik) 30 Db 31
Zağra-i Cedid (Nova Zagora) 31 Db
Zagreb 34 Aa
Zagros mts. 19 Eb
Zagros seismic zone 18 Cb
Zahran 22 Gg
Zaidis 8 Cd 9
Zaila' 7 Cd 9–12 19 44 45 46
Zaire R. 11 Be
Zaiton (Zaitun, Ch'üan-chou) 8 Ec 9 10 45
Zaječar 34 Cb
Zallaca 39 Cc
Zamakh 15 Ca
Zamakhshar 24 Bb
Zamboanga 55 Fa 56
Zamin 24 Cc
Zamora 36 Db 37 38 39
Zanagas 35 Hh
al-Zandj 1.7.i 8 Cd 11 44 45
Zandjān (Zendjan) 16 Ab 20 22 25
Zanzibar (Zandjibar) 5 Ce 9 11 12 13 44-46
Zara (Anat.) 28 Db 31 34
Zara (Dalmatia) 31 Aa 34
Zarafshān R. (N. Ṣughd) 17 Fa 24
Zaragoza (Saragossa) 36 Fb 38, see Saraḳusṭa
Zarandj 7 Dc 8 17 19 20 24 Ig 25, see Zabul
Zarih, Buḥ. 17 Dc
Zarīn Isl. 45 Ce, see Seychelles
Zarzis 40 Eb 43
Zāwa 16 Db
al-Zawia 43 Fb
Zawzan 17 Db
Zayan 43 Bb
Zaybak 17 Gb
Zayinda-Rūd 16 Bc
Zazzau 41 Cc
Zebetra 20 Bb
Zeitun Behesni 31 Gc
Zeltern 43 Gc
Zemmour 42 Ab
Zendjan, see Zandjān
Zengids 22 Cb
Zenobii 14 Gd
Zeugma (Apameia, Birecik) 28 Db
Zeytun 31 Fb 34
Ziḥne 31 Cb 34
Zile 31 Fb 33 34
Zilfi 22 He
Zimbabwe 9 Cf 11
Beni Ziri 38 Ed
Ziştovī (Svishtov) 31 Db 34
Zivid Emirates 9 Bc
Ziyāfa 23 Ff
Ziyanids 10 Bc 11
Ziyārids 16 Bb
W. Ziz 40 Bb
Zlatica 34 Db, see Izlādī
Zliten 43 Fb
Zughba 40 Ca
Zuila 41 Db
Zujar 39 Hc
Zuḳāḳ al-Suwāḳ 23 Bcd
Zuṭṭ 16 Ac
Zuwāra (Persia) 16 Bc
Zuwāra (Zuāra, Tripolitania) 40 Eb Le 43
Zvornik (İzvornik) 30 Ba 34
Zwawa 40 Ca

ASTRONOMICAL INDEX (reference to pages 2/3)

(*Latin constellations* in italics)

al-Adlā' 3 Vd
Ākhir al-Nahr 3 Wj
al-'Aḳrab 2 Gi 3 Hh
al-'Anāḳ 3 Kc
Andromeda 2 Xd
al-'Anḳā 2 Xj
Aquarius 2 Cg
Aquila 2 Ef
Ara 2 Gj
Argo Navis 2 OPj
Aries 2 Ve
'Arḳuwat al-Dalū 3 Ae
al-Arnab 2 Sh
al-Asad 2 Ne
Auriga 2 Sd
al-'Awā'id 3 Gc
al-Awhakān 3 Ic
al-'Awwā' 2 Jd 3 Lf
al-'Ayyūḳ, al-'Ayyūḳ al-bār 3 Sc

Banāt al-Na'sh 3 Lc
Barshā'ush 2 U–Vc
al-Bāṭi'a 2 Mg
Baṭn al-Ḥūt 3 Wd/We
Baṭn al-Nāḳa 3 Wc
Boötes 2 Jd
al-Bulda 3 Eh
al-Buṭain 3 Ve

Canis major 2 Rh, *minor* 2 Qf
Capricornus 2 Ch
Carina 2 Qj
Cassiopeia 2 Xbc
Centaurus 2 Jij
Cepheus 2 Bb
Cetus 2 Wg
Columba 2 Si
Corona australis 2 Fi
Corona borealis 2 Ie
Corvus 2 Lh
Crater 2 Mh
Crux 2 Lk
Cygnus 2 Dd

al-Dabarān 3 Te
al-Dadjādja 2 Dd 3 Dd
al-Dafīra 3 Le
al-Dalfīn 2 De
al-Dalū 2 Cg
Delphinus 2 Df
Dhanb al-Ḥūt 3 Bk
Dhat al-Kursi 2 Xbc
al-Dhībān 3 Hb
al-Dhirā' al-mabsūṭa 3 Qd
al-Dhirā' al-maḳbūḍa 3 Qf
al-Dhirā'ān 3 Qe
Dhubbān al-'Ayyūḳ 3 Sc
Dhubbān al-Dhubbān 3 Sd
Dhubbān Suhail 3 Qj
al-Ḍifda' al-awwal 3 Bh
al-Ḍifda' al-thānī 3 Xh
al-Dil' al-munīr 3 Vd
al-Djabbār 2 Sf
al-Djabha 3 Ne
al-Djadī 2 Ch
al-Djāh 3 Wa
al-Djāthī 2 Hd
al-Djawzā' 3 Sf
Djūn 3 Lc
Draco 2 G–Jb
al-Dubb al-akbar 2 K–Oc
al-Dubb al aṣghar 2 a

Equuleus 2 Df
Eridanus 2 Uh Vj

al-Fakka 3 Ie
Fam al-Nāka 3 Ad
al-Fargh al-mu'akhkhar 3 Xf
al-Fargh al-muḳaddam 3 Af
al-Faras al-aṣghar 2 Df
al-Faras al-a'ẓam 2 Be
al-Fard 3 Mc
al-Farḳadān 3 Kb
Fu'ad al-Asad 3 Ld

Gemini 2 Qe
al-Ghafr 3 Jg
al-Ghumaiṣa 3 Qf
al-Ghurāb 2 Lh 3 Lh
Grus 2 Bj
al-Haḳ'a 3 Se
Ḥalḳ al-Nāḳa 3 Wc
al-Hamal 2 Ve
al-Han'a 3 Re
al-Ḥauḍ 3 Oc
al-Ḥawwā' 2 Hf
al-Ḥayya 2 Gg
al-Ḥayya 2 If
Hercules 2 Ge
al-Ḥimārān 3 Kj
al-Hindī 2 Dj
al-Hudjra 3 Ie
Humsik al-'Inān 2 Sd
al-Ḥūt al-djanūbī 2 Bi
Hydra 2 Nh

al-Iklīl 2 Fi
al-Iklīl al-shamālī 2 Id 3 Ie Ih

al-Kalb, Kalb al-'Aḳrab 3 Hh
al-Kalb al-akbar 2 Rh
Kalb al-Asad 3 Nf
al-Kalb al-aṣghar 2 Qf
al-Ḳā'id 3 Kc
Kaifā'us 2 Bb
Ḳanṭurus 2 Ji
al-Karīna 2 Qj
al-Ḳaws 2 Eh
al-Ḳayṭūs 2 Wg
al-Kilā' 2 Nj
al-Kurkī 2 Bj

Leo 2 Nf
Lepus 2 Sh
Libra 2 Jh
Lupus 2 Ii
Lyra 2 Fd

al-Maʻḳal 3 Kj
al-Midjmara 2 Gj
al-Mīkh 3 Aa
al-Mira' al-musalsala 2 Xd
al-Mirzam 3 Sf
al-Mīzān 2 Jh
al-Murabbaʻ 3 Lk
al-Muthallath 2 Vd

al-Naʻāʼim al-Sādira 3 Eh
al-Naʻāʼim al-Wārida 3 Fh
Nādjid al-Barrāḳ 3 Sg
al-Nadjm 3 Ue
Nadjm al-Dadjādja 3 Dc
al-Nahr 2 Vj Uh
al-Naʻsh 3 Lc
al-Nasr al-Ṭāʼir 3 Ef
al-Nasr al-Wāḳiʻ 3 Fd
al-Nathra 3 Pe

Ophiucus 2 Hg
Orion 2 Sg

Pavo 2 Ek
Pegasus 2 Bf
Perseus 2 Ud
Phoenix 2 Xj

al-Rāmih 3 Je
Ridf al-Wāḳiʻ 3 Fc
al-Rishā 3 Wd

al-Sabʻ 2 Ii
Saʻd al-Akhbīya 3 Bg
Saʻd Bulʻ 3 Dg
Saʻd al-Dhābiḥ 3 Dg
Saʻd al-Suʻūd 3 Cg
al-Safīna 2 Pi
Safīnat Nūḥ 3 Lc
Sagitta 2 Ee
Sagittarius 2 Ei
al-Saḥābatān 3 Sk
al-Sāhiḳān 3 Hh
al-Sahm 2 Ee
Sahm al-Awwal 3 Dj
Sahm al-Ḳaws 3 Bj
al-Ṣalīb al-djanūbī 2 Lj
al-Ṣalibān 3 Gc
al-Salyāḳ 2 Fd 3 Dc
al-Samakatān 2 Xe
Sanām al-Nāḳa 3 Xc
al-Ṣarfa 3 Me
al-Sarīr 3 Mc
Scorpius 2 Gi
Serpens 2 Gg
al-Sharaṭān 3 Ve
al-Shudjāʻ 2 Og
al-Shūla 3 Gh
al-Simāk al-aʻzal 3 Kg
al-Simāk al-Rāmih 3 Je
Suhail 3 Rj
al-Sulbār al-muḥannith 3 Wj
al-Sunbula 2 Kg

al-Ṭāʼir 3 Ef
al-Ṭarf 3 Oe
Taurus 2 Tf
Tawābiʻ al-ʻAyyūk 3 Td
al-Ṭāwūs 2 Ek
al-Thānī 3 Nc
al-Thaūr 2 Te
al-Thurayyā 3 Ue
al-Tinnīn 2 G–Jb 3 Gb
Triangulum 2 Vd
al-Tu'amān 2 Qd
Tucana 2 Bk
al-Tūkān 2 Bk

al-Uḥaimir 3 Kf
al-ʻUḳāb 2 Ef
Ursa major 2 K–Oc
Ursa minor 2 a

Vela 2 Nj
Virgo 2 Kg

al-Wākiʻ (al-kathīr) 3 Fd

al-Zabra 3 Me
al-Zalīm al-fard 3 Bh
Zalīm al-Maʻḳal 3 Jj
al-Zarāfa 2 Xbc
Zāwiyat al-ʻAwwā' 3 Lg
al-Zubānān 3 Ih

ECONOMIC INDEX

alfa 42
aloes 7 20 44–46
amber 5–9 20
ambergris 10 15 44 45
apples 17 41
areca 51
arms, see weapons
aromatics 7 10 14 44 45
asafoetida 17 20
asbestos 17
attar of roses 20

balm 26
bamboo 20 44 45
barley 31
beads 10
beaver furs 26
benzamine (benzoin) 26 45
betel-nuts 44 45
birds' nests 55
bitumen 20
bows 24
brass 53
brocades 10 16 17 26 37 41

calicos 26
camels 13 15 42–45
camphor 6 7 10 13 20 44 45 48 54
cardamom 14 44 50 51
carpets 7 13 16 26 27 44 45 51 53
cassia 26 44 45
cattle 5 6 8 13 29
cedar 42
ceramics, see pottery
cereals 13 29 40 42
Chinese wares 44 45
cinnabar 10
cinnamon 5 13 26 44 49
citrus 25
cloth 5 12 26 29
cloves 5 10 44 48 54
coal 55 56
cochineal 25 37
coconuts 5 25 44 45 48 53
codfish 12
coffee 12 13 26 53 56
condiments 20
copper 5–9 12 13 17 28 45 53
copra 44
coral 5 10 13 27 40 42
coriander 50
cork 13 42
corms 5
corn 7 9, see grain, wheat
cotton 5 13 16 20 22 25 27 29 37 45 53
cowries 10
crystal 51

dates 15 16 17 20 22 26 40 42 43
diamonds 5 8 45 51 53 55 56
drugs 7 10 20 27
dyes 12 13 16, see cochineal, indigo, saffron

earth, edible 16
ebony 7 13 14 20 44 45 48
elephants 44
esparto grass 13 37

fabrics 29, see brocades, cloth, cotton, silk, velvet
feathers 13
figs 25 29
fish 8 9 13 16 17 22 24 41 42
flax 12 13 52 56
foodstuffs 44 45
fowls 22
frankincense 14 15
fruit 13 16 17 25 26 29 40 42 44
furs 5 7–9 12 24–26

galls 13 26
garnets 17
gas 43
gems 7 20 26 44 45, see stones, precious
ginger 8 10 13 14 50 51
glass 5 10 11 12 37
goats 13 27 29 34 40 42
gold 5–13 17 24 26 34 37 41 44 45 55
grain 5 44 45
grapes 17 25 29 37, see wines
gum resin 5 15
guns 48, see weapons

hair, goats' 27
hardware 11 26, see metalwork
hardwoods 11 26, see ebony, timber, teak
hawks 24
hemp 12 13 32
hides 7 24, see leather
honey 9 13 16 26 34 37 44
horses 6 7 11 13 17 34 42 44 45, horse-breeding 24

incense 5 17 44 45, see frankincense
indigo 7 13 16 20 25 26 44 45 49 51
iron ore 6 9 12 13 16 32 42 44 45
iron tools 5 6 16 45
iron weapons 5
ivory 5–10 12 13 20 24 44 45 53

jade 24 51
jet 17
jewels 5 48
jute 13 48

knives 48
kohl 16
kola nuts 9 11 41

lambskins 13
lapis lazuli 17 24 40
lead 9 12 16 28 37 42 43
leather 8 11 15 26 37
linen 16 26 37 41
liquorice 13
livestock 17
luxuries 37

madder 25 37
manganese 43
manna 26
marble 28
marten furs 26
mats 22
melons 17 22 24 25
mercury (quicksilver) 9 16 28
metalwork 45 50 53
metals 5 7 44 45
millet 6 9
minerals 13 24
monkeys 5

nard 44
nutmeg 10 49 54 55

oak galls 13 26
oil (mineral) 41 56
oils (vegetable) 20, see olive, palm
olives 29 40 42 43
olive oil 13 25 26 37
onyx 44
oranges 37, see citrus
opium 26 27

palms 42
palm-oil 12 13
paper 5 17 20 24 37
pearls 5 7 8 10 13 14 15 20 27 44 45 49
pears 16
pepper 5 8 10 13 44 45 49 50 51 54–56
perfume 7 16 20 25 44 45 48
pistachios 17
pitch (mineral) 35
pitch (wood) 35, see tar
platinum 13
pomegranates 17
porcelain 7–10 13 44 45
pottery 10 16

raisins 17
reclamation 5
relics 6
rhinoceros horn 5 44 45
rhubarb 10 17
rice 13 16 25 26 29 32 44 45 55
rosebuds 27
rosewater 16 22
rubber 13 56
rubies 5 8 14 17

sables 7 44
saddles 44
saffron 16 25 37 44
sailcloth 32
salt (mined) 5 7–11 13 20 37 40 41, (marine) 40
sandalwood 5 8 14 20 44 45 54
satin 10 16
shawls 54
sheep 13 29 34
shellfish 10
silk 7 8 10 12 13 16 17 25 26 29 37 44 45 52 53
silver 5 9 16 24 34 44 45
skins 13 26, see leather
slaves 5–10 12 24 41 45 51
soap 16 17
sorghum 44 45
specie 5 26
spices 5 10 13 14 26 29 37 44 45 47 52
spikenard 5
sponges 5
steel 17 44 45
stones, precious 5 10 12 44 45, see gems
stoneware 17
sugar 9 10 12 13 16 17 20 25 29 32 37 44 45 49 56
sulphur 13
swords 24

taffeta 10
tallow 9 13 32
tar 13 40
tea 7 10 12 13 26 45 56
teak 13 44 45
tents 24
textiles 7 11 16 17 24 37 44 45 49
tiles 16 37
timber 9 11 12 13 32 34 37 44 45
tin 44 45 56
tobacco 12 13 26 42 56
tortoise shells 5 10 44 45
town-building 5
turmeric 45 48
turquoises 16 24 26
tutty 16

velvets 25 26 53
vines 42 43

wax 9 11 13 16 26 42
weapons 8 9 24 37
wheat 13 28 29 37 44 45
wines 5 12 13 17 26 45
woad 37
wood 7 13 29 51
wool 10 11 13 20 27 29 50
woollens 41

yaks 24

zinc 42 43

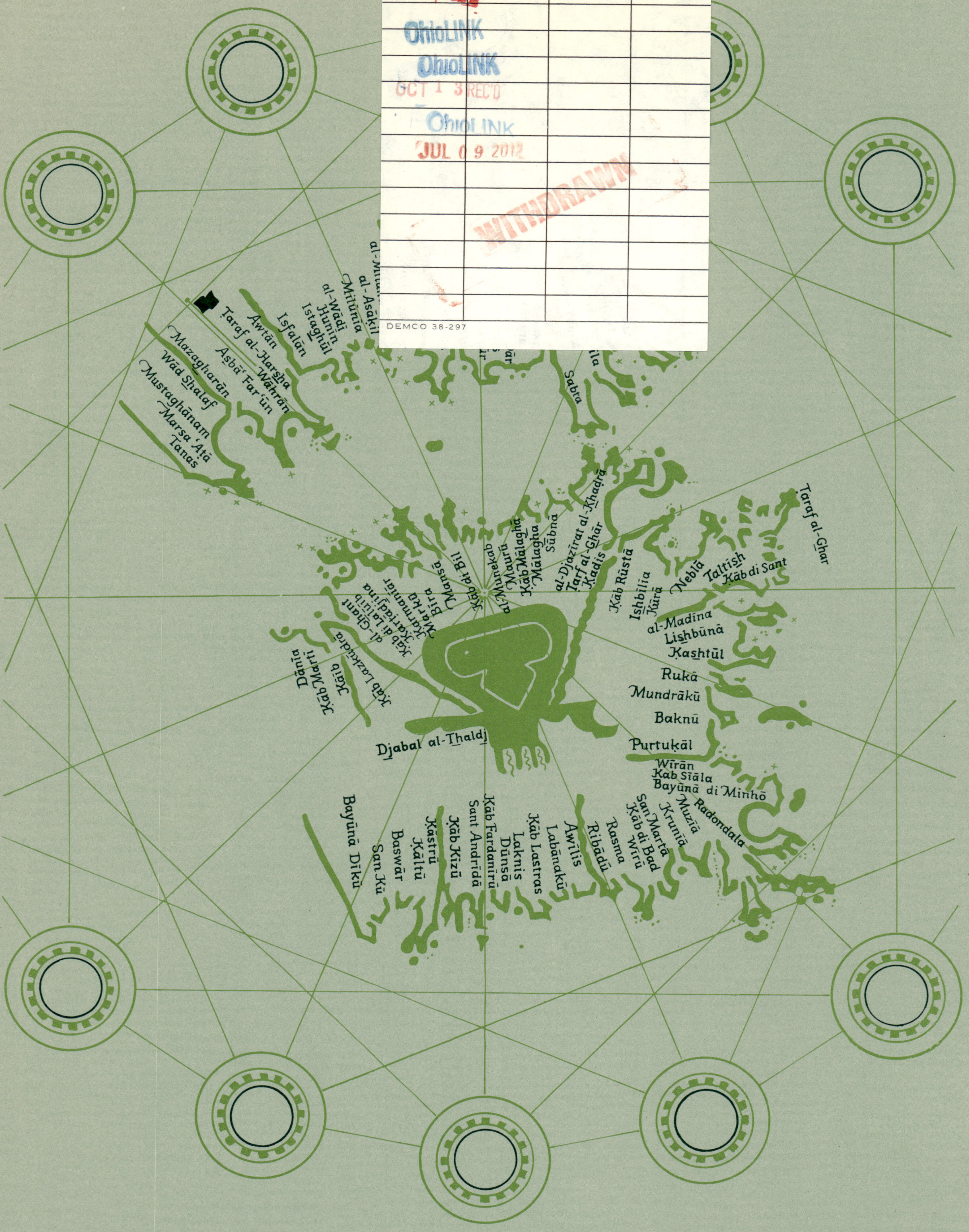

Chart of the coasts of Spain and Morocco.
Transcribed from the Sea Atlas of Ahmad al-Sharfī
of Sfax, A.D. 1571/72 (MS. Marsh No. 294)
by courtesy of the Bodleian Library, Oxford